Project Management for Small and Medium Size Businesses

Project Management for Small and Medium Size Businesses

HAROLD KERZNER
HANS J. THAMHAIN

VAN NOSTRAND REINHOLD COMPANY
NEW YORK CINCINNATI TORONTO LONDON MELBOURNE

Copyright © 1984 by Van Nostrand Reinhold Company Inc.

Library of Congress Catalog Card Number: 83-5776
ISBN: 0-442-24660-9

All rights reserved. No part of this work covered by the copyright hereon may be reproduced or used in any form or by any means – graphic, electronic, or mechanical, including photocopying, recording, taping, or information storage and retrieval systems – without permission of the publisher.

Manufactured in the United States of America

Published by Van Nostrand Reinhold Company Inc.
135 West 50th Street
New York, N.Y. 10020

Van Nostrand Reinhold Company Limited
Molly Millars Lane
Wokingham, Berkshire, England

Van Nostrand Reinhold
480 Latrobe Street
Melbourne, Victoria 3000, Australia

Macmillan of Canada
Division of Gage Publishing Limited
164 Commander Boulevard
Agincourt, Ontario M1S 3C7, Canada

15 14 13 12 11 10 9 8 7 6 5 4 3 2 1

Library of Congress Cataloging in Publication Data

Kerzner, Harold.
   Project management for small and medium-size businesses.

   Bibliography: p.
   Includes index.
   1. Industrial project management. 2. Small business–Management. I. Thamhain, Hans. II. Title.
HD69.P75K49   1983   658.4'04   83-5776
ISBN 0-442-24660-9

Preface

With the general acceptance of project management during the past ten years, corporations of all sizes have begun to examine its relative merits, advantages, and limitations. Small companies, which would have once considered it suitable only for FORTUNE 1000 corporations, are now putting its principles into practice. As an example, an Ohio-based company with 38 employees is now utilizing matrix management in the same way that a corporation with 10,000 employees would.

Most textbooks, lectures, and seminars on the subject continue to emphasize the problems of large corporations with project management. This is to be expected since the pioneers in project management were large aerospace, defense, and construction companies. Almost all problems facing large corporations, however, can be scaled down to apply to smaller organizations. In the experience of the authors, project management in smaller companies is much more difficult than it is in large ones.

The thrust of this text is geared to the needs of small and medium-sized businesses. Most of the material has been extracted from previous writings of the authors and adapted for use by smaller companies. The text stresses the behavioral aspects of project management since smaller organizations, with their limited resources, may have a greater need for understanding organizational behavior.

Readers wishing to study any of these topics more thoroughly should review the proceedings of the Annual Seminar/Symposiums of the Project Management Institute. Information can be obtained by writing

>The Project Management Institute
>P.O. Box 43
>Drexel Hill, PA 19026
>(215-622-1796)

HAROLD KERZNER
HANS J. THAMHAIN

Contents

Preface / v

I. CONCEPTS AND PRINCIPLES

1. Evolution, Growth, and Understanding of Project Management / 1
2. Programs, Projects, Tasks, and Life Cycles / 14
3. Understanding the Role of the Project Manager and His Environment / 27
4. Effective Project Management in the Small Business Organization / 41

II. ORGANIZING, PLANNING, AND CONTROL / 45

5. Organizing for Project Work / 47
6. Problem Areas in Organizing the Small Business for Project Management / 79
7. The Executive's Role in Project Management / 92
8. General Planning / 114
9. Project Planning / 131
10. Program Plan / 138
11. Detailed Schedules and Charts / 146
12. Cost Control / 152
13. Variances and Earned Value / 169

III. NEW BUSINESS DEVELOPMENT / 193

14. New Contracts: The Lifeblood for Project Management / 195

15. Planning for Growth / 198
16. Types of Solicitations and Contracts / 205
17. Developing the New Contract Opportunity / 214
18. Creating Winning Proposals / 219
19. Pricing Strategies / 222
20. Closing the Contract / 228

IV. **PROGRAM MANAGEMENT LEADERSHIP / 231**

21. People Are Your Most Valuable Asset / 233
22. The Art of Interpersonal Compliance / 235
23. The Power Spectrum in Project Management / 242
24. Leadership Effectiveness in Project Management / 248
25. How to Manage Change / 254
26. Skill Requirements for Program Managers / 263
27. Effective Conflict Management / 273
28. Conflict Resolution Approaches / 281
29. Recommendations for Improving Project Management Effectiveness / 286

V. **TEAM BUILDING / 289**

30. Selecting Key Personnel / 291
31. Organizing the Project Team / 294
32. Developing the Project Team / 302
33. Financial Compensation and Rewards / 326
34. Handling Project Phaseouts and Transfers / 316
35. Career Development in Project Management / 331

VI. Bibliography / 343

VII. Index / 363

Project Management for Small and Medium Size Businesses

PART I
CONCEPTS AND PRINCIPLES

1
Evolution, Growth, and Understanding of Project Management

Executives of both small and large companies will be facing increasingly complex challenges in the 1980s. These challenges are the result of high escalation factors for salaries and raw materials, increased union demands, pressure from stockholders, and the possibility of long term, high inflation accompanied by a mild recession and a lack of borrowing power with financial institutions. These environmental conditions have existed before, but not to the degree that they do today.

In the past, companies have attempted to ease the impact of these environmental conditions by embarking on massive cost-reduction programs. The usual results of these programs have been early retirement, layoffs, and a reduction in manpower through attrition. As jobs become vacant, executives pressure line managers to accomplish the same amount of work with fewer resources, either by improving efficiency or by upgrading performance requirements to a higher position on the learning curve. Because people costs are more inflationary than the cost of equipment or facilities, executives are funding more and more capital equipment projects in an attempt to increase or improve productivity without increasing labor.

Unfortunately, modern companies are somewhat limited in how far they can go to reduce manpower without running a high risk to corporate profitability. Capital equipment projects are not always the answer. Thus, companies have been forced to look elsewhere for the solutions to their problems.

Almost all of today's executives agree that the solution to the majority of corporate problems involves obtaining better control and use of existing corporate resources. Emphasis is being placed on looking internally rather than externally for the solution to these problems. As part of the attempt to achieve an internal solution, executives are taking a hard look at the ways corporate activities are being managed. Project management is one of the techniques now under consideration.

The project management approach is relatively modern. It is characterized by new methods of restructuring management and adapting special management techniques with the purpose of obtaining better control and use of existing resources. Twenty years ago project management was confined to the Department of Defense contractors and construction companies. Today, the concept behind project management is being applied in such diverse industries and organizations as defense, construction, pharmaceuticals, chemicals, banking, hospitals, accounting, advertising, law, state and local governments, and the United Nations. Small as well as large companies are now considering project management as a way of life.

The rapid rate of change in both technology and the marketplace has created enormous strains upon existing organizational forms. The traditional structure is highly bureaucratic, and experience has shown that it cannot respond rapidly enough to a changing environment. Thus, the traditional structure must be replaced by project management, or other temporary management structures that are highly organic and can respond very rapidly as situations develop inside and outside the company.

Project management has long been discussed by corporate executives and academics as one of several workable possibilities for organizational forms of the future that could integrate complex efforts and reduce bureaucracy. The acceptance of project management has not been easy, however. Many executives are not willing to accept change and are inflexible when it comes to adapting to a different environment. The project management approach requires a departure from the traditional business organizational form, which was basically vertical and which emphasized a strong superior-subordinate relationship.

Project management can mean different things to different people. Quite often, executives misunderstand the concept because they have ongoing projects within their company and feel that they are using project management to control these activities. In such a case, the following might be considered an appropriate definition:

- Project management is the art of creating the illusion that any outcome is the result of a series of predetermined, deliberate acts when, in fact, it was dumb luck.

Although this might be the way that some companies are running their projects, this is not project management. Project management is designed to make better use of existing resources by getting work to flow horizontally as well as vertically within the company. This approach does not really destroy the vertical, bureaucratic flow of work, but simply requires that line organizations talk to one another horizontally so work will be accomplished more smoothly throughout the organization. The vertical flow of work is still the responsibility of the line managers. The horizontal flow of work is the responsibility of the project managers, and their primary effort is to communicate and coordinate activities horizontally between the line organizations. The following would be an overview definition of project management:

- Project management is the planning, organizing, directing, and controlling of company resources for a relatively short-term objective that has been established to complete specific goals and objectives. Furthermore, project management utilizes the systems approach to management by having functional personnel (the vertical hierarchy) assigned to a specific project (the horizontal hierarchy).

The above definition requires further comment. Classical management is usually considered to have five functions or principles:

- Planning
- Organizing
- Staffing

4 CONCEPTS AND PRINCIPLES

- Controlling
- Directing

You will notice that, in the above definition, the staffing function has been omitted. This was intentional, because the project manager does not staff the project. Staffing is a line responsibility. The project manager has the right to request specific resources, but the final decision of what resources will be committed rests with the line managers.

We should also comment on what is meant by a "relatively" short-term project. Not all industries have the same definition for a short-term project. In engineering, it might be a six-month to two-year project; in construction, three to five years; in nuclear components, ten years; and in insurance, two weeks. For small and medium-size companies, short-term projects are normally on the low end of the scale, namely three months to one year.

Figure 1 is a pictorial representation of project management. The objective of the figure is to show that project management is designed to manage or control company resources on a given activity, within time, within cost, and within performance. Time, cost, and perfor-

Figure 1. Overview of project management.

mance are the constraints on the project. If the project is to be accomplished for an outside customer, then the project has a fourth constraint; good customer relations. Executives should immediately realize that it is possible to manage a project internally within time, cost, and performance and then alienate the customer to such a degree that no further business will be forthcoming. Executives in both large and small companies often select the project managers based upon who the customer is and what kind of customer relations will be necessary.

We have made reference to the fact that the project manager must control company resources within time, cost, and performance. Most companies have six resources:

- Money
- Manpower
- Equipment
- Facilities
- Materials
- Information/technology

Actually, the project manager does not control any of these resources directly, except perhaps money (i.e., the project budget). Resources are controlled by the line managers, functional managers, or, as they are often called, resources managers. The project managers must therefore negotiate with the line managers for all project resources. When we say that a project manager controls project resources, we really mean that he controls those resources (that are temporarily loaned to him) through the line managers. In large organizations, this approach works fine because there is usually a continuous stream of projects, creating the need for full-time, dedicated project managers. In the small company, a line manager may have to act as project manager as well. Now, one person controls the project as well as the line resources, and a conflict of interest may occur.

Classical management has often been defined as a process in which the manager does not necessarily perform things for himself, but accomplishes objectives through others in a group situation. This basic definition also applies to the project manager. In addition, a project manager must help himself. There is nobody to help him.

If we take a close look at project management, we will see that the project manager actually works for the line managers, not vice versa. Many people do not realize this. They have a tendency to put a halo around the head of the project manager and give him a bonus at project termination when, in fact, the credit should really go to the line managers who are continuously pressured to make better use of their resources. The project manager is simply the agent through whom this is accomplished. So, why do some companies glorify the project management position?

When the project management/line management relationship begins to deteriorate, the project almost always suffers. Executives must promote a good working relationship between line and project management. One of the most common ways of destroying this relationship is by asking, "Who contributes to profits — the line or project manager?" Project managers feel that they control all project profits because they control the budget. The line managers, on the other hand, argue that they must staff with appropriately budgeted-for personnel, supply the resources at the desired time, and supervise the actual performance. Actually, both the vertical and horizontal lines contribute to profits. These types of conflicts can destroy the entire project management structure.

The previous examples should indicate that project management is more behavioral than quantitative. Effective project management requires an understanding of:

- Quantitative tools and techniques
- Organizational structures
- Organizational behavior

Most companies understand well the quantitative tools for planning, scheduling, and controlling work. It is also imperative that project managers understand totally the operations of each line organization. This is usually easier to accomplish in small companies than in larger ones. In addition, the project manager must understand his own job description, especially where his authority begins and ends. During an in-house seminar on engineering project management, one of the project engineers was asked to provide a description of his job as a project engineer. During the discussion that followed, several project managers, and line managers, said that there was a great deal of overlapping between their job descriptions and that of the project engineer.

Organizational behavior is important because the functional employees at the interface position find themselves reporting to more than one boss — a line manager and one project manager for each project they are assigned to. Executives must provide proper training so functional employees can report effectively to multiple managers.

The slow growth rate and acceptance of project management were related to the fact that the limitations of project management were readily apparent, yet the advantages were not completely recognizable. Project management requires organizational restructuring. The question, of course, is, "How much restructuring?" Executives have avoided the subject of project management for fear that "revolutionary" changes must be made to the organization. As will be seen in Chapter 6, project management can be achieved with little departure from the existing traditional structure.

Project management restructuring permitted companies to:

- Accomplish tasks that could not be effectively handled by the traditional structure
- Accomplish one-time activities with minimum disruption of routine business

The second item implies that project management is a temporary management structure and therefore causes minimum organizational disruption. The major problems identified by those managers who endeavored to adapt to the new system all revolved about conflicts in authority and resources.

Three major problems were identified by Killian.[1]

- Project priorities and competition for talent may interrupt the stability of the organization and interfere with its long-range interests by upsetting the normal business of the functional organization.

---

[1] William P. Killian, "Project Management — Future Organizational Concepts," *Marquette Business Review*, 2, 90–107 (1971).

- Long-range planning may suffer as the company gets more involved in meeting schedules and fulfilling the requirements of temporary projects.
- Shifting people from project to project may disrupt the training of new employees and specialists. This may hinder their growth and development within their fields of specialization.

Another major concern was the fact that project management required upper-level managers to relinquish some of their authority through delegation to the middle managers. In several situations, middle management soon became the power positions, even more so than upper-level management.

Despite these limitations, there were several driving forces behind the project management approach. According to John Kenneth Galbraith, these forces stem from "the imperatives of technology." The six imperatives are:[2]

- The time span between project initiation and completion appears to be increasing.
- The capital committed to the project prior to the use of the end item appears to be increasing.
- As technology increases, the commitment of time and money appears to become inflexible.
- Technology requires more and more specialized manpower.
- The inevitable counterpart of specialization is organization.
- The above five "imperatives" identify the necessity for more effective planning, scheduling, and control.

As the driving forces overtook the restraining forces, project management began to mature. Executives began to realize that the approach was in the best interest of the company. Project management, if properly implemented, can make it easier for executives to overcome such internal and external obstacles as:

- Unstable economy
- Shortages

---

[2]John Kenneth Galbraith, *The New Industrial State,* New York: New American Library: 1968, pp. 25-28.

EVOLUTION, GROWTH, AND UNDERSTANDING OF PROJECT MANAGEMENT

- Soaring costs
- Increased complexity
- Heightened competition
- Technological changes
- Societal concerns
  - Consumerism
  - Ecology
  - Quality of work

Project management may not eliminate these problems, but may make it easier for the company to adapt to a changing environment. If these obstacles are not controlled, the results can be:

- Decreased profits
- Increased manpower needs
- Cost overruns, schedule delays, and penalty payments occurring earlier and earlier
- An inability to cope with new technology
- R&D results too late to benefit existing product lines
- New products introduced into the marketplace too late
- Temptation to make hasty decisions that prove to be costly
- Management insisting on earlier and greater return on investment
- Greater difficulty in establishing on-target objectives in real time
- Problems in relating cost to technical performance and scheduling during the execution of the project

Project management became a necessity for many companies. They began to expand into multiple product lines, many of which were often dissimilar, and organizational complexities grew almost without bound. The reasons for this can be attributed to:

- Technology increasing at an astounding rate
- More money invested in R&D
- More information available
- Shortening of project life cycles

To satisfy the requirements imposed by the above four factors, management was "forced" into organizational restructuring; the traditional organizational form which had survived for so many decades was now found to be inadequate for integrating activities across functional "empires." The seeds for the organizational revolution were planted, but acceptance by small organizations was slow.

The organizational revolution was characterized by the acceptance of project management as a way of life. And as could be expected, the exact degree of acceptance varied with the nature of the company's business, the maturity and experience of the company's top management, and the risks that the company was willing to incur in the investigation of new organizational structures that were dynamic in nature.

Project management can take on many forms and shapes such as:[3]

- Fragmented
- Formalized matrix
- Informal matrix
- Partial project management
- Task force management

There are many (if not infinite) versions of project management, perhaps one for each company, and dating back to the late forties and early fifties. It was not until the late fifties that project management came into the limelight, and even then, the growth rate was relatively slow. There were three reasons for this slow rate of acceptance:

- Executives appeared to be afraid of change and preferred the status quo.
- Many companies operated in an environment where technology changed very slowly, and therefore project management was deemed unnecessary.
- Companies that needed project management wanted to be followers rather than leaders, and preferred to learn from the mistakes of others.

By 1960, only the aerospace, defense, and construction industries were readily willing to accept project management as a way of life.

---

[3] Further definitions of these structures will be provided later.

EVOLUTION, GROWTH, AND UNDERSTANDING OF PROJECT MANAGEMENT

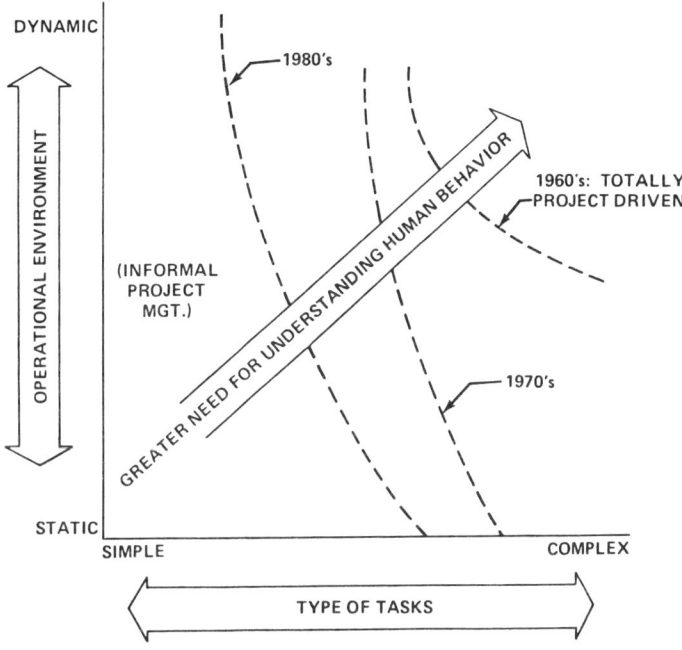

Figure 2. Matrix implementation scheme.

The reason for this can best be seen from Figure 2. Companies that were heavily burdened with complex tasks and that operated in a highly dynamic environment were the first to readily accept project management. These industries (namely construction, aerospace, and defense), which were the pioneers in project management, were almost entirely project-driven organizations.[4]

---

[4] Clarification should be made of the terminology. A project-driven organization is one where each horizontal project has its own profit and loss statement and is considered a separate horizontal cost center within the company. In the project-driven organization, the functional units exist solely to support the projects, and corporate profitability is measured on the horizontal rather than the vertical line. In the nonproject-driven organization (such as manufacturing), profits are measured on the vertical line and the projects exist to support the functional departments.

The significant fact about these pioneering industries is that, once having realized the necessity for project management, they plunged head-first into complete, formalized project management rather than in a piecemeal manner. The majority of the companies even went so far as to implement the full-blown matrix form of project management with total cost control on the horizontal line.

As could be expected, many of the companies found it extremely difficult to implement project management, especially due to lack of training in the area of interpersonal skills. Again returning to Figure 2, we see that the necessity for improved interpersonal skills increases as we approach the totally project-driven organizations. Unfortunately, the training in the area of interpersonal skills and communicative skills followed rather than preceded this massive organizational restructuring. Yet many companies took their lumps and survived, mainly because the employees (primarily the white-collar workers) were willing to give the new system a chance realizing that project management was a necessity to continue to conduct business.

The 1960s proved to be both feast and famine. In the early sixties, funding was plentiful for aerospace, construction, and defense industry contractors and subcontractors. By the late sixties, however, much of the money supply for project-driven organizational subcontractors dried up and several industries that had contemplated the acceptance of full project management postponed their plans.

Yet even with the feast and famine conditions of the sixties, more and more companies adopted the project management approach. The majority of the companies following the "pioneering industries" were high-technology companies which maintained a continuous stream of complex tasks. This can be identified in Figure 2. The matrix form of project management was being readily accepted as a necessity for doing business, and yet few companies realized the true value of the matrix.

During the fifties and sixties, literature on project/matrix management was scarce, and those articles that did appear in the literature were almost entirely construction, aerospace, or defense oriented.

Full implementation of project management, specifically matrix management, may take as much as two to three years. Organizational restructuring and interpersonal skills training can be accomplished within one year, but the establishment of a (computerized) project management cost and control system often required departure from existing cost control systems and usually brought with it the greatest resistance to change.

By the 1970s, matrix and project management took its position in the center stage and the word "matrix" became common. The full advantages and disadvantages of the matrix were now becoming clear as more and more companies began searching for ways to implement the matrix, even if fragmented.

By the mid-1970s, journals began to abound with literature on matrix management and project management as identified below:

- Project teams and task forces will become more common in tackling complexity.... There will be more of what some people call temporary management systems as project management systems where the men who are needed to contribute to the solution meet, make their contribution, and perhaps never become a permanent member of any fixed and permanent group.[5]

Articles such as this made it clear that project management was a viable tool to achieve complex corporate objectives, by simply defining a project as a group of people thrown together temporarily to achieve a corporate goal or objective. The literature identified the project manager as the "leader" of the project team even though there could have been assigned employees that were a higher rank or pay grade than the project managers.

By the mid-1970s, more and more small businesses began restructuring towards project management. Some companies accepted it willingly while others were forced into acceptance in order to remain qualified vendors or subcontractors. Unfortunately, many of the principles of project management are not easily scaled down to the small companies, and many small and medium-sized organizations found it extremely difficult to implement a project management organization. These difficulties will be discussed in later chapters.

---

[5] "Business Says It Can Handle Bigness," *Business Week,* October 17, 1970, p. 115. Reprinted from October 17, 1970 issue of *Business Week* by special permission. © 1970 by McGraw-Hill Inc., New York, N.Y. 10020. All rights reserved.

2
Programs, Projects, Tasks, and Life Cycles

A major reason for the increasing acceptance of the project management approach has been the recognition that the traditional organizational structure is too inflexible in adapting to a changing environment. Project management is an outgrowth of systems management. Systems management has emerged as a means of unifying the entire organization toward common goals and objectives. Figure 3 shows why systems management is needed to organize and unify the individual "islands" of the company. Simply stated, general systems theory attempts to integrate and unify scientific information across

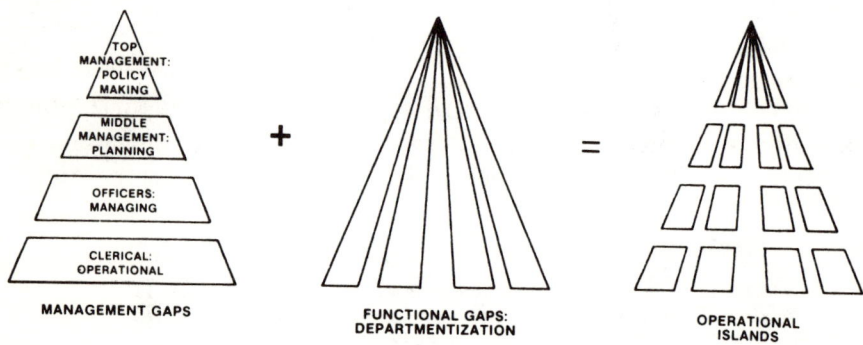

Figure 3. Why are systems necessary?

many fields of knowledge. It is an approach to solving problems by looking at the total picture rather than through analyzing individual components.

A system is generally regarded as an ongoing entity whereas a project has a finite time duration. Unfortunately, many executives today do not recognize this close relationship between systems theory and project management.

Executives as well as practitioners appear to have relatively poor definitions of systems, programs, and projects. The exact definition of each depends upon the user's environment and ultimate goal. Because there can be situations where programs, projects, and systems have different organizational structures, executives should understand the basic definitions.

Military and government organizations were the first to attempt to define clearly the boundaries of systems, programs, and projects. Below are two such definitions for systems:

- Air Force
  A composite of equipment, skills, and techniques capable of performing and/or supporting an operational role. A complete system includes related facilities, equipment, material services, and personnel as a self-sufficient unit in its intended operational and/or support environment.
- NASA
  One of the principal functioning entities comprising the project hardware within a project or program area. Ordinarily a "system" is the first major subdivision of project work; for example, spacecraft systems, launch vehicle systems, etc. . . .

Systems tend to imply an infinite lifetime, but with constant upgrading. Programs can be construed as the necessary, first-level elements of a system. Two representative definitions of programs are given below:

- Air Force
  The integrated, time-phased tasks necessary to accomplish a particular purpose.

- NASA

    A related series of undertakings that continue over a period of time (normally years), and are designed to accomplish a broad scientific or technical goal in the NASA long-range plan; for example, lunar and planetary exploration, manned spacecraft systems, etc. . . .

Programs can be regarded as subsystems. However, they are generally defined as time-phased efforts, whereas systems exist on a continuous basis. Projects are also time-phased efforts (much shorter than programs) and are the first level of breakdown of a program. A typical definition would be:

- NASA/Air Force

    A project is within a program as an undertaking with a scheduled beginning and end, and normally involves some primary purpose.

The government sector usually refers to its efforts as programs, headed by a program manager. Industries, on the other hand, prefer to call their efforts projects, headed by a project manager. The distinction is inconsequential because the same policies, procedures, and guidelines that regulate programs most often apply to projects also. For the remainder of this text, programs and projects will be discussed interchangeably. However, the reader should be aware that projects are normally the first-level subdivision of a program. This breakdown will be discussed in Chapters 15 and 16.

Once a group of tasks is selected and considered to be a project, the next step is to define the kinds of project units. There are four categories:

- Individual projects — short-duration projects normally assigned to a single individual who may be acting as both a project manager and functional manager.
- Staff projects — these are projects that can be accomplished by one organizational unit, a department, for example. A staff or task force is developed from each section involved. This works best if only one functional unit is involved.

- Special projects — very often special projects occur that require a certain primary function and/or authority to be assigned temporarily to other individuals or units. This works best for short-duration projects.
- Matrix of aggregate projects — these require input from a large number of functional units and usually control vast resources.

Each of these categories can require different responsibilities, job descriptions, policies, and procedures, and all can exist simultaneously.

For all practical purposes, there is no basic difference between program management and project management. But what about product management? Project management and product management are similar, with one major exception: the project manager focuses on the end date of his project, whereas the product manager is not willing to admit that his product line will ever end. The product manager wants his product to be as long-lived and profitable as possible. Even when the demand for the product diminishes, the product manager will always look for spin-offs to keep his product alive.

Figure 4 shows the relationship between project and product management. When the project is in the R&D phase, a project manager is involved. Once the product is developed and introduced into the marketplace, control is taken over by the product manager. Both product and project management can, and do, exist concurrently within companies.

Figure 4 identifies the fact that product management can operate horizontally as well as vertically. When a product is shown horizontally on the organizational chart, it implies that the product line is not big enough to control its own resources full-time and therefore shares key functional personnel similar to project management. If the product line were large enough to control its own resources full-time, it would be shown as a separate division or vertical line on the organizational chart.

Also shown in Figure 4 is the remarkable fact that the project manager (or project engineer) is reporting to a marketing-type person. Should executives permit project managers and project engineers to report to a marketing-type individual even if the project entails a great amount of engineering? Many executives today would attest

18 CONCEPTS AND PRINCIPLES

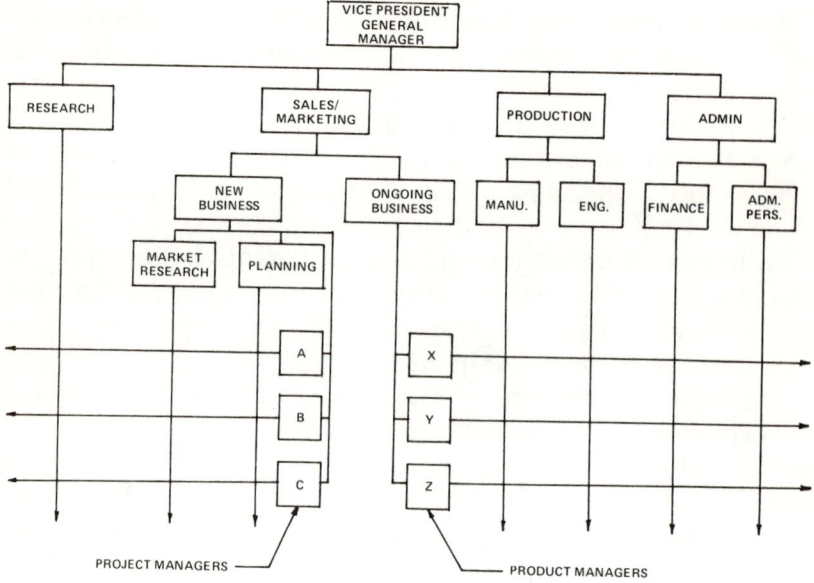

Figure 4. Organizational chart.

that the answer is yes. The reason for this is that technically oriented project leaders get too involved with the technical details of the project and lose insight as to when and how to "kill" a project. Remember, most technical leaders have been trained in an academic rather than a business environment. Their commitment to success often does not take into account such important parameters as return on investment, profitability, competition, and marketability.

To alleviate these problems, project managers and project engineers, especially on R&D-type projects, are now reporting to marketing so that marketing input will be included in all R&D decisions. Many executives have been forced into this position because of the high costs incurred during R&D, especially since, in case of a severe need to reduce costs, the R&D organization is usually the first to feel the pinch. Executives must exercise caution with regard to this structure where both product and project managers report to the marketing function. The marketing executive could become the focal point of the entire organization, with the capability of building a very large empire.

Every program, project, or product has certain phases of development. A clear understanding of these phases permits managers and executives to better control total corporate resources in the achievement of desired goals. The phases of development are known as life cycle phases. However, the breakdown and terminology of these phases differ, depending upon whether we are discussing products or projects.

During the past few years, there has been at least partial agreement about the life cycle phases of a product. They include:

- Research and development
- Market introduction
- Growth
- Maturity
- Deterioration
- Death

Today, there is no agreement among industries, or even companies within the same industry, about the life cycle phases of a project. This is understandable because of the complex nature and diversity of projects.

The theoretical definitions of the life cycle phases of a system, as defined by Cleland and King, can be applied to a project.[6] These include:

- Conceptual
- Definition
- Production
- Operational
- Divestment

The first phase is the conceptual phase and includes the preliminary evaluation of an idea. Table 1 defines the efforts attributed to this phase. Most important in this phase is a preliminary analysis of risk and the resulting impact on the time, cost, and performance requirements, together with the potential impact on company resources.

---

[6] D.I. Cleland and W.R. King, *Systems Analysis and Project Management*, New York: McGraw-Hill, 1975, pp. 187–190.

Table 1. Conceptual Phase.[a]

- Determine existing needs or potential deficiencies of existing systems
- Establish system concepts which provide initial strategic guidance to overcome existing or potential deficiencies
- Determine initial technical, environmental, and economic feasibility and practicability of the system
- Examine alternative ways of accomplishing the system objectives
- Provide initial answers to the questions
  - What will the system cost?
  - When will the system be available?
  - What will the system do?
  - How will the system be integrated into existing systems?
- Identify the human and nonhuman resources required to support the system
- Select initial system designs which will satisfy the system objectives
- Determine initial system interfaces
- Establish a system organization

[a]From *Systems Analysis and Project Management* by David I. Cleland and William Richard King. Copyright © 1968, 1975 by McGraw-Hill, Inc. Used with permission of McGraw-Hill Book Company. (P. 187.)

Table 2. Definition Phase.[a]

- Firm identification of the human and nonhuman resources required
- Preparation of the final system performance requirements
- Preparation of the detailed plans required to support the system
- Determination of realistic cost, schedule, and performance requirements
- Identification of those areas of the system where high risk and uncertainty exist, and delineation of plans for further exploration of these areas
- Definition of intersystem and intrasystem interfaces
- Determination of necessary support subsystems
- Identification and initial preparation of the documents required to support the system, such as policies, procedures, job descriptions, budget and funding papers, letters, memoranda, etc.

[a]From *Systems Analysis and Project Management* by David I. Cleland and William Richard King. Copyright © 1968, 1975 by McGraw-Hill, Inc. Used with permission of McGraw-Hill Book Company. (P. 188.)

The conceptual phase also includes a "first cut" at the feasibility of the effort.

The second phase, the definition phase, as shown in Table 2, is mainly a refinement of the elements described under the conceptual phase. The definition phase requires a firm identification of the resources to be required together with the establishment of realistic time, cost, and performance parameters. This phase also includes the initial preparation of all documentation necessary to support the system. For a project based upon competitive bidding, the conceptual phase would include the decision of whether or not to bid, and the definition phase would include the development of the total bid package (i.e., time, schedule, cost, and performance).

Analyzing system costs during the conceptual and definition phases is not an easy task because of the amount of estimating involved. Most project or system costs can be broken down into operating (recurring) and implementation (nonrecurring) categories. The implementation costs include one-time expenses such as construction of a new facility, purchasing of computer hardware, or detailed planning. Operating costs, on the other hand, include recurring expenses such as manpower. The operating costs may be reduced if personnel perform at a higher position on the learning curve. The identification of learning curve position is vitally important during the definition phase, when firm cost positions must be established. Of course, it is not always possible to know what individuals will be available or how soon they can perform at a higher learning curve position.

Once the approximate total cost of the project is determined, a cost-benefit analysis should be conducted to determine if the estimated value of the information obtained from the system exceeds the costs of obtaining the information. This analysis is often included as part of a feasibility study. There are several situations, such as in competitive bidding, where the feasibility study is actually the conceptual and definition phases. Because of the costs that can be incurred during these two phases, top-management approval is almost always necessary before the initiation of such a feasibility study.

The third phase is the production (or acquisition) phase and includes such items as those listed in Table 3. This phase is predominantly a testing and final standardization effort so that operation can begin. Almost all documentation must be completed in this phase.

Table 3. Production Phase.[a]

- Updating of detailed plans conceived and defined during the preceding phases
- Identification and management of the resources required to facilitate the production processes such as inventory, supplies, labor, funds, etc.
- Verification of system production specifications
- Beginning of production, construction, and installation
- Final preparation and dissemination of policy and procedural documents
- Performance of final testing to determine adequacy of the system to do the things it is intended to do
- Development of technical manuals and affiliated documentation describing how the system is intended to operate
- Development of plans to support the system during its operational phase

[a]From *Systems Analysis and Project Management* by David I. Cleland and William Richard King. Copyright © 1968, 1975 by McGraw-Hill, Inc. Used with permission of McGraw-Hill Book Company. (P. 188.)

The fourth phase is the operational phase, and as shown in Table 4, it integrates the project's product or services into the existing organization. If the project were developed for establishment of a marketable product, then this phase could include the product life cycle phases of market introduction, growth, maturity, and a portion of deterioration.

Table 4. Operational Phase.[a]

- Use of the system results by the intended user or customer
- Actual integration of the project's product or service into existing organizational systems
- Evaluation of the technical, social, and economic sufficiency of the project to meet actual operating conditions
- Provision of feedback to organizational planners concerned with developing new projects and systems
- Evaluation of the adequacy of supporting systems

[a]From *Systems Analysis and Project Management* by David I. Cleland and William Richard King. Copyright © 1968, 1975 by McGraw-Hill, Inc. Used with permission of McGraw-Hill Book Company. (P. 189.)

Table 5. Divestment Phase.[a]

- System phasedown
- Development of plans transferring responsibility to supporting organizations
- Divestment or transfer of resources to other systems
- Development of "lessons learned from system" for inclusion in qualitative-quantitative data base to include:
  - Assessment of image by the customer
  - Major problems encountered and their solution
  - Technological advances
  - Advancements in knowledge relative to department strategic objectives
  - New or improved management techniques
  - Recommendations for future research and development
  - Recommendations for the management of future programs, including interfaces with associate contractors
  - Other major lessons learned during the course of the system

[a]From *Systems Analysis and Project Management* by David I. Cleland and William Richard King. Copyright © 1968, 1975 by McGraw-Hill, Inc. Used with permission of McGraw-Hill Book Company. (P. 190.)

The final phase, as shown in Table 5, is divestment and includes the reallocation of resources. The question to be answered is:

- Where should the resources be reassigned?

Consider a company that sells products on the open consumer market. As one product begins the deterioration and death phases of its life cycle (i.e., divestment phase of a system), then new products or projects must be established. Such a company would therefore require a continuous stream of projects in order to survive. In the ideal situation these new projects will be established at such a rate that total revenue will increase and company growth will be clearly visible.

The divestment phase evaluates the efforts on the total project and serves as input to the conceptual phases for new projects and systems. This final phase also has an impact on other ongoing projects with regard to priority identification.

The phases of a project and those of a product are compared in Figure 5. Notice that the life cycle phases of a product generally

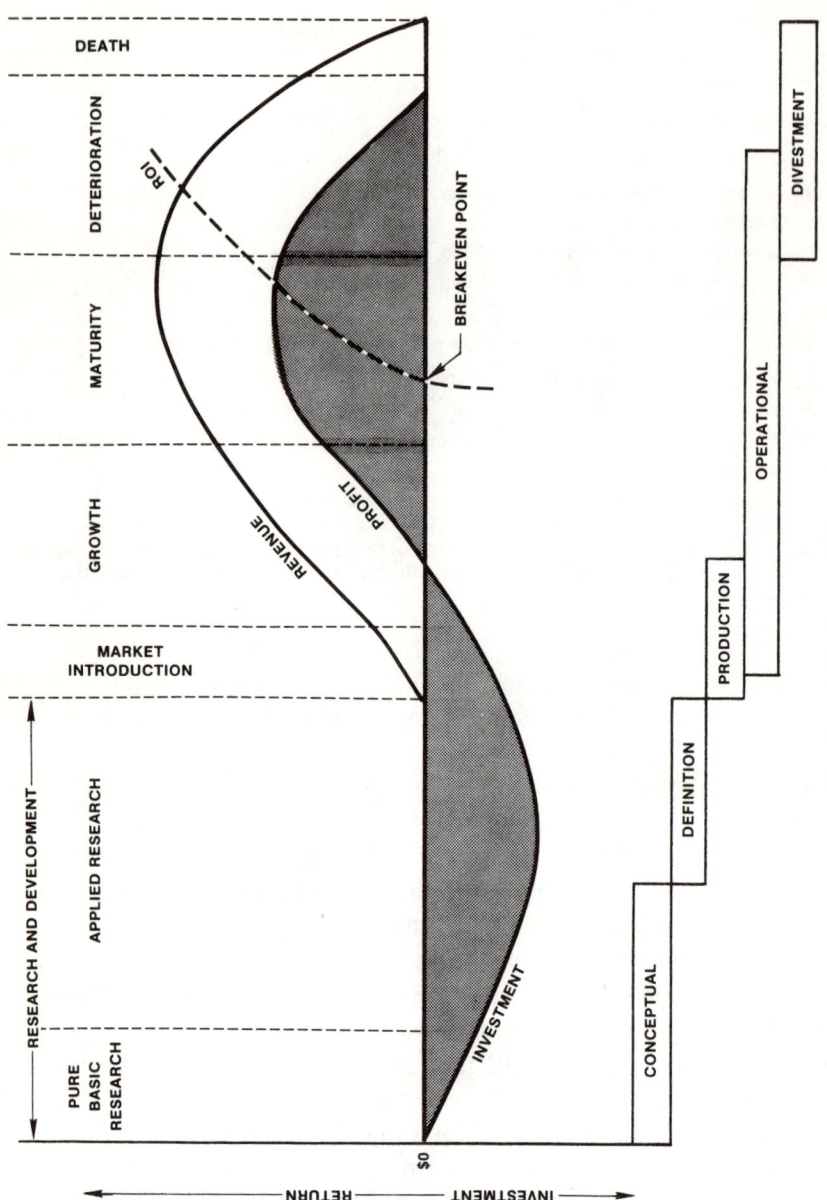

Figure 5. System/product life cycles.

Table 6. Life Cycle Phase Definitions.

ENGINEERING	MANUFACTURING	COMPUTER PROGRAMMING	CONSTRUCTION
• Start-up	• Formation	• Conceptual	• Planning, data gathering, and procedures
• Definition	• Buildup	• Planning	• Studies and basic engineering
• Main	• Production	• Definition and design	• Major review
• Termination	• Phaseout	• Implementation	• Detail engineering
	• Final audit	• Conversion	• Detail engineering/construction overlap
			• Construction
			• Testing and commissioning

26 CONCEPTS AND PRINCIPLES

do not overlap, whereas the phases of a project can and often do overlap.

Table 6 identifies the various project life cycle phases that are commonly used. Even in mature project management industries, such as construction, one could survey ten different construction companies and find ten different definitions for the life cycle phases.

The life cycle phases for computer programming, as listed in Table 6, are also shown in Figure 6 to illustrate how manpower resources can build up and decline during a project. In Figure 6, PMO is the present method of operations and PMO' will be the "new" present method of operations after conversion. This life cycle would probably be representative of a 12-month activity. Most executives prefer short data processing life cycles because computer technology changes at a very rapid rate. An executive of a major utility commented that his company was having trouble determining how to terminate a computer programming project to improve customer service because by the time a package is ready for full implementation, an updated version appears on the scene. Should the original project be canceled and a new project begun? The solution appears to be in establishing short data processing project life cycle phases, perhaps through segmented implementation.

As a final note, executives should realize that even within the same company, it is possible for different life cycle phase definitions to exist. This is because some projects are longer than others, more complex, or simply more difficult to manage.

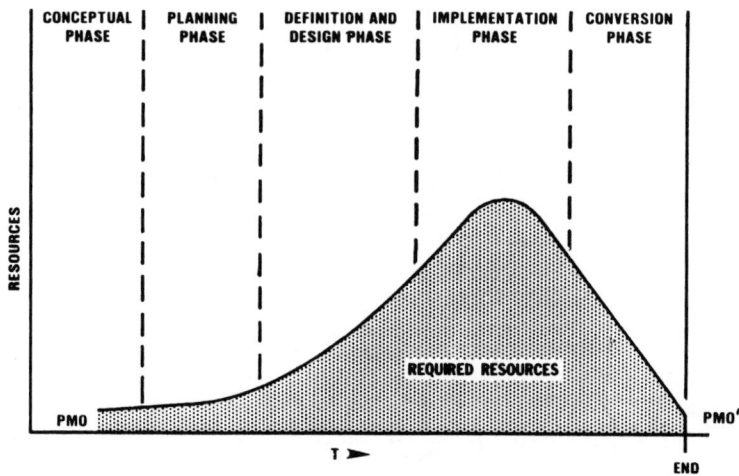

Figure 6. Definition of a project life cycle.

3
Understanding the Role of the Project Manager and His Environment

Because current organizational structures are unable to accommodate the wide variety of interrelated tasks necessary for successful project completion, the need for project management has become apparent. It is usually first identified by those lower-level and middle managers who find it impossible to control their resources effectively for the diverse activities within their line organization. Quite often middle managers feel the impact of a changing environment more than upper-level executives.

Once the need for change is identified, middle management must convince upper-level management that such a change is actually warranted. If top-level executives cannot recognize the problems with resource control, then project management will not be adopted, at least formally. Informal acceptance, however, is another story.

In 1978, one of the authors received a request from an automobile equipment manufacturer who was considering formal project management. The author was permitted to speak with several middle managers. The following comments were made:

- "Here at ABC Company (a division of XYZ Corporation), we have informal project management. By this, I mean that work flows the same as it would in formal project management except that the authority, responsibility, and accountability are im-

plied rather than rigidly defined. We have been very successful with this structure, especially when you consider that the components we sell cost 30 percent more than our competitors, and that our growth rate has been in excess of 12 percent each year for the past six years. The secret of our success has been our quality and our ability to meet schedule dates."
- "Our informal structure works well because our department managers do not hide problems. They aren't afraid to go into another department manager's office and talk about the problems they're having controlling resources. Our success is based upon the fact that *all* of our department managers do this. What's going to happen if we hire just one or two people who won't go along with this approach? Will we be forced to go to formalized project management?"
- "This division is a steppingstone to greatness in our corporation. It seems that all of the middle managers who come to this division get promoted either within the division, to higher management positions in other divisions, or to a higher position at corporate headquarters."

At this point the author conducted two three-day seminars on engineering project management for 75 of the lower-, middle-, and upper-level managers. The seminar participants were asked whether or not they wanted to adopt formal project management. The following concerns were raised by the participants:

- "Will I have more or less power and/or authority?"
- "How will my salary be affected?"
- "Why should I permit a project manager to share the resources in my empire?"
- "Will I get top-management visibility?"

Even with these concerns, the majority of the attendees felt that formalized project management would alleviate a lot of their present problems.

Although the middle levels of the organization, where resources are actually controlled on a day-to-day basis, felt positive about project management, convincing the top levels of management was another story. If you were the chief executive officer of this division, earning a salary in six figures, and looking at a growth rate of 12 percent per year for the last five years, would you "rock the boat" simply because your middle managers wanted project management?

This example highlights three major points:

- The final decision for the implementation of project management does (and will always) rest with executive management, regardless of company size.
- Executives must be willing to listen when middle management identifies a crisis in controlling resources. This is where the need for project management should first appear.
- Executives are paid to look out for the long-range interests of the corporation and should not be swayed by near-term growth rate or profitability.

Today, ABC Company is still doing business the way it was done in the past — with informal project management. The company is a classic example of how informal project management can be made to work successfully. The author agrees with the company executives that, in this case, formal project management is not necessary.

Once the need for project management has been defined, the next logical question is, "How long a conversion period will be necessary before a company can operate in a project management environment?" To answer this question we must first look at Figure 7. Technology, as expected, has the fastest rate of change, and the overall environment of a business must adapt to this rapidly changing technology.

In an ideal situation, the organizational structure of a company would immediately adapt to the changing environment. In a real situation, this will not be a smooth transition, but more like the erratic line shown in Figure 7. This erratic line is a trademark or characteristic of the traditional structure. Project management structures, however, can, and often do, adapt to a rapidly changing environment with a relatively smooth transition.

Even though an executive can change the organizational structure with the stroke of a pen, people are responsible for its implementation. However, it can be seen in Figure 7 that people have the slowest rate of change. Edicts, documents signed by executives, and training

30 CONCEPTS AND PRINCIPLES

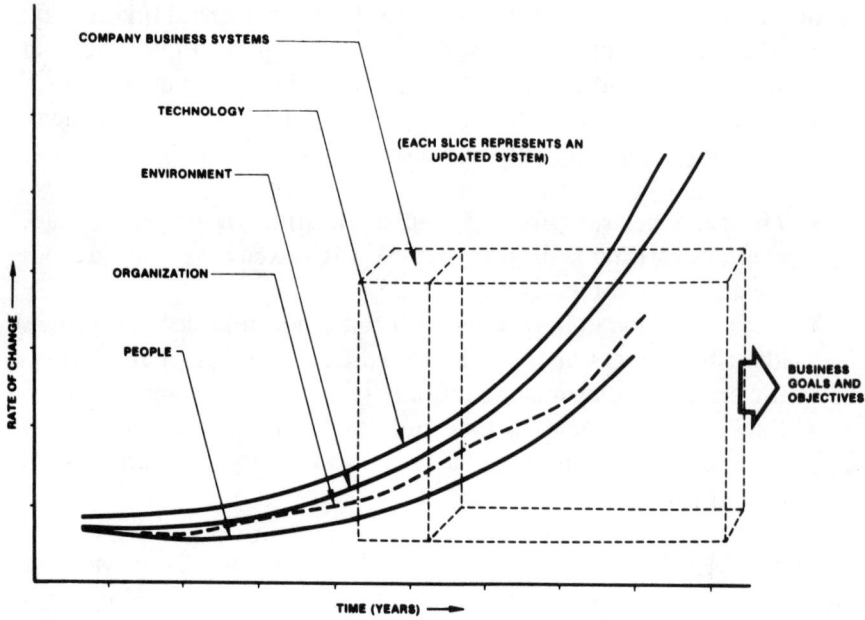

Figure 7. Systems in a changing environment.

programs will not convince employees that a new organizational form will work. Employees will be convinced only after they see the new system in action, and this takes time.

As a ground rule, it often takes two to three years to convert from a traditional structure to a project management structure. The major reason for this is that in a traditional structure the line employee has one and only one boss; in a project management structure the employee reports vertically to his line manager and horizontally to every project manager to whose activities he is assigned either temporarily or full-time. Employees will perform in a new system because they are directed to do so, but will not have confidence in it or become dedicated until after they have been involved in several different projects and believe that they can effectively report to more than one boss.

When an employee is told that he will be working horizontally as well as vertically, his first concern is his take-home pay. Employees always question whether or not they can be evaluated fairly if they report to several managers during the same time period. One of the major reasons why project management fails is because top-level executives neglect to consider that any organizational change must be explained in terms of the wage and salary administration program. This must be given *before* change is made. If change comes first, and employees are not convinced that they can be evaluated correctly, they may very likely try to sabotage the whole effort. From then on, it will probably be a difficult, if not impossible, task to rectify the situation. However, once the organizational employees accept project management and the procedure of reporting in two directions, the company can effectively and efficiently convert from one project management organizational form to another.

Not all companies need two to three years to convert to project management. The ABC Company described earlier would probably have very little trouble in converting because informal project management is well accepted. In the early sixties, TRW was forced to convert to a project management structure almost overnight. They were highly successful in this, mainly because of the loyalty and dedication of the employees. The TRW employees were willing to give the system a chance. Any organizational structure, no matter how bad, will work if the employees are willing to make it work. Yet other companies can spend three to five years trying to implement changes and drastically fail. The literature describes many cases where project management has failed because:

- There was no need for project management.
- Employees were not informed about how project management should work.
- Executives did not select the appropriate projects or project managers for the first few projects.
- There was no attempt to explain the effect of the project management organizational form on the wage and salary administration program.

- Employees were not convinced that executives were in total support of the change.

Some companies (and executives) are forced into project management before they realize what has happened, and if recognition at the top levels of management does not occur within a short time period thereafter, chaos seems inevitable. As an example, consider a highly traditional company that purchased a computer a few years ago. The company has five divisions: engineering, finance, manufacturing, marketing, and personnel. Not knowing where to put the computer, the chief executive officer created an electronic data processing (EDP) department and placed it under finance and accounting. The executive's rationale was that since the purpose for buying the computer was to eliminate repetitive tasks and the majority of these were in accounting and finance, that was where EDP belonged. The vice-president for accounting and finance might not be qualified to manage the EDP department, but that seemed beside the point.

The EDP department has a staff of scientific and business computer programmers, and systems analysts. The scientific programmers spend almost all of their time working in the engineering division writing engineering programs; they must learn engineering in order to do this. In this company, the engineer does not consider himself a computer programmer, but does the computer programmer consider himself an engineer?

The company's policy is that merit and cost-of-living increases are given out in July of each year. This year the average salary increase will be 7 percent. However, the president wants the increase given according to merit, and not as a flat rate across the board. After long hours of deliberation, it was decided that engineering, manufacturing, and marketing would receive 8 percent raises and finance and personnel 5.5 percent.

After announcement of the salary increases, the scientific programmers began to complain because they felt they were doing engineering-type work and should, therefore, be paid according to the engineering pay scale. Management tried to resolve this problem by giving each division its own computer and personnel. However, this resulted in duplication of effort and inefficient use of personnel.

With the rapid advancements in computer technology of recent years, management realized the need for timely access to information for executive decision-making. In a rather bold move, executives created a new division called management information systems (MIS). The MIS division now has full control of all computer operations and gives the EDP personnel the opportunity to show that they actually contribute to corporate profits.

Elevating the computer to the top levels of the organization was a significant step toward project management. Unfortunately, many executives did not fully realize what had happened. Because of the need for a rapid information retrieval system that can integrate data from a variety of line organizations, the MIS personnel soon found that they were working horizontally, not vertically. Today MIS packages cut across every division of the company. Thus, the emergence of the project management concept to handle a horizontal flow of work appeared on the scene.

With the emergence of data processing project management, executives were forced to find immediate answers to such questions as:

- Can we have project management strictly for data processing projects?
- Should the project manager be the programmer or the user?
- How much authority should be delegated to the project manager, and will this delegated authority cause a shift in the organizational equilibrium?

The answers to these questions have not been and still are not easy to solve. Today, IBM provides its customers with the opportunity to hire IBM as the in-house data processing project management team. This partially eliminates the necessity for establishing internal project management relationships that could easily become permanent.

The implementation problems identified here are not restricted solely to large companies but to small companies as well. And as described previously, project management in small companies may be much more difficult to administer than in larger organizations.

As project management developed, some essential factors in its successful implementation were recognized. The major factor was the role of the project manager, which became the focal point of integrative responsibility.

Providing the project manager with integrative responsibility resulted in:

- Total accountability assumed by a single person
- Project rather than functional dedication
- A requirement for coordination across functional interfaces
- Proper utilization of integrated planning and control

Those executives who chose to accept project management soon found the advantages of the new technique:

- Easy adaptation to an ever-changing environment
- Ability to handle a multidisciplinary activity within a specified period of time
- Horizontal as well as vertical work flow
- Better orientation toward customer problems
- Easier identification of activity responsibilities
- A multidisciplinary decision-making process
- Better work relationships with prime contractors

Executives must be cautious in implementing project management. If the new approach is not closely supervised during the implementation phase, it may create problems that have a direct bearing upon corporation profits. As an example, consider the effects and probable causes shown below:[7]

- Effects
    - Late completion of activities
    - Cost overruns
    - Substandard performance
    - High turnover in project staff
    - High turnover in functional staff
    - Two functional departments performing the same activities on one project

---

[7] This has been adapted from Russell D. Archibald, *Managing High-Technology Programs and Projects,* New York: Wiley, 1976, p. 10.

- Causes
  - Top management not recognizing this activity as a project
  - Too many projects going on at once
  - Impossible schedule commitments
  - No functional input into the planning phase
  - No one person responsible for the total project
  - Poor control of design changes
  - Poor control of customer changes
  - Poor understanding of the project manager's job
  - No integrated planning and control
  - Company resources overcommitted
  - Unrealistic planning and scheduling
  - No project cost-accounting ability
  - Conflicting project priorities
  - Poorly organized project office
  - Wrong person assigned as the project manager

Many of these causes and effects can occur within any organizational structure. However, they are more pronounced with project management. Therefore, companies both large and small must exercise due caution and make sure that the implementation is correctly *planned* for.

The project manager is responsible for coordinating and integrating activities across multiple, functional lines. In order to do this, the project manager needs strong communicative and interpersonal skills, must become familiar with the operations of each line organization, and should have general knowledge of the technology.

An executive with a computer manufacturer stated that his company was looking externally for project managers. When asked if the executive expected candidates to have a command of computer technology, the executive remarked: "You give me an individual who has good communicative skills and interpersonal skills and I'll give him a job. I can teach people the technology and give them technical experts to assist them in decision-making. But I cannot teach somebody how to work with people."

The project manager's job is not an easy one. Project managers may have increased authority and responsibility, but very little power. This lack of power can force them to "negotiate" with upper-level manage-

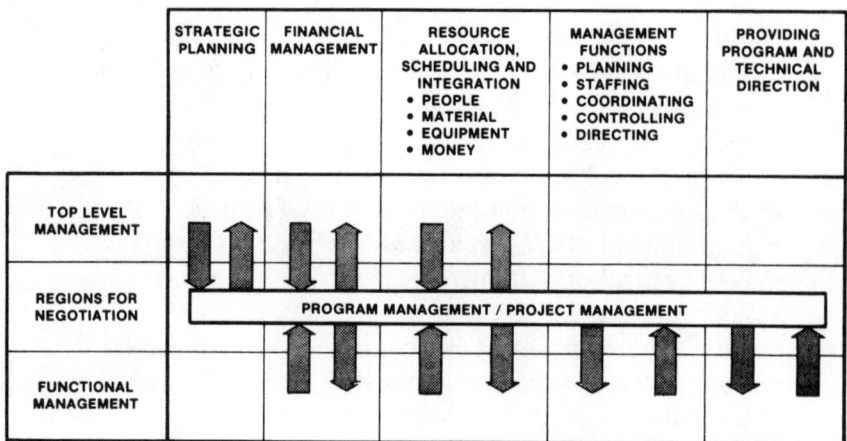

Figure 8. The negotiation activities of systems management.

ment as well as functional management for control of company resources, as shown in Figure 8. They may often be treated as outsiders by the formal organization. Yet, even with these problems and roadblocks, they have managed to survive. J. Robert Fluor has described the new responsibilities of project managers at Fluor Corporation:[8]

> Project management continues to become more challenging and we think this trend will continue. This means we have to pay special attention to the development of project managers who are capable of coping with jobs that range from small to mega projects and with life spans of several months to ten years. At Fluor, a project manager must not only be able to manage the engineering, procurement and construction aspects of a project, he or she must also be able to manage aspects relating to finance, cost engineering, schedule, environmental considerations, regulatory agency requirements, inflation and cost escalations, labor problems, public and client relations, employee relations and changing laws. That's primarily on the domestic side. On international projects, the list of additional functions and considerations adds totally different complications.

---

[8] J. Robert Fluor, "Development of Project Managers," keynote address to the Project Management Institute, Ninth International Seminar Symposium, Chicago, Illinois, October 24, 1977.

The domestic considerations identified above hold true today even for some of the smallest construction companies.

In the project environment, everything seems to revolve about the project manager. Although the project organization is a specialized task-oriented entity, it cannot exist apart from the traditional structure of the organization. The project manager, therefore, must walk the fence between the two organizations. The term *interface management* is often used for this role, which can be described as:[9]

- Managing human interrelationships in the project organization
- Maintaining the balance between technical and managerial project functions
- Coping with risk associated with project management
- Surviving organizational restraints

Organizational restraints have a tendency to develop into organizational conflict, often requiring that top management take an active role in conflict resolution by:

- Setting a selection criteria for projects
- Establishing priorities among projects

To be effective as a project manager, an individual must have management as well as technical skills. Unfortunately, businessmen sometimes find it difficult to think as engineers, and engineers find it difficult at times to think as businessmen. Executives have found that it is usually easier to train engineers rather than businessmen to fill project management positions.

Because the engineers often consider their careers limited in the functional disciplines, they look toward project management and project engineering as career path opportunities. But becoming a manager entails learning about psychology, human behavior, organizational behavior, interpersonal relations, and communications. MBA programs have come to the rescue of individuals desiring the background to be effective project managers.

---

[9] David L. Wilemon and John P. Cicero, "The Project Manager – Anomalies and Ambiguities," *Academy of Management Journal* (September 27, 1970).

The average age of project managers in industry is between 32 and 38. There are three reasons for this:

- An individual often makes his most profitable contribution to society between 30 and 40. If individuals do not begin climbing the corporate ladder by the time they are 40, they may be severely limited in career growth.
- When is an individual most concerned about money? (All the time is not an acceptable answer!) It is not between the ages of 20 and 30 because to a person coming right out of college, any money looks good. It is not between the ages of 40 and 50 because, by that time, individuals are fairly set in their ways and living styles. But between the ages of 30 and 40, the individual is thinking about financial security and the future.
- The younger individual in most cases is willing to take more risks than the older individual in order to meet the project objective. Furthermore, the individual is often willing to work long hours on overtime and weekends.

Actually, the age of the project manager varies from industry to industry. Data processing project managers are usually younger than the average because current knowledge of computer technology is a necessity. R&D project managers also fall into this category because of technology requirements. Manufacturing and construction project managers are often older because experience is so important.

Today, even the smallest of companies are trying to hire and hold on to at least one or two top-notch project managers. The reason for this is simple; the company does not want to be caught unprepared when and if that one large project comes along.

In the past, executives motivated and retained qualified personnel primarily with financial incentives. Today other ways are being used. Some people are more title-oriented than money-oriented. For example, changing an individual's title sometimes motivates people to stay with the company simply because they want to put this new title on their resumes at a later date.

Another method, and by far the best, is work challenge. The project manager is actually a general manager and gets to know the total operation of the company. In fact, the project managers get to know more about the total operation of the company than do most executives. This is why project management is often used as a training ground to prepare future general managers who will be capable of filling top management positions. This is not a bad idea, provided that executives know that the general management aspect is the result of experience in integrating work horizontally. Placing an individual into project management for the sole purpose of training a future general manager is not recommended.

The major responsibility of the project manager is planning. If project planning is performed correctly, then it is conceivable that the project manager will work himself out of a job because the project can run itself. This rarely happens, however. Few projects are ever completed without some conflict for the project manager to resolve.

In most cases, the project manager provides detailed definitions of the work to be accomplished, but the line managers (the true experts) do the detailed planning. Although project managers cannot control or assign line resources, they must make sure that the resources are adequate and scheduled to satisfy the needs of the project, not vice versa. As the architect of the project plan, the project manager must provide:

- Complete task definitions
- Resource requirement definitions
- Major timetable milestones
- Definition of end-item quality and reliability requirements
- The basis for performance measurement

These factors, if properly established, result in:

- Assurance that functional units will understand their total responsibility toward achieving project needs
- Assurance that problems resulting from scheduling and allocation of critical resources are known beforehand
- Early identification of problems that may jeopardize successful project completion so that effective corrective action can be taken to prevent or resolve problems

Project managers are responsible for project administration and must therefore have the right to establish their own policies, procedures, rules, guidelines, and directives — provided these conform to overall company policy. Companies with mature project management structures usually have rather loose company guidelines so that project managers have some degree of flexibility in how to control their projects. However, there are certain administrative requirements project managers cannot establish. As an example, the project manager cannot make any promises to a functional employee concerning:

- Promotion
- Grade
- Salary
- Bonus
- Overtime
- Responsibility
- Future work assignments

These seven items can be administered by line managers only. However, the project manager can have indirect involvement by telling the line manager how well an employee is doing (and putting it in writing), requesting overtime because the project budget will permit it, and offering individuals the opportunity to perform work above their current pay grade. The latter can cause severe managerial headaches if coordination with the line manager does not take place because the individual will expect immediate rewards if he performs well.

The establishment of project administrative requirements is part of project planning. Executives must either work with the project managers at project initiation or act as resource persons. Improper project administrative planning can create a situation that requires:

- A continuous revision and/or establishment of company and/or project policies, procedures, and directives
- A continuous shifting in organizational responsibility and possible unnecessary restructuring
- A need for staff to acquire new knowledge and skills

If these situations occur simultaneously on several projects, there could be confusion throughout the organization. This situation quite often occurs in smaller companies.

4
Effective Project Management in the Small Business Organization

In the previous three chapters, we have described the art and science of project management and the role of the project manager. The acceptance of project management for the large companies has been relatively easy because of the abundance of published literature that identifies the potential pitfalls and problems. But for the smaller organizations, there exist major differences.

- *In small companies, the project manager has to wear multiple hats and may have to act as a project manager and line manager at the same time.* Large companies may have the luxury of a single full-time project manager for the duration of a project. Smaller companies may not be able to afford a full-time project manager and therefore may require that functional managers wear two hats. This poses a problem in that the functional manager may be more dedicated to his own functional unit than to the project and, as can be expected, the project may suffer. There is also the risk that when the line manager also acts as project manager, then the line manager may keep the best resources for his own project. The line manager's project may be a success at the expense of all the other projects for which he must supply resources.

In the ideal situation, the project manager works horizontally and has project dedication whereas the line manager works vertically and has functional (or company) dedication. If the working relationship between the project and functional manager is a good one, then decision-making will be made in a manner that is in the best interest of both the project and the company. Unfortunately, this may be difficult to accomplish in small companies when an individual wears multiple hats.

- *In a small company, the project manager handles multiple projects, each with perhaps a different priority.* In a large company, project managers normally handle only one project at a time. Handling multiple projects becomes a serious problem if the priorities are not close together. For this reason, many small companies avoid the establishing of priorities for fear that the lower-priority activities will never be accomplished.
- *In a small company, the project manager has limited resources.* In a large company, if the project manager is unhappy with resources that are provided, he may have the luxury of returning to the functional manager and either demanding or negotiating for other resources. In a small organization, the resources assigned may be simply the only resources available.
- *In a small company, project managers must generally have a better understanding of interpersonal skills than in a larger company.* This is a necessity because a project manager in the small company has limited resources and must motivate the employees as best he can.
- *In the smaller company, the project manager generally has shorter lines of communications.* In small organizations, the project managers almost always report to a top-level executive, whereas in larger organizations, the project managers can report to any level of management. Small companies tend to have fewer levels of management.
- *Small companies do not have a project office.* Large companies, especially in aerospace or construction, can easily support a project office of 20 to 30 people, whereas in the smaller company the project manager may have to be the entire project office. This implies that project managers in small companies may be required to have more general and specific information about all company activities, policies, and procedures than their counterparts in the larger companies.
- *In a small company, there may be a much greater risk to the total company with the failure of as little as one project.* Large

companies may be able to afford the loss of a multimillion-dollar program whereas the smaller company may be in serious financial trouble. For example, a machine tool company in the Midwest has almost 70 percent of its business generated by one of the big three automotive manufacturers. The risk to the small company arises when one project becomes a large percentage of their business. For this reason, many smaller companies avoid bidding on projects that could place the company in such a delicate position because, with the acceptance of such a project, the company would have to either hire additional resources or give up some of its smaller accounts.

- *In a small company, there might be tighter monetary controls but less sophisticated control techniques.* Because the smaller company incurs greater risk with the failure (or cost overrun) of as little as one project, costs are generally controlled much more tightly and more frequently than in larger companies. However, the smaller companies generally rely upon manual or partially computerized systems whereas the larger organizations rely heavily upon sophisticated software packages. Today, more and more small companies are being forced to completely computerize their cost control procedures so as to adhere to requirements imposed by customers and prime contractors.
- *In a small company, there usually exists more upper-level management interference.* This is expected, because in the small company there is a much greater risk with the failure of a single project. In addition, executives in smaller companies "meddle" more than executives in larger companies, and quite often delegate as little as possible to project managers.
- *Evaluation procedures for individuals are usually easier in a smaller company.* This holds true because the project manager gets to know the people better and, as stated above, there exists a greater need for interpersonal skills on the horizontal line in a smaller company.
- *In a smaller company, project estimating is usually more precise and based upon either history or standards.* This type of planning process is usually manual as opposed to computerized. In addition, functional managers in a small company usually feel morally obligated to live up to their commitments, whereas in the larger companies, much more lip service is given.

These arguments are presented here not necessarily to discourage the small company, but to identify the additional problems that may have to be encountered and resolved. Project management, when implemented correctly, will generate a smoother flow of work and better control of resources, on the horizontal as well as vertical lines.

PART II
ORGANIZING, PLANNING, AND CONTROL

5
Organizing for Project Work

During the past ten years there has been a so-called hidden revolution in the introduction and development of new organizational structures. Management has come to realize that organizations must be dynamic in nature, that is, they must be capable of rapid restructuring should environmental conditions dictate. These environmental factors evolved from the increasing competitiveness of the market, changes in technology, and a requirement for better control of resources for multiproduct firms.

Small businesses generally respond faster to changes in the environment than do larger businesses. This is primarily due to the fact that the smaller businesses may not be able to withstand the risks associated with nonadaptability or slow change. Unfortunately for the small business, the adaptability to a new environment is usually accomplished within the framework of the existing organizational structure. Small and medium sized companies tend to change organizational forms only as a last resort.

Much has been written about how to identify and interpret those signs which indicate that a new organizational form may be necessary. According to Grinnell and Apple, there are five general indications that the traditional structure may not be adequate for managing projects.[10]

---

[10] S.K. Grinnell, and H.P. Apple, "When Two Bosses Are Better Than One," *Machine Design*, 84–87 (January, 1975).

- Management is satisfied with its technical skills, but projects are not meeting time, cost, and other project requirements.
- There is a high commitment to getting project work done, but there are great fluctuations in how well performance specifications are met.
- Highly talented specialists involved in the project feel exploited and misused.
- Particular technical groups or individuals constantly blame each other for failure to meet specifications or delivery dates.
- Projects are on time and to specifications, but groups and individuals are not satisfied with the achievement.

Unfortunately many companies do not realize the necessity for organizational change until it is too late. Management continually looks externally (i.e., to the environment) for solutions to problems rather than internally. A typical example would be that new product costs are continually rising while the product life cycle may be decreasing. Should emphasis be placed on lowering costs or developing new products?

If we assume that an organizational system is composed of both human and nonhuman resources, then we must analyze the sociotechnical subsystem whenever organizational changes are being considered. The social system is represented by the organization's personnel and their group behavior. The technical system includes the technology, materials, and machines necessary to perform the required tasks.

Behavioralists contend that there is no one best structure to meet the challenges of tomorrow's organizations. The structure used, however, must be one that optimizes company performance by achieving a balance between the social and the technical requirements. According to Sadler:[11]

> Since the relative influence of these (sociotechnical) factors change from situation to situation, there can be no such thing as an ideal structure making for effectiveness in organizations of all kinds, or even appropriate to a single type of organization at different stages in its development.

---

[11] Philip Sadler, "Designing an Organizational Structure," *Management International Review*, 11, 6, 1933 (1971).

There are often real and important conflicts between the type of organizational structure called for if the tasks are to be achieved with minimum cost, and the structure that will be required if human beings are to have their needs satisfied. Considerable management judgement is called for when decisions are made as to the allocation of work activities to individuals and groups. High standardization of performance, high manpower utilization and other economic advantages associated with a high level of specialization and routinization of work have to be balanced against the possible effects of extreme specialization in lowering employee attitudes and motivation.

Even the simplest type of organizational change can induce major conflicts. The creation of a new position, the need for better planning, the lengthening or shortening of the span of control, the need for additional technology (knowledge), and centralization or decentralization can result in major changes in the sociotechnical subsystem. Argyris has defined five conditions that form the basis for organizational change requirements:[12]

> These requirements... depend upon (1) continuous and open access between individuals and groups, (2) free, reliable communication, where (3) independence is the foundation for individual and departmental cohesiveness and (4) trust, risk-taking and helping each other is prevalent so that (5) conflict is identified and managed in such a way that the destructive win-lose stances with their accompanying polarization of views are minimized.... Unfortunately these conditions are difficult to create.... There is a tendency toward conformity, mistrust and lack of risk-taking among the peers that results in focusing upon individual survival, requiring the seeking out of the scarce rewards, identifying one's self with a successful venture (be a hero) and being careful to avoid being blamed for or identified with a failure, thereby becoming a "bum." All these adaptive behaviors tend to induce low interpersonal competence and can lead the organization, over the long-run, to become rigid, sticky,

---

[12] Chris Argyris, "Today's Problems with Tomorrow's Organizations," *The Journal of Management Studies,* 31–55 (February, 1967).

and less innovative, resulting in less than effective decisions with even less internal commitment to the decisions on the part of those involved.

Today, organizational restructuring is a compromise between the traditional (classical) and the behavioral schools of thought; management must consider the needs of the individuals as well as the needs of the company. After all, is the organization structured to manage people or to manage work?

There is a wide variety of organizational forms for restructuring management. The exact method depends upon the people in the organization, the company's product lines, and management's philosophy. A poorly restructured organization can sever communication channels that may have taken months or years to cultivate; cause a restructuring of the informal organization, thus creating new power, status, and political positions; and eliminate job satisfaction and motivational factors to such a degree that complete discontent is the result.

Sadler defines three tasks that must be considered because of the varied nature of organizations: control, integration, and external relations.[13] If the company's position is very sensitive to the environment, then management may be more concerned with the control task. For an organization with multiple products, each requiring a high degree of engineering and technology, the integration task can become primary. Finally, for situations with strong labor unions and repetitive tasks, external relations can predominate, especially in strong technological and scientific environments where strict government regulations must be adhered to.

In the sections that follow, a variety of organizational forms will be presented. Obviously, it is an impossible task to describe all possible organizational structures. Each of the organizational forms included is used to describe how the project management organization evolved from the classical theories of management. For each organizational form, advantages and disadvantages are listed in terms of both technology and social systems. Sadler has prepared a six-question checklist that explores a company's tasks, social climate, and relationship to the environment:[14]

[13,14] Philip Sadler, "Designing an Organizational Structure," *Management International Review*, 11, 6, 1933 (1971).

- To what extent does the task of organization call for close control if it is to be performed efficiently?
- What are the needs and attitudes of the people performing the tasks? What are the likely effects of control mechanisms on their motivation and performance?
- What are the natural social groupings with which people identify themselves? To what extent are satisfying social relationships important in relation to motivation and performance?
- What aspect of the organization's activities needs to be closely integrated if the overall task is to be achieved?
- What organizational measures can be developed that will provide an appropriate measure of control and integration of work activities, and at the same time meet the needs of people and provide adequate motivation?
- What environmental changes are likely to affect the future trend of company operations? What organizational measures can be taken to insure that the enterprise responds to these effectively?

The answers to these questions are not easy. For the most part, they are a matter of the judgment exercised by organizational and behavioral managers. These considerations apply to the small as well as the large company.

Organizations are continuously restructured to meet the demands of the environment. Restructuring can produce a major change in the role of individuals both in the formal and informal organization. Many researchers believe that the greatest usefulness of behavioralists lies in their ability to help the informal organization adapt to changes and resolve the resulting conflicts. Unfortunately, behavioralists cannot be totally effective unless they have an input into the formal organization as well. Conflicts arise out of changes in the formal structure. Whatever organizational form is finally selected, formal channels must be developed so that each individual has a clear description of the authority, responsibility, and accountability necessary for the flow of work to proceed.

In the discussion of organizational structures, the following definitions will be used:

- *Authority* is the power granted to individuals (possibly by their position) so that they can make final decisions for others to follow.

- *Responsibility* is the obligation incurred by individuals in their roles in the formal organization in order to perform assignments effectively.
- *Accountability* is the state of being totally answerable for the satisfactory completion of a specific assignment.

Authority and responsibility can be delegated (downward) to lower levels in the organization. Accountability usually rests with the individual.

Yet, even with these clearly definable divisions of authority, responsibility, and accountability, establishing good interface relationships between the project and functional managers can take a great deal of time, especially during the conversion from a traditional to a project organizational form. Trust is the key to success here, and can overcome any problems in authority, responsibility, or accountability. When trust exists, the normal progression in the growth of the project-functional interface bond is as follows:

- Even though a problem exists, both the project and functional managers deny that any problem exists.
- When the problem finally surfaces, each manager blames the other.
- As trust develops, both managers readily admit responsibility for several of the problems.
- The project and functional managers meet face-to-face to work out the problem.
- The project and functional managers begin to formally and informally anticipate the problems that can occur.

Problems with poorly defined authority, responsibility, and accountability are usually more pronounced in larger rather than smaller companies because of the struggle for power and empire-building. In small companies, roles and responsibility are usually well understood by all, without the need for vast amounts of documentation.

For each of the organizational structures described below, advantages and disadvantages are listed. Many of the disadvantages stem from possible conflicts arising from problems in authority, responsibility, and accountability.

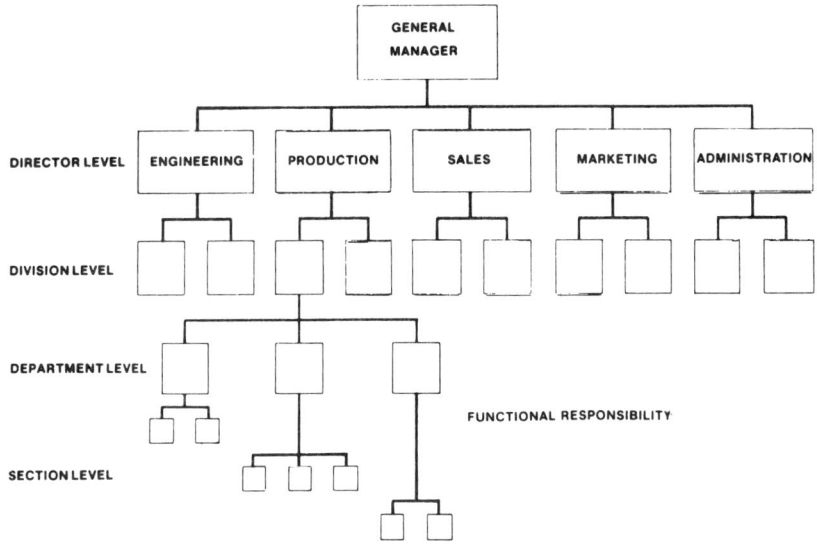

Figure 9. The traditional management structure.

For more than two centuries the traditional management structure has survived. However, recent business developments, such as the rapid rate of change in technology and position in the marketplace, as well as increased stockholder demands, have created strains on the existing organizational forms. Fifty years ago companies could survive with only one or perhaps two product lines. The classical management organization, as shown in Figure 9, was found to be satisfactory for control, and conflicts were at a minimum.[15]

However, as time progressed, companies found that survival depended upon multiple product lines (i.e., diversification) and vigorous integration of technology into the existing organization. As organizations grew and matured, managers found that company activities were not being integrated effectively, and that new conflicts were arising in the well-established formal and informal channels. Managers began searching for more innovative organization forms that would alleviate the integration and conflict problems.

---

[15] Many authors refer to classical organizations as pure functional organizations. This can be seen from Figure 9. Also, note that the department level is below the division level. In some organizations these titles are reversed.

Table 7. Advantages of the Classical/Traditional Organization.

- Provides easier budgeting and cost control
- Provides better technical control
  - Specialists can be grouped to share knowledge and responsibility
  - Personnel can be used on many different projects
  - All projects will benefit from the most advanced technology (better utilization of scarce personnel)
- Provides flexibility in the use of manpower
- Provides broad manpower base to work with
- Provides continuity in the functional disciplines; policies, procedures, and lines of responsibility are more easily defined and understandable
- Readily admits mass production activities within established specifications
- Provides good control over personnel since each employee has one and only one person to report to
- Provides vertical and well-established communication channels
- Allows quick reaction capability, but reaction may be dependent upon the priorities of the functional managers

Before a valid comparison can be made with the newer forms, the advantages and disadvantages of the traditional structure must be shown. Table 7 lists the advantages of the traditional organization. As seen in Figure 9, the general manager has beneath him all of the functional entities necessary to either perform R&D or develop and manufacture a product. All activities are performed within the functional groups and are headed by a department (or, in some cases, a division) head. Each department maintains a strong concentration of technical expertise. Since all of the project must flow through the functional departments, each project can benefit from the most advanced technology, thus making this organizational form well suited for mass production. Functional managers can hire a variety of specialists and provide them with easily definable paths for career progression.

The functional managers maintain absolute control over the budget. They establish their own budgets, upon approval from above, and specify requirements for additional personnel. Because the functional manager has manpower flexibility and a broad base from which to work, most projects are normally completed within cost.

Both the formal and informal organizations are well established, and levels of authority and responsibility are clearly defined. Since each person reports to only one individual, communication channels are well structured. If a structure has this many advantages, then why are we looking for other structures?

For each advantage, there is almost always a corresponding disadvantage. Table 8 lists the disadvantages of the traditional structure. The majority of these are related to the fact that there is no strong central authority or individual responsible for the total project. As a result, integration of activities that cross functional lines becomes a difficult chore and top-level executives must get involved in the daily routine. Conflicts occur as each functional group struggles for power. The strongest functional group dominates the decision-making process. Functional managers tend to favor what is best for their functional group rather than what is best for the project. Many times, ideas will remain functionally oriented with very little regard for ongoing projects. In addition, the decision-making process is slow and tedious.

Because there exists no customer focal point, all communications must be channeled through upper-level management. Upper-level managers then act in a customer relations capacity and refer all complex problems down through the vertical chain of command to the functional managers. The response to the customer's needs therefore becomes a slow and aggravating process because the information must be filtered through several layers of management. If problem-solving and coordination are required to cross functional lines, then additional

Table 8. Disadvantages of the Traditional/Classical Organization.

- No one individual is directly responsible for the total project (i.e., no formal authority; committee solutions)
- The project-oriented emphasis necessary to accomplish the project tasks is not provided
- Coordination becomes complex and additional lead time is required for approval of decisions
- Decisions normally favor the strongest functional groups
- There is no customer focal point
- Response to customer needs is slow
- There is difficulty in pinpointing responsibility; this is the result of little or no direct project reporting, very little project-oriented planning, and no project authority
- Motivation and innovation are decreased
- Ideas tend to be functionally oriented with little regard for ongoing projects

lead time is required for the approval of decisions. All trade-off analysis must be accomplished through committees chaired by upper-level management.

Projects have a tendency to fall behind schedule in the classical organizational structure. Completing all projects and tasks on time, with a high degree of quality and efficient use of available resources, is all but impossible without continuous involvement of top-level management. Incredibly large lead times are required. Functional managers attend to those tasks that provide better benefits to themselves and their subordinates first. Priorities may be dictated by requirements of the informal as well as formal departmental structure.

As companies grew in size, more and more emphasis was placed upon multiple ongoing programs with high-technology requirements. Organizational pitfalls soon appeared, especially in the integration of the flow of work. As management discovered that the critical point in any program is the interface between functional units, the new theories of "interface management" developed.

Because of the interfacing problems, management began searching for innovative methods to coordinate the flow of work between functional units without modification to the existing organizational structure. This coordination was achieved through several integrating mechanisms:[16]

- Rules and procedures
- Planning processes
- Hierarchical referral
- Direct contact

By specifying and documenting management policies and procedures, management attempted to eliminate conflicts between functional departments. Management felt that, even though many of the projects were different, the actions required by the functional personnel were repetitive and predictable. The behavior of the individuals should therefore be easily integrated into the flow of work with min-

---

[16] Jay R. Galbraith, "Matrix Organization Designs," *Business Horizons,* 29–40 (February, 1971). Galbraith defines a fifth mechanism, liaison departments, which will be discussed later in this section.

imum communication necessary between individuals or functional groups.

Another method for reducing conflicts and minimizing the need for communication was through detailed planning. Functional representation would be present at all planning, scheduling, and budget meetings. This method worked best for nonrepetitive tasks and projects.

In the traditional organization, one of the most important responsibilities of upper-level management was the resolution of conflicts through hierarchical referral. The continuous conflicts and struggle for power between the functional units consistently required that upper-level personnel resolve those problems resulting from situations that were either nonroutine or unpredictable and for which no policies or procedures existed.

The fourth method was direct contact and interaction by the functional managers. The rules and procedures, as well as the planning process method, were designed to minimize ongoing communications between functional groups. The quantity of conflicts that executives had to resolve forced key personnel to spend a great percentage of their time as arbitrators, rather than as managers. To alleviate problems of hierarchical referral, upper-level management requested that all conflicts be resolved at the lowest possible levels. This required that functional managers meet face-to-face to resolve conflicts.

In many organizations, these new methods proved ineffective, primarily because there still existed a need for a focal point for the project to insure that all activities would be properly integrated.

When the need for project managers was acknowledged, the next logical question was where in the organization to place them. Executives preferred to keep project managers as low as possible in the organization. After all, if they reported to someone high up, they would have to be paid more and would pose a continuous threat to top management.

The first attempt to resolve this problem was to develop project leaders or coordinators within each functional department, as shown in Figure 10. Section-level personnel were temporarily assigned as project leaders and would return to their former positions at project termination. This is why the term *project leader* is used rather than *project manager;* the word "manager" implies a permanent relationship. This proved effective for coordinating and integrating work

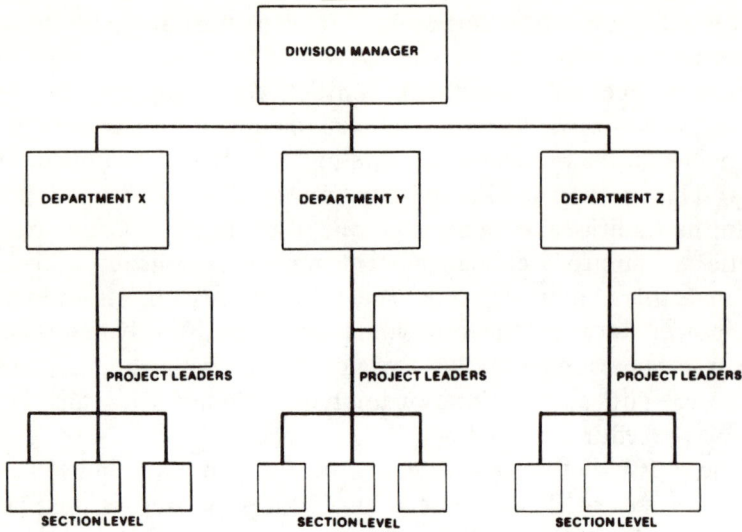

Figure 10. Departmental project management.

within one department, provided that the correct project leader was selected. Some employees considered this position an increase in power and status, and conflicts arose about whether assignments should be based upon experience, seniority, or capability. Several employees wanted the title merely so they could use it on their resumes. Furthermore, the project leaders had almost no authority, and section-level managers refused to take directions from them. Many section managers were afraid that if they did take direction, they were admitting that the project leaders were next in line for the department manager's position.

When the activities required efforts that crossed more than one functional boundary, say two or more sections or departments, conflicts arose. The project leader in one department did not have the authority to coordinate activities in any other department. Furthermore, the creation of this new position caused internal conflicts within each department.

Even though we have criticized this organizational form, it does not mean that it cannot work. Any organizational form (yes, *any* form) will work if the employees want it to work. As an example, a computer manufacturer has a Midwestern division with three departments within it, as in Figure 10, and approximately 14 people per department. When a project comes in, the division manager determines which department will handle most of the work. Let us say that the work load is 60 percent department X, 30 percent department Y, and 10 percent department Z. Since most of the effort is in department X, the project leader is selected from that department. When the project leader goes into the other two departments to get resources, he will almost always get the resources he wants. There are two reasons why this organizational form works here:

- The other department managers know that they may have to supply the project leader on the next activity.
- There are only three functional boundaries or departments involved (i.e., a small organization).

The next step in the evolution of project management was the task force concept. The rationale behind the task force concept was that integration could be achieved if each functional unit placed a representative on the task force. The group could then jointly solve problems as they occurred, provided that budget limitations were still adhered to. Theoretically, decisions could now be made at the lowest possible levels, thus expediting information and reducing, or even eliminating, delay time.

The task force was composed of both part-time and full-time personnel from each department involved. Daily meetings were held to review activities and discuss potential problems. Functional managers soon found that their task force employees were spending more time in unproductive meetings than at functional activities. In addition, the nature of the task force position caused many individuals to shift membership within the informal organization. Many functional managers then placed nonqualified and inexperienced individuals on task forces. The result was that the group soon became ineffective because they either did not have the information necessary to make the decisions, or lacked the authority (delegated by the functional managers) to allocate resources and assign work.

Development of the task force concept was a giant step toward conflict resolution: Work was being accomplished on time, schedules were being maintained, and costs were usually within the budget. But integration and coordination were still problems because there were no specified authority relationships or individuals to oversee the entire project through completion. Many attempts were made to overcome this by placing various people in charge of the task force; functional managers, division heads, and even upper-level management had opportunities to direct task forces. However, without formal project authority relationships, task force members maintained loyalty to their functional organizations, and, when conflicts came about between the project and functional organization, the project always suffered.

Although the task force concept was a step in the right direction, the disadvantages strongly outweighed the advantages. A strength of the approach was that it could be established very rapidly and with very little paperwork. Integration, however, was complicated; work flow was difficult to control; and functional support was difficult to obtain, because it was almost always strictly controlled by the functional manager. In addition, task forces were found to be grossly ineffective on long-range projects.

The next step in the evolution of work integration was the establishment of liaison departments, particularly in engineering divisions that performed multiple projects involving a high level of technology (see Figure 11). The purpose of the liaison department was to handle

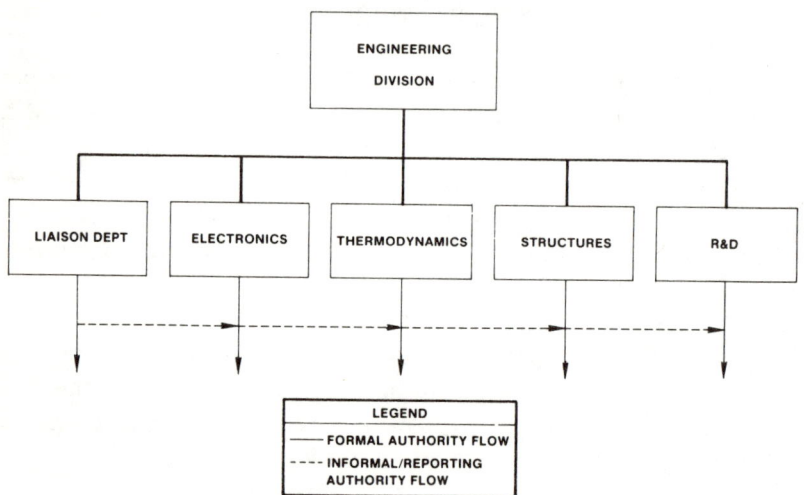

Figure 11. Engineering division with liaison department.

transactions between functional units within the division. The liaison personnel received their authority through the division head. The liaison department did not actually resolve conflicts, however; their prime function was to assure that all departments would work toward the same requirements and goals. Liaison departments are still in existence in many large companies and typically handle engineering change and design problems.

Unfortunately, the liaison department is simply a scale-up of the project coordinator within the department. The authority given to the liaison department extends only to the outer boundaries of the division. If a conflict came about between the manufacturing and engineering divisions, for example, hierarchical referral would still be needed for resolution. Today, liaison departments are synonymous with project engineering and systems engineering departments.

It soon became obvious that control of a project must be given to personnel whose first loyalty is directed toward the completion of the project. To do this, the project management position must be separated from any controlling influence of the functional managers. Figure 12 shows a typical line-staff organization.

Two possible situations can exist with this form of line-staff project control. In the first situation, the project manager serves only as the focal point for activity control, that is, a center for information. The prime responsibility of the project manager is to keep the division manager informed of the status of the project and to harass or attempt to influence managers into completing activities on time. As stated

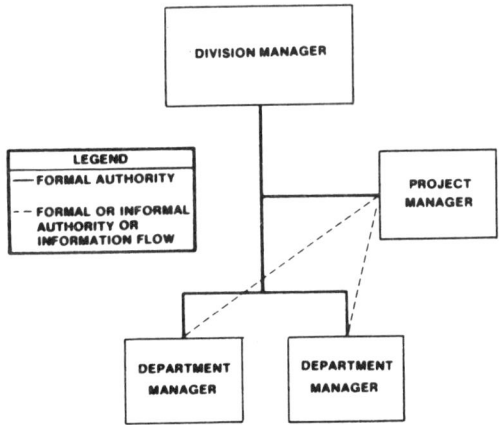

Figure 12. Life-staff organization.

by Galbraith, "since these men had no formal authority, they had to resort to their technical competence and their interpersonal skills in order to be effective."[17]

The project manager maintained monitoring authority only, despite the fact that both he and the functional manager reported to the same individual. Both work assignments and merit reviews were made by the functional managers. Department managers refused to take direction from the project managers because this would seem like an admission that the project manager was next in line to be the division manager.

The amount of authority given to the project manager posed serious problems. Almost all upper-level and division managers were from the classical management schools and therefore maintained serious reservations about how much authority to relinquish. Many of these managers considered it a demotion if they had to give up any of their long-established powers.

The second situation involves the amount of authority given to the project manager. The project manager (using the authority vested in him by the division manager) can assign work to individuals in the functional organizations. The functional manager, however, still maintains the authority to perform merit reviews, but cannot enforce both professional and organizational standards in the completion of an activity. The individual performing the work is now caught in a web of authority relationships, and additional conflicts develop because functional managers are forced to share their authority with the project manager.

Although this second situation did occur during the early stages of matrix project management, it did not last because:

- Upper-level management was not ready to cope with the problems arising from shared authority.
- Upper-level management was reluctant to relinquish any of their power and authority to project managers.
- Line-staff project managers who reported to a division head did not have any authority or control over those portions of a project in other divisions; that is, the project manager in the engineering division could not direct activities in the manufacturing division.

---

[17] Jay R. Galbraith, "Matrix Organization Designs," *Business Horizons*, 29–40, (February, 1971).

The pure project organization, as shown in Figure 13, is similar to departmental project management and develops as a division within a division. As long as there exists a continuous flow of projects, work becomes stable and conflicts are at a minimum. The major advantage of this organizational flow is that one individual, the program manager, maintains complete authority over the entire project. Not only does he assign work, but he also conducts merit reviews. Because each individual reports to only one person, strong communication channels develop and result in a very rapid reaction time.

Long lead times became a thing of the past. Trade-off studies could be conducted as fast as time would permit without having to look at the impact on other projects (unless, of course, identical facilities or equipment were required). Functional managers were able to maintain qualified staffs for new-product development without sharing personnel with other programs and projects.

The responsibilities attributed to the project manager were entirely new. First of all, his authority was now granted by the vice-president and general manager. The program manager handled all conflicts, both those within his organization and those involving other projects. Interface management was conducted at the program manager level. Upper-level management was now able to spend more time on executive decision-making rather than conflict arbitration.

The major disadvantage with the pure project form is the cost of maintaining the organization. There is no chance for sharing an indi-

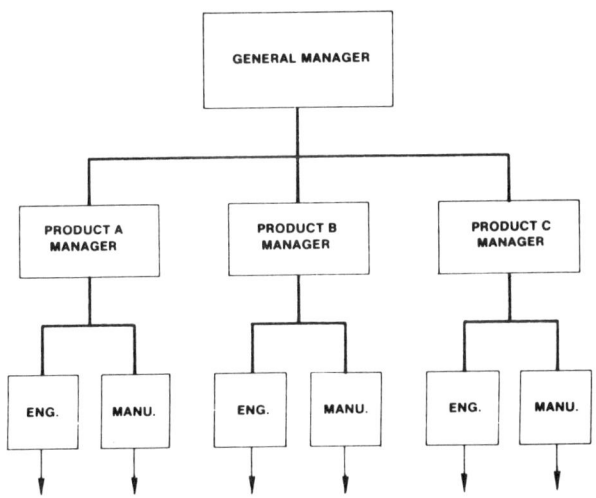

Figure 13. Pure product structure.

vidual with another project in order to reduce costs. Personnel are usually attached to these projects long after they are needed, because once an employee is given up, the product manager might never be able to get him back. Motivating personnel becomes a problem. At project completion, functional personnel do not have a "home" to return to. Many organizations place these individuals into an overhead labor pool from which selection can be made during new-project development. People who remain in the labor pool for a certain period of time may be laid off indefinitely. As each project comes to a close, people become uneasy and often strive to prove their worth to the company by over-achieving, a condition that is only temporary. It is very difficult for management to convince key functional personnel that they do, in fact, have career opportunities in this type of organization.

In pure functional structures, technologies are well developed but project schedules often fall behind. In the pure project structure, the fast reaction time keeps activities on schedule, but technology suffers because without strong functional groups, which maintain interactive technical communication, the company's outlook for meeting the competition may be severely hampered. The engineering department for one project might not communicate with their counterparts on other projects, and duplication of efforts can easily occur.

The last major disadvantage of this organizational form is the control of facilities and equipment. The most common conflict occurs

Table 9. Advantages of the Product Organizational Form.

- This form provides complete line authority over the project (i.e., strong control through a single project authority)
- The project participants work directly for the project manager; unprofitable product lines are more easily identified and can be eliminated
- There are strong communications channels
- Expertise can be maintained on a given project without sharing of key personnel
- Very rapid reaction time is provided
- Personnel demonstrate loyalty to the project; better morale with product identification
- A focal point can be developed for out-of-company customer relations
- There is flexibility in determining time (schedule), cost, and performance trade-offs
- Interface management becomes easier as unit size is decreased
- Upper-level management maintains more free time for executive decision-making

Table 10. Disadvantages of the Product Organizational Form.

- Cost of maintaining this form in a multiproduct company would be prohibitive due to duplication of effort, facilities, and personnel; inefficient usage
- There exists a tendency to retain personnel on a project long after they are needed. Upper-level management must balance work loads as projects start up and are phased out
- Technology suffers because, without strong functional groups, outlook of the future to improve company's capabilities for new programs would be hampered (i.e., no perpetuation of technology)
- Control of functional (i.e., organizational) specialists requires top-level coordination
- There is a lack of opportunities for technical interchange between projects
- There is a lack of career continuity and opportunities for project personnel

when two projects require use of the same piece of equipment or facilities at the same time. Hierarchical referral is required to alleviate this problem. Upper-level management can assign priorities to these projects. This is normally accomplished by defining certain projects as strategic, tactical, or operational, the same definitions usually given to plans.

Table 9 summarizes the advantages of this organizational form and Table 10 lists the disadvantages.

The organizational form of the future is the matrix structure. The matrix organizational form is an attempt to combine the advantages of the pure functional (traditional) structure and the product organizational structure and is ideally suited for companies, such as construction, that are "project driven." Figure 14 shows a typical matrix structure. Each project manager reports directly to the vice-president and general manager. Since each project represents a potential profit center, the power and authority used by the project manager come directly from the general manager. The project manager has total responsibility and accountability for project success. The functional departments, on the other hand, have functional responsibility to maintain technical excellence on the project. Each functional unit is headed by a department manager whose prime responsibility is to insure that a unified technical base is maintained and that all available information can be exchanged for each project. Department managers must also keep their people aware of the latest technical accomplishments in the industry.

66 ORGANIZING, PLANNING, AND CONTROL

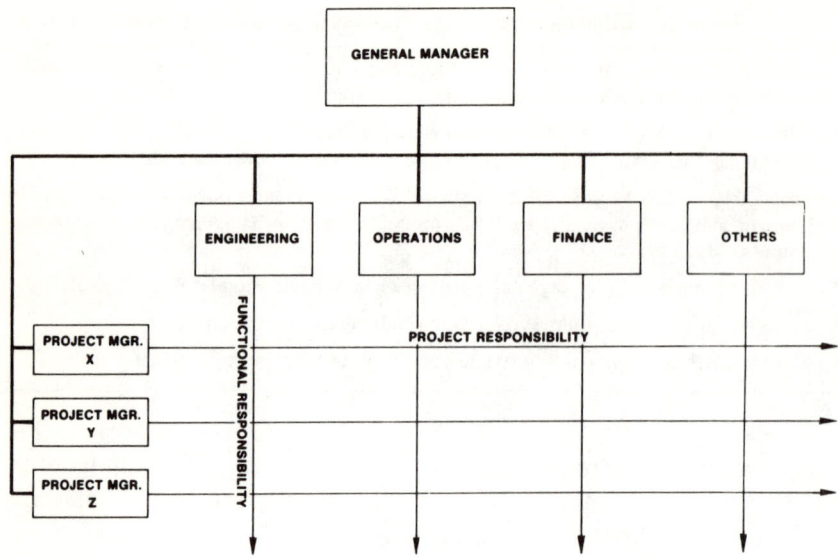

Figure 14. Pure matrix structure.

Certain ground rules exist for matrix development:

- For large projects, participants must spend full time on the project; this insures a degree of loyalty.
- Horizontal as well as vertical channels must exist for making commitments.
- There must be a quick and effective method for conflict resolution.
- There must be communication channels and free access between managers.
- All managers must have an input into the planning process.
- Both horizontally and vertically oriented managers must be willing to negotiate for resources.
- The horizontal line must be permitted to operate as a separate entity except for administrative purposes.

These ground rules simply state some of the ideal conditions that matrix structures should possess. Each ground rule brings with it advantages and disadvantages.

Before the advantages and disadvantages of this structure are described, the organization concepts must be introduced. The basis for the matrix approach is the attempt to create synergism through shared responsibility between project and functional management. Yet this is easier said than done. The following questions must be answered before successful operations of a matrix structure can be achieved.

- If each functional unit is responsible for one aspect of a project, and other parts are conducted elsewhere (possibly subcontracted to other companies), how can a synergistic environment be created?
- Who decides what element of a project is more important?
- How can a functional unit (operating in a vertical structure) answer questions and achieve project goals and objectives that are compatible with other projects?

The answers to these questions depend upon the mutual understanding between the project and functional managers. Since both individuals maintain some degree of authority, responsibility, and accountability on each project, they must continuously negotiate. Unfortunately, the program manager might only consider what is best for his project (disregarding all others), whereas the functional manager might consider the organization as being more important than each project.

In the matrix,

- There should be no disruption due to dual accountability.
- A difference in judgment should not delay work in progress.

In order to get the job done, project managers sometimes need adequate organizational status and authority. A corporate executive contends that the organizational chart shown in Figure 14 can be modified to show that the project managers have adequate organizational authority by placing the department manager boxes at the tips of the functional arrowheads. The executive further contends that, with this approach, the project managers appear to be higher in the organization than their departmental counterparts but are actually equal in status. Executives who prefer this method must exercise due caution because the line and project managers may not feel that there still exists an equality in the balance of power.

Problem-solving in this type of environment is a fragmented and diffused process. The project manager acts as a unifying agent for project control of resources and technology. He must maintain open channels of communication between himself and functional units as well as between functional units themselves so as to prevent suboptimization of individual projects. The problems of routine administration can and do become a cost-effective requirement.

In many situations, functional managers have the power and means of making a project manager look good, provided that they can be motivated enough to think in terms of what is best for the project. Unfortunately, this is not always accomplished. As stated by Mantell:[18]

> There exists an inevitable tendency for hierarchically arrayed units to seek solutions and to identify problems in terms of scope of duties of particular units rather than looking beyond them. This phenomenon exists without regard for the competence of the executive concerned. It comes about because of authority delegation and functionalism.

This concept of "tunnel vision" can exist at all levels of management.

The project environment and functional environment cannot be separated; they must interact. The location of the project and functional unit interface is the focal point for all activities.

The functional manager controls departmental resources (i.e., people). This poses a problem in that, although the project manager maintains the maximum control (through the line managers) over all resources including cost and personnel, the functional manager must provide staff for the project's requirements. It is therefore inevitable that conflicts occur between functional and project managers.

> These conflicts revolve about items such as project priority, manpower costs, and the assignment of functional personnel to the project manager. Each project manager will, of course, want the

---

[18] Leroy H. Mantell, "The Systems Approach and Good Management," *Business Horizons* (October, 1972).

ORGANIZING FOR PROJECT WORK 69

best functional operators assigned to his program. In addition to these problems, the accountability for profit and loss is much more difficult in a matrix organization than in a project organization. Project managers have a tendency to blame overruns on functional managers, stating that the cost of the function was excessive. Whereas functional managers have a tendency to blame excessive costs on project managers with the argument that there were too many changes, more work required than defined initially and other such arguments.[19]

The individual placed at the interface position has two bosses: He must take direction from both the project manager and the functional manager. The merit review and hiring and firing responsibilities still rest with the department manager. Merit reviews are normally made by the functional manager after discussions with the program manager. The functional manager may not have the time necessary to continuously measure the progress of this individual. He must rely upon the word of the program manager for merit review and promotion. The interface members generally give loyalty to the person signing their merit reviews. This poses a problem, especially if conflicting orders are given by the functional and project managers. The simplest solution is for the individual at the interface to ask the functional and project managers to communicate with each other to resolve the problem. This type of situation poses a problem for project managers:

- How does a project manager motivate an individual working on a project (either part-time or full-time) so that his loyalties are with the project?
- How does a project manager convince an individual to perform work according to project direction and specifications when these requests may be in conflict with department policy, especially if the individual feels that his functional boss may not look upon him too favorably?

There are many advantages to matrix structures, as shown in Table 11. Functional units exist primarily as support for a project. Because

---

[19]William P. Killian, "Project Management – Future Organizational Concepts," *Marquette Business Review*, 2, 90–107 (1971).

70 ORGANIZING, PLANNING, AND CONTROL

Table 11. Advantages of a Pure Matrix Organizational Form.

- The project manager maintains maximum project control over all resources, including cost and personnel (through the line managers)
- Policies and procedures can be set up independently for each project provided that they do not contradict company policies and procedures
- The project manager has the authority to commit company resources provided that scheduling does not cause conflicts with other projects
- Rapid responses are possible to change conflict resolution and project needs
- The functional organizations exist primarily as support for the project
- Each person has a "home" after project completion. People are more susceptible to motivation and end-item identification. Each person can be shown a career path
- Because key people can be shared, program cost is minimized. People can work on a variety of problems (i.e., better people control)
- A strong technical base can be developed and much more time can be devoted to complex problem-solving. Knowledge is available to all projects on an equal basis
- Conflicts are minimal, and those requiring hierarchical referral are more easily resolved
- There is better balance between time, cost, and performance

of this, key people can be shared and costs can be minimized. People can be assigned to a variety of challenging problems. Each person, therefore, has a "home" after project completion. Each person can be shown a career path in the company. People are more susceptible to motivation and end-item identification. Functional managers find it easier to develop and maintain a strong technical base and can therefore spend more time on complex problem-solving. Knowledge can be shared for all projects.

The matrix structure can provide rapid response to changes, conflicts, and other project needs. Conflicts are normally minimal, but those requiring resolution are easily resolved using hierarchical referral.

This rapid response is a result of the project manager's authority to commit company resources, provided that scheduling conflicts with other projects can be eliminated. Furthermore, the project manager has the authority to independently establish his own project policies and procedures, provided that they do not conflict with company policies. This can do away with much red tape and permits a better balance between time, cost, and performance.

The matrix structure provides us with the best of two worlds: the traditional structure and the matrix structure. The advantages of the matrix structure eliminate almost all of the disadvantages of the traditional structure. The word "matrix" often brings fear into the hearts of executives because it implies radical change, or at least they think it does. If we take a close look at Figure 14, we can see that the traditional structure is still there. The matrix is simply horizontal lines superimposed over the traditional structure. The horizontal lines will come and go as projects start up and terminate, but the traditional structure will remain forever.

Matrix structures are not without their disadvantages, as shown in Table 12. The main disadvantage of the matrix organization is that more administrative personnel are needed to develop policies and procedures, and therefore both direct and indirect administrative costs will increase. Each project organization operates independently. This poses a problem in that duplication of effort can easily occur; for example, two projects might be developing the same cost-accounting procedure or functional personnel may be doing similar R&D efforts on different projects. Both vertical and horizontal communication is a must in the project matrix organization.

Functional managers are only human and therefore may be biased according to their own set of priorities. Project managers, on the other hand, must realize that their project is not the only one, and that a proper balance is needed; this includes a balance of power between functional and project units as well as a proper balance between time, cost, and performance.

Table 12. Disadvantages of a Pure Matrix Organizational Form.

- Company-wide, the organizational structure is not cost effective because more people than necessary are required, primarily administrative
- Each project organization operates independently. Care must be taken that duplication of efforts does not occur
- More effort and time are needed initially to define policies and procedures
- Functional managers may be biased according to their own set of priorities
- Although rapid response time is possible for individual problem resolution, matrix response time is slow, especially on fast-moving projects
- Balance of power between functional and project organizations must be watched
- Balance of time, cost, and performance must be monitored

One of the advantages of the matrix is a rapid response time for problem resolution. This rapid response generally applies to slow-moving projects where problems occur within each functional unit. On fast-moving projects, the reaction time can become quite slow, especially if the problem spans more than one functional unit.

The matrix structure therefore becomes a compromise in an attempt to obtain the best of two worlds. In pure product management, technology suffered because there did not exist any single group for planning and integration. In the pure functional organization, time and schedule are sacrificed. Matrix project management is an attempt to obtain maximum technology and performance in a cost-effective manner and within time and schedule constraints.

We should note that with proper executive-level planning and control, all of the disadvantages can be eliminated. This is the only organizational form where this is possible. However, care must be taken with regard to the first disadvantage listed in Table 12. There is a natural tendency when going to a matrix to create more positions in executive management than are actually necessary in order to get better control, and this will drive up the overhead rates. This may be true in some companies, but there is a point where the matrix will become mature and fewer people will be required at the top levels of management. When executives wish to reduce cost, they normally begin *at the top* by combining positions when slots become vacant. This is a natural fallout of having mature project and line managers, and with less top-level interference.

Previously, we identified the necessity for the project manager to be able to establish his own policies, procedures, rules, and guidelines. Obviously, with personnel reporting in two directions and to multiple managers, conflicts over administration can easily occur. According to Shannon:[20]

> When operating under a matrix management approach, it is obviously extremely important that the authority and responsibility of each manager be clearly defined, understood and accepted by both functional and program people. These relationships need to be

---

[20] Robert Shannon, "Matrix Management Structures," *Industrial Engineering*, 27-28 (March, 1972). Published and copyright 1972 by the American Institute of Industrial Engineers, Inc., Norcross, Georgia 30092.

spelled out in writing. It is essential that in the various operating policies, the specific authority of the program manager be clearly defined in terms of program direction, and that the authority of the functional executive be defined in terms of operational direction.

Most practitioners consider the matrix to be a two-dimensional system where each project represents a potential profit center and each functional department represents a cost center. (This interpretation can also create conflict because functional departments may feel that they no longer have an input into corporate profits.) For large corporations with multiple divisions, the matrix is no longer two-dimensional, but multidimensional.

William C. Goggin has described geographical area and space and time as the third and fourth dimension of the Dow Corning Matrix:[21]

> Geographical areas — business development varied widely from area to area, and the profit-center and cost-center dimensions could not be carried out everywhere in the same manner. . . . Dow Corning area organizations are patterned after our major U.S. organizations. Although somewhat autonomous in their operation, they subscribe to the overall corporate objectives, operating guidelines, and planning criteria. During the annual planning cycle, for example, there is a mutual exchange of sales, expense, and profit projections between the functional and business managers headquartered in the United States and the are managers around the world.
>
> Space and time — a fourth dimension of the organization denotes fluidity and movement through time. . . . The multi-dimensional organization is far from rigid; it is constantly changing. Unlike centralized or decentralized systems that are too often rooted deep in the past, the multi-dimensional organization is geared toward the future. Long-term planning is an inherent part of its operation.

Goggin then went on to describe the advantages that Dow Corning expected to gain from the multidimensional organization:

---

[21] William C. Goggin, "How the Multidimensional Structure Works at Dow Corning," *Harvard Business Review*, 56-57 (January–February, 1974). Copyright © 1973 by the President and Fellows of Harvard College; all rights reserved.

- Higher profit generation even in an industry (silicones) price-squeezed by competition. (Much of our favorable profit picture seems due to a better overall understanding and practice of expense controls throughout the company.)
- Increased competitive ability based on technological innovation and product quality without a sacrifice in profitability
- Sound, fast decision-making at all levels in the organization, facilitated by stratified but open channels of communications, and by a totally participative working environment
- A healthy and effective balance of authority among the businesses, functions, and areas
- Progress in developing short- and long-range planning with the support of all employees
- Resource allocations that are proportional to expected results
- More stimulating and effective on-the-job training
- Accountability that is more closely related to responsibility and authority
- Results that are visible and measurable
- More top-management time for long-range planning and less need to become involved in day-to-day operations

Obviously, the matrix structure is the most complex of all organizational forms. Careful consideration must be given as to where and how the matrix organization fits into the total organization. Grinnell and Apple define four situations where it is most practical to consider a matrix:[22]

- When complex, short-run products are the organization's primary output
- When a complicated design calls for both innovation and timely completion
- When several kinds of sophisticated skills are needed in designing, building, and testing the products — skills then need constant updating and development
- When a rapidly changing marketplace calls for significant changes in products, perhaps between the time they are conceived and delivered

---

[22] S.K. Grinnell and H.P. Apple, "When Two Bosses Are Better Than One," *Machine Design*, 84–87 (January, 1975).

The matrix can take many forms, but there are basically three common varieties. Each type represents a different degree of authority attributed to the program manager and indirectly identifies the relative size of the company. As an example, in the matrix of Figure 14, all program managers report directly to the general manager. This type of arrangement works best for small companies that have a minimum number of projects, and assumes that the general manager has sufficient time to coordinate activities between the project managers. In this type of arrangement, all conflicts between projects are hierarchically referred to the general manager for resolution.

As companies grew in size and in number of projects, the general manager found it increasingly difficult to act as the focal point for all projects. A new position was created, that of director of programs or manager of programs or projects. This is shown in Figure 15. The director of programs was responsible for all program management. This freed the general manager from the daily routine of having to monitor all programs himself.

Beck has elaborated on the basic role of this new position, the manager of project managers (M.P.M.):[23]

> The M.P.M. is a project manager, a people manager, a change manager and a systems manager. In general, one role cannot be considered more important than the other. The M.P.M. has responsibilities for managing the projects, directing and leading people and the project management effort, and for planning for change in the operation. The Manager of Project Managers is a liaison between the Project Management Department and upper management as well as functional department management and acts as a systems manager when serving as a liaison.

Executives contend that an effective span of control is five to seven people. Does this apply to the director of project management as well? Consider a company that has 15 projects going on at once. Three are over $5 million, seven are between $1 and $3 million, and five projects are under $700,000. Each project has a full-time

---
[23] Dale R. Beck, "The Role of the Manager of Project Managers," *Proceedings of the Ninth Annual International Seminar/Symposium on Project Management,* October 24-26, 1977, Chicago, Illinois, p. 141.

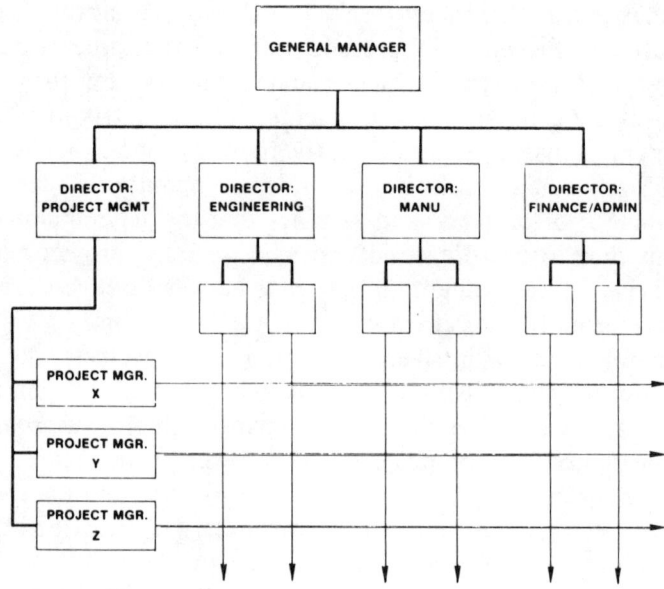

Figure 15. Development of a director of project management.

project manager. Can all 15 project managers report to the same person? The company solved this problem by creating a deputy director of project management. All projects over $1 million reported to the director and all projects under $1 million went to the deputy director. The director's rationale soon fell by the wayside when he found that the more severe problems that were occupying his time were occurring on the smaller dollar-volume projects. If the project manager is actually a general manager, then the director of project management should be able to supervise effectively more than seven project managers. The desired span of control, of course, will vary from company to company and must take into account:

- The demands imposed on the organization by task complexity
- Available technology
- The external environment
- The needs of the organizational membership

These variables influence the internal functioning of the company. Executives must realize that there is no one best way to organize under all conditions. This includes span of control.

As companies expand, it is inevitable that new and more complex conflicts arise. The control of the engineering functions poses such a problem.

- Should the project manager have ultimate responsibility for the engineering functions of a project, or should there be a deputy project manager who reports to the director of engineering and controls all technical activity?

Although there are pros and cons for both arrangements, the problem resolved itself in the company mentioned above when the projects grew so large that the project manager became unable to handle both the project management and the project engineering functions. Therefore, as shown in Figure 16, a chief project engineer was assigned to each project as deputy project manager, but remained functionally

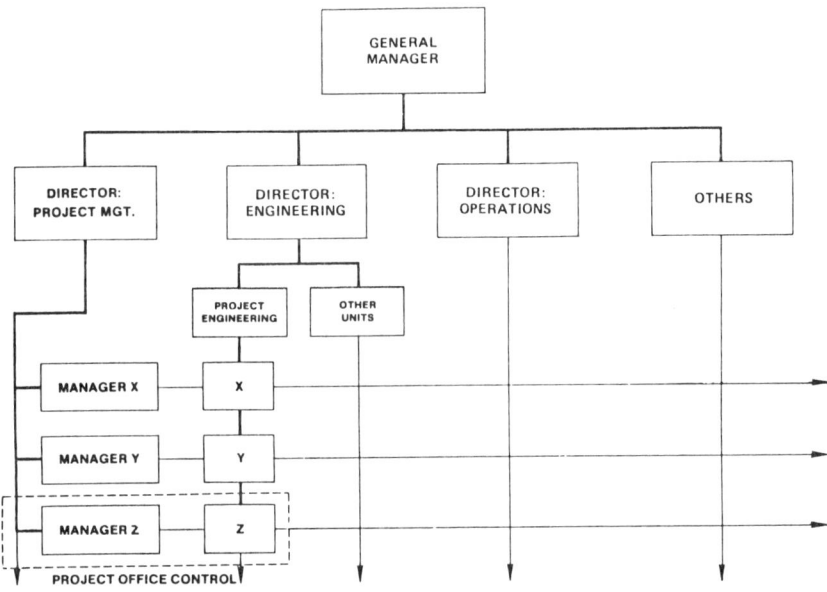

Figure 16. Placing project engineering in the project office.

assigned to the director of engineering. The project manager was now responsible for time and cost considerations, whereas the project engineer was concerned with technical performance. The project engineer can be either "solid" vertically and "dashed" horizontally, or vice versa. There are also situations where the project engineer may be "solid" in both directions. This decision usually rests with the director of engineering. Of course, in a project where the project engineer would be needed on a part-time basis only, he would then be "solid" vertically and "dashed" horizontally.

This subdivision of functions is necessary in order to control large projects adequately. However, for small R&D projects, say $100,000 or less, it is quite common for an engineer to serve as the project manager as well as the project engineer. Here, the project manager must have technical expertise, not merely understanding. Furthermore, this individual can still be attached to a functional engineering support unit other than project engineering. As an example, the mechanical engineering department receives a government contract for $75,000 to perform tests on a new material. The proposal is written by an engineer attached to this department. When the contract is awarded, this individual, although not in the project engineering department, can fulfill the role of project manager and project engineer while still reporting to the manager of the mechanical engineering department. This arrangement works best (and is cost-effective) for short-duration projects that cross a minimum number of functional units.

6
Problem Areas in Organizing the Small Business for Project Management

Project management has matured as an outgrowth of the need to develop and produce complex and/or large projects in the shortest possible time, within anticipated cost, with required reliability and performance, and (when applicable) to realize a profit. Based upon the realization that modern organizations have become so complex that traditional organizational structures and relationships no longer allow for effective management, how can a company determine which organizational form is best, especially since some projects last for only a few weeks or months while others may take years?

To answer such a question, we must first determine whether or not the necessary characteristics exist for warranting a project management organizational form. Generally speaking, the project management approach can be effectively applied to a one-time undertaking that is:[24]

- Definable in terms of a specific goal
- Infrequent, unique, or unfamiliar to the present organization
- Complex with respect to interdependence of detailed tasks
- Critical to the company

---

[24] John M. Stewart, "Making Project Management Work," *Business Horizons,* 54 (Fall, 1965).

Once a group of tasks is selected and considered to be a project, the next step is to define the kinds of projects, described in Chapter 2. These include individual, staff, special, and matrix or aggregate projects.

Unfortunately, many companies do not have a clear definition of what a project is. As a result, large project teams are often constructed for small projects when they could be handled more quickly and effectively by some other structural form. All structural forms have their advantages and disadvantages, but the project management approach, even with its disadvantages, appears to be the best possible alternative.

Four fundamental parameters must be analyzed when implementation of a project organizational form is considered:

- Integrating devices
- Authority structure
- Influence distribution
- Information system

Project management is a means of integrating all company efforts, especially research and development, by selecting an appropriate organizational form. Two questions arise when we think of designing the organization to facilitate the work of the integrators:[25]

- Is it better to establish a formal integration department, or simply to set up integrating positions independent of one another?
- If individual integrating positions are set up, how should they be related to the larger structure?

Informal integration works best if, and only if, effective collaboration can be achieved between conflicting units. Without any clearly defined authority, the role of the integrator is simply to act as an exchange medium across the interface of two functional units. As the size of the organization increases, formal integration positions

---

[25] William P. Killian, "Project Management – Future Organizational Concepts," *Marquette Business Review*, 2, 90–107 (1971).

must exist, especially in situations where intense conflict can occur (e.g., research and development).

Not all organizations need a pure matrix structure to achieve this integration. Many problems can be solved simply through the scalar chain of command, depending upon the size of the organization and the nature of the project. The actual size of organizations needed to achieve project control can vary from one person to several thousand. The organizational structure needed for effective project control is governed by the desires of top management and project circumstances.

Unfortunately, integration and specialization appear to be diametrically opposed. As described by Davis:[26]

> When organization is considered synonymous with structure, the dual needs of specialization and coordination are seen as inversely related, as opposite ends of a single variable, as the horns of a dilemma. Most managers speak of this dilemma in terms of the centralization-decentralization variable. Formulated in this manner, greater specialization leads to more difficulty in coordinating the differentiated units. This is why the (de)centralization pendulum is always swinging, and no ideal point can be found at which it can come to rest.
>
> The division of labor in a hierarchical pyramid means that specialization must be defined either by function, by product, or by area. Firms must select one of these dimensions as primary and then subdivide the other two into subordinate units further down the pyramid. The appropriate choice for primary, secondary and tertiary dimensions is based largely upon the strategic needs of the enterprise.

Top management must decide upon the authority structure that will control the integration mechanism. The authority structure can range from pure functional authority (traditional management), to product authority (product management), and finally to dual authority (matrix management). From a management point of view, organizational forms are often selected based upon how much authority top management wishes to delegate or surrender.

---

[26] Stanley M. Davis, "Two Models of Organization: Unity of Command Versus Balance of Power," *Sloan Management Review*, 30 (Fall, 1975). Reprinted by permission.

Integration of activities across functional boundaries can also be accomplished by influence. Influence includes such factors as participation in budget planning and approval, design changes, location and size of offices, and salaries. Influence can also cut administrative red tape and develop a much more unified informal organization.

Information systems also play an important role. Previously we stated that one of the advantages of several project management structures is the ability to make both rapid and timely decisions with almost immediate response to environmental changes. Information systems are designed to get the right information to the right person at the right time in a cost-effective manner. Organizational functions must facilitate the flow of information through the management network.

Galbraith has described additional factors that can influence organizational selection. These factors are:[27]

- Diversity of product lines
- Rate of change of the product lines
- Interdependencies among subunits
- Level of technology
- Presence of economies of scale
- Organizational size

A diversity of product lines requires both top-level and functional managers to maintain knowledge in all areas. Diversity makes it more difficult for managers to make realistic estimates concerning resource allocations and the control of time, cost, schedules, and technology. The systems approach to management requires that sufficient information and alternatives be available so that effective trade-offs can be established. For diversity in a high-technology environment the organizational choice might, in fact, be a trade-off between the flow of work and the flow of information. Diversity tends toward strong product authority and control.

Many functional organizations consider themselves companies within a company and pride themselves on their independence. This

---

[27] Jay R. Galbraith, "Matrix Organization Designs," *Business Horizons,* 29–40 (February, 1971).

poses a severe problem in trying to develop a synergistic atmosphere. Successful project management requires that functional units recognize the interdependence that must exist in order for technology to be shared and schedule dates to be met. Interdependency is also required in order to develop strong communications channels as well as coordination.

The use of new technologies poses a serious problem in that technical expertise must be established in all specialities, including engineering, production, material control, and safety. Maintaining technical expertise works best in strong functional disciplines, provided the information is not purchased outside the organization. The main problem, however, is how to communicate this expertise across functional lines. Independent R&D units can be established as opposed to integrating R&D into each functional department's routine efforts. Organizational control requirements are much more difficult in high-technology industries with ongoing research and development than with pure production groups.

The economies of scale and size can also affect organizational selection. The economies of scale are most often controlled by the amount of physical resources that a company has available. For example, a company with limited facilities and resources might find it impossible to compete with other companies on production or competitive bidding for larger dollar-volume products. Such a company must rely heavily on maintaining multiple projects (or products), each of low cost or volume, whereas a larger organization may need only three or four projects large enough to sustain the organization. The larger the economies of scale, the more the organization tends to favor pure functional management.

The size of the organization is important in that it can limit the amount of technical expertise in the economies of scale. While size may have little effect on the organizational structure, it does have a severe impact on the economies of scale. Small companies, for example, cannot maintain large specialist staffs and therefore incur a larger cost for lost specialization and lost economies of scale.

The four factors described previously for organizational form selections together with the six alternatives of Galbraith can be regarded as universal in nature. Beyond these universal factors, we must look at the company in terms of its product, business base, and personnel. Goodman has defined a set of subfactors related to R&D groups:[28]

- Clear location of responsibility
- Ease and accuracy of communication
- Effective cost control
- Ability to provide good technical supervision
- Flexibility of staffing
- Importance to the company
- Quick reaction capability to sudden changes in the project
- Complexity of the project
- Size of the project with relation to other work in-house
- Form desired by customer
- Ability to provide a clear path for individual promotion

Goodman asked various managers to select from the above list and rank the factors from most important to least important in terms of how they would be considered in designing an organization. Both general management and project management personnel were queried. With one exception — the flexibility of staffing — the responses from both groups correlated to a coefficient of 0.811. Clear location of responsibility was seen as the most important factor, and a path for promotion the least important.

Middleton conducted a mail survey to aerospace firms in an attempt to determine how well the companies using project management met their objectives. Forty-seven responses were received. Tables 13 and 14 identify the results. Middleton stated: "In evaluating the results of the survey, it appears that a company taking the project organization approach can be reasonably certain that it will improve controls and customer (out-of-company) relations, but internal operations will be more complex."[29]

The way in which a company operates its project organization is bound to affect the organization, both during the operation of the project and after the project has been completed and personnel disbanded. The overall effects on the company must be looked at

---

[28] Richard A. Goodman, "Organizational Reference in Research and Development," *Human Relations*, 3, 4, 279-298 (1970).
[29] C.J. Middleton, "How to Set Up a Project Organization," *Harvard Business Review*, 73-82 (March–April, 1967). Copyright © 1967 by the President and Fellows of Harvard College; all rights reserved.

Table 13. Major Company Advantages of Project Management.[a]

ADVANTAGES	PERCENT OF RESPONDENTS
• Better control of projects	92
• Better customer relations	80
• Shorter product development time	40
• Lower program costs	30
• Improved quality and reliability	26
• Higher profit margins	24
• Better control over program security	13

OTHER BENEFITS

- Better project visibility and focus on results
- Improved coordination among company divisions doing work on the project
- Higher morale and better mission orientation for employees working on the project
- Accelerated development of managers due to breadth of project responsibilities

[a] *Source:* C. J. Middleton, "How to Set Up a Project Organization," *Harvard Business Review,* 73-82 (March-April, 1967). Copyright © 1967 by the President and Fellows of Harvard College; all rights reserved.

Table 14. Major Company Disadvantages of Project Management.[a]

DISADVANTAGES	PERCENT OF RESPONDENTS
• More complex internal operations	51
• Inconsistency in application of company policy	32
• Lower utilization of personnel	13
• Higher program costs	13
• More difficult to manage	13
• Lower profit margins	2

OTHER DISADVANTAGES

- Tendency for functional groups to neglect their job and let the project organization do everything
- Too much shifting of personnel from project to project
- Duplication of functional skills in project organization

[a] *Source:* C. J. Middleton, "How to Set Up a Project Organization," *Harvard Business Review,* 73-82 (March-April, 1967). Copyright © 1967 by the President and Fellows of Harvard College; all rights reserved.

from a personnel and cost-control standpoint. This will be accomplished, in depth, in later chapters. Although project management is growing, the creation of a project organization does not necessarily insure that an assigned objective will be accomplished successfully. Furthermore, weaknesses can develop in the areas of maintaining capability and structure changes.

Middleton has listed four undesirable results that can develop from the use of project organizations and can affect company capabilities:[30]

- Project priorities and competition for talent may interrupt the stability of the organization and interfere with its long-range interests by upsetting the traditional business of functional organizations.
- Long-range plans may suffer as the company gets more involved in meeting schedules and fulfilling the requirements of temporary projects.
- Shifting people from project to project may disrupt the training of employees and specialists, thereby hindering the growth and development within their fields of specialization.
- Lessons learned on one project may not be communicated to other projects.

An almost predictable result of using the project management approach is the increase in management positions. Killian describes the results of two surveys:[31]

One company compared its organization and management structure as it existed before it began forming project units with the structure that existed afterward. The number of departments had increased from 65 to 106, while total employment remained practically the same. The number of employees for every supervisor had dropped from 13.4 to 12.8. The company concluded that a major cause of this change was the project groups.

Another company uncovered proof of its conclusion when it counted the number of second-level and higher management positions. It found that it has 11 more vice-presidents and directors, 35 more managers, and 56 more second-level supervisors. Although

---
[30] Ibid.
[31] William P. Killian, "Project Management – Future Organizational Concepts," *Marquette Business Review*, 2, 90–107 (1971).

the company attributed part of this growth to an upgrading of titles, the effect of the project organization was the creation of 60 more management positions.

Although the project organization is a specialized, task-oriented entity, it seldom, if ever, exists apart from the traditional structure of the organization.[32] All project management structures overlap the traditional structure. Furthermore, companies can have more than one project organizational form in existence at one time. A major steel producer, for example, has a matrix structure for R&D and a product structure elsewhere.

Perhaps the most serious problem in organizing the small business is the location of the project manager. Ideally, the project manager should be at the same organizational level as the person he must negotiate with for resources. However, there are good reasons for placing him elsewhere in the organization. According to Martin:[33]

Projects should be located wherever in the organization they can function most effectively. Several reasons for having the project manager report directly to a high level in the organization may be mentioned:

- The project manager is charged with getting results from the coordinated efforts of many functions. He should therefore report to the man who directs all those functions.
- The project manager must have adequate organizational status to do his job effectively.
- To get adequate and timely assistance in solving problems that inevitably appear in any important project, the project manager needs direct and specific access to an upper echelon of management.
- The customer, particularly in a competitive environment, will be favorably impressed if his project manager reports to a high organizational echelon.

---

[32] Allen R. Janger, "Anatomy of the Project Organization," *Business Management Record*, 12-18 (November, 1963).
[33] Charles C. Martin, *Project Management: How to Make It Work,* New York: Amacom, A Division of American Management Associations, 1976, p. 80.

Good reasons may also exist for having the project manager report to a lower echelon:

- It is organizationally and operationally inefficient to have too many projects, especially small ones, diverting senior executives from more vital concerns.
- Although giving a small project a high place in the organization may create the illusion of executive attention, its real result is to foster executive neglect of the project.
- Placing a junior project manager too high in the organization will alienate senior functional executives on whom he must rely for support.

Small and medium-sized companies generally prefer to have the project managers report fairly high up in the chain of command, even though the project manager may be working on a relatively low priority project. Project managers are usually viewed as less of a threat in the small organization than in the larger ones, thus creating less of a problem for the project manager to report high up.

Accepting a project management structure is a giant step from which there may be no return. The company may have to create more management positions without changing the total employment levels. In addition, incorporation of a project organization is almost always accompanied by the upgrading of jobs. In any event, management must realize that whichever project management structure is selected, a dynamic state of equilibrium will be necessary.

Organizing the small company for projects involves two major questions:

- Where should the project manager be placed within the organization?
- Are the majority of our projects internal or external to the organization?

These two questions are implicitly related. For either large, complex projects or those involving outside customers, project managers generally report to a high level in the organization. For small or internal projects, the project manager reports to a middle or lower-level manager.

Small and medium-sized companies have been very successful in managing internal projects using departmental project management (see Figure 10) especially when only a few functional groups must interface with one another. More than often, line managers may be permitted to wear multiple hats and also act as project managers, thereby reducing the need for hiring additional project managers.

Customers external to the organization are usually favorably impressed if a small company identifies a project manager who is dedicated and committed to their project, even if on a part-time basis. As a result, outside customers, particularly through a competitive bidding environment, respond favorably towards a matrix structure, even if the matrix structure is simply eyewash for the customer. As an example, consider the matrix structure shown in Figure 17. Both large and small companies that operate on a matrix usually develop a separate organizational chart for each customer.

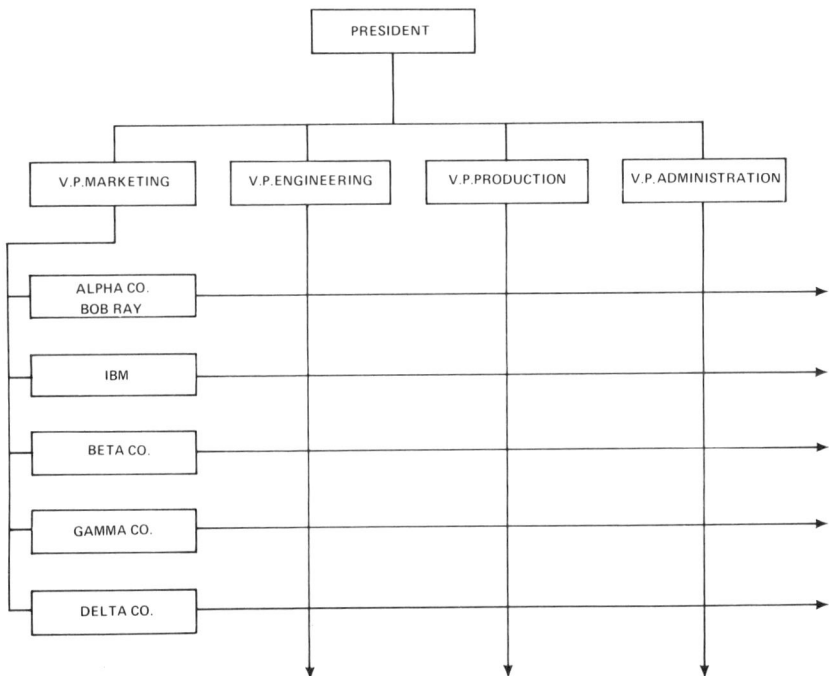

Figure 17. Organizational matrix.

Figure 17 represents the organizational chart that would be presented to Alpha Company. The Alpha Company project would be identified with bold lines and would be placed immediately below the vice-president, regardless of the priority of the project. After all, if you were the Alpha Company customer, would you want your project to appear at the bottom of the list?

Figure 17 also identifies two other key points that are important to small companies. First, only the name of the Alpha Company project manager, Bob Ray, need be identified. The reason for this is because Bob Ray may also be the project manager for one or more of the other projects and it is usually not a good practice to identify to the customer that Bob Ray will have split loyalties among several projects. Actually, the organization in the chart shown in Figure 17 is a machine tool company employing 280 people, and with 5 major projects and 30 minor projects. The company has only two full-time project managers. Bob Ray manages the projects for Alpha, Gamma, and Delta Companies; the Beta Company project has the second full-time project manager; and the IBM project is being managed

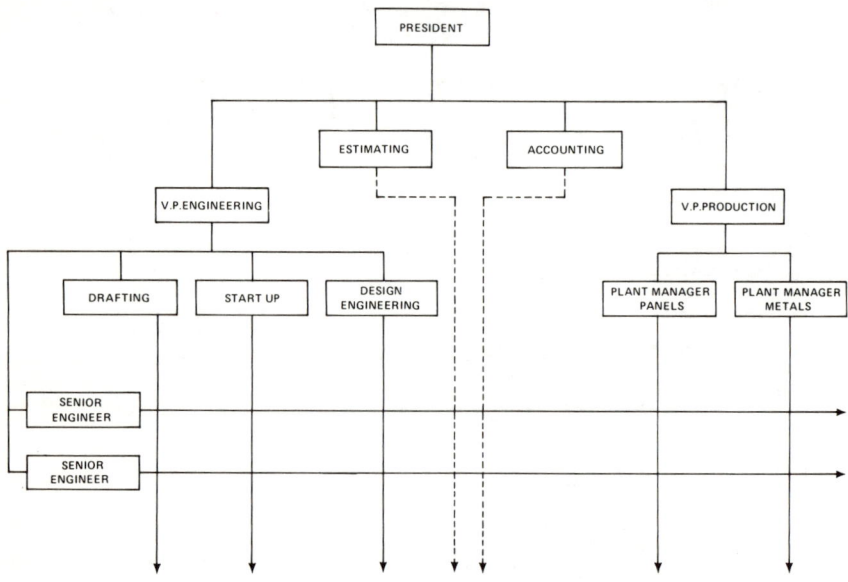

Figure 18. Simple matrix structure.

personally by the vice-president of engineering, who happens to be wearing two hats.

The second key point is that small companies generally should not identify the names of functional employees because

- The functional employees are probably part-time.
- It is usually best in small companies for all communications to be transmitted through the project manager.

Another example of how a simple matrix structure can be used to impress the customer is shown in Figure 18. The company identified here actually contains only 38 employees. Very small companies normally place the estimating department reporting directly to the president as shown in Figure 18. In addition, the senior engineers, which appear to be acting in the role of project managers, may simply be the department managers for drafting, startup, and/or design engineering. Yet, from an outside customer's perspective, this company has a dedicated and committed project manager for the project.

7
The Executive's Role in Project Management

Project management cannot succeed without the support of executive management. Although the need for project management is first detected by the line managers who control the resources on a day-to-day basis, executives must be sold on the concept and convinced that it is in the best interest of the company for the executive to change his method of management.

The job description of the executive, regardless of company size, must include strategic planning, defining the policies and procedures necessary to achieve the goals and objectives, and insuring the growth and survival of the company over the next several years. From a project management point of view, the executive's role includes

- Establishing priorities
- Resolving conflicts (which could not be resolved at lower positions within the organization)
- If necessary, acting as the project sponsor
- Being actively involved during the planning and conceptual phases of a project
- Being passively involved in the implementation phases of a project as long as there exists a structured feedback mechanism so that the executive will be informed concerning the true status of the project

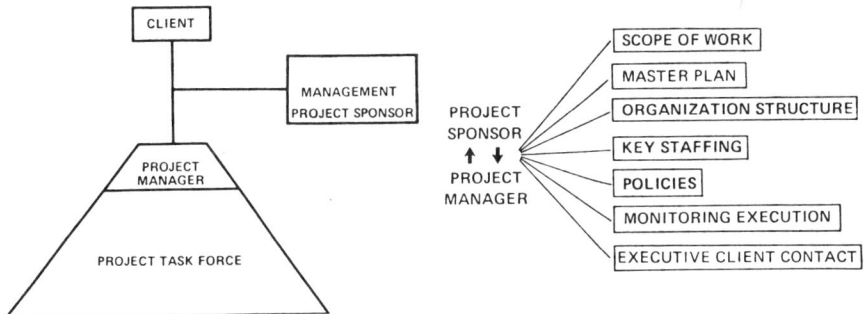

Figure 19. Functions of a project sponsor. (From L.J. Weber, W. Riethmeier, A.F. Westergard, and K.O. Hartley, "The Project Sponsor's View," Proceedings of the Ninth Annual Seminar/Symposium, October 22-26, 1977, Chicago, Illinois; reprinted by permission of the Project Management Institute. Pp. 67-81.)

The last item requires further comment. For small companies in which the revenue of the firm is spread over a small number of projects, active executive involvement can be expected because of the risk to the company. The failure of as little as one project could easily result in bankruptcy or receivership.

Acting as a project sponsor is a key role for executives of both small and large companies. The various functions for the role of a project sponsor are shown in Figure 19. The most important function identified is that of executive-client contact. In this role, the project sponsor must convince the customer that the contractor's executive management is actively involved in analysis of the time, cost, and performance parameters of the project. Because of this, the project sponsor is usually staffed by executive management. In large companies, the project sponsor can be any vice-president who, in addition to his normal line function, must also act in the role of the project sponsor. This is shown in Figure 20, where any vice-president (except perhaps the vice-president of operations) may take on the role of project sponsor for one or more projects.

The project sponsor is actually a high-level staff assistant to the project manager, as was shown in Figure 19. The project manager still maintains maximum control over the project task force and can communicate as needed with the customer or client. Customers usually feel better if the project cost and scheduling information is

94 ORGANIZING, PLANNING, AND CONTROL

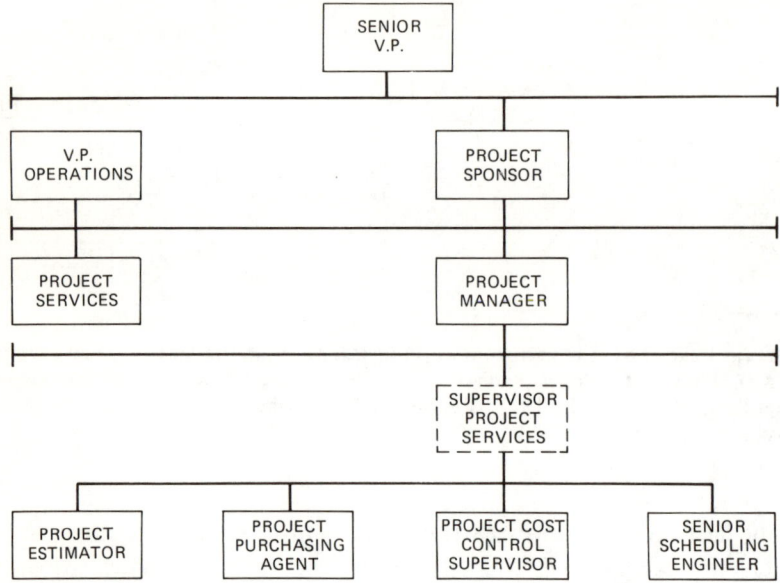

Figure 20. Department/project organization interface. (From L.J. Weber, W. Riethmeier, A.F. Westergard, and K.O. Hartley, "The Project Sponsor's View," Proceedings of the Ninth Annual Seminar/Symposium, October 22-26, 1977, Chicago, Illinois; reprinted by permission of the Project Management Institute.)

transmitted through the project sponsor with the technical data coming from the project manager/project engineer.

In small companies, the project sponsor may even be the president of the company. In large companies, because the project manager normally reports pretty high up, and even though a project sponsor may be assigned, project decision-making and strategy may be handled between the customer's and contractor's project managers. However, in small companies strategic decision-making will almost always occur at the project sponsor level rather than the project manager level. This is shown in Figure 21, which identifies the necessity for communications above the project management level.

For small projects, the project sponsor role may be filled by marketing, new business development, or even a division manager. This is shown in Figure 22. Lower and middle-level managers can act as project sponsors if the customer recognizes these people as experts in their field and wishes communications to take place at this level.

THE EXECUTIVE'S ROLE IN PROJECT MANAGEMENT 95

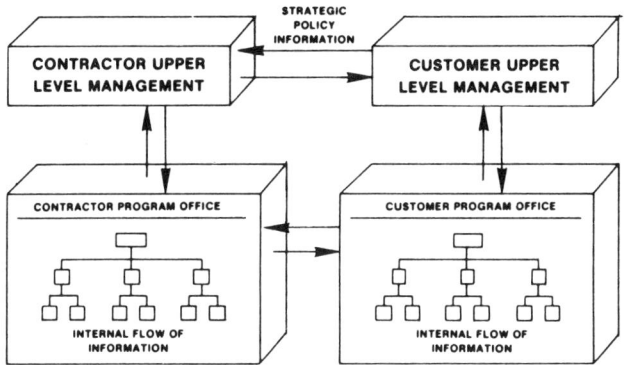

Figure 21. Information flow pattern from contractor program office.

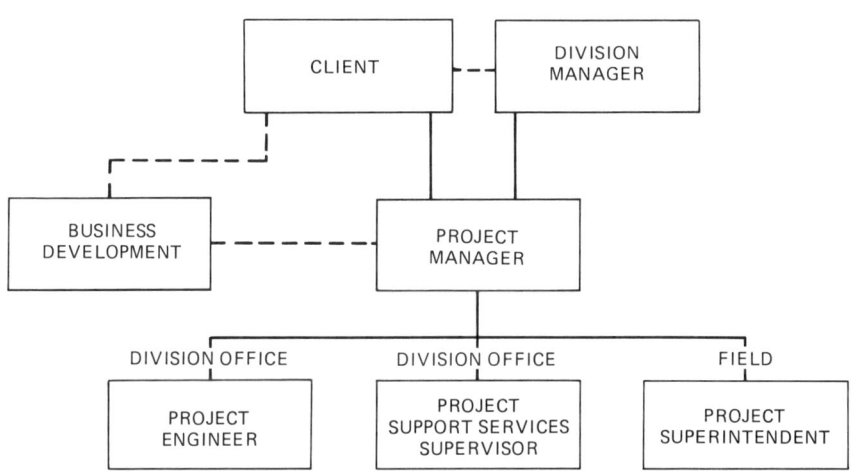

Figure 22. Typical project. (From D.A. MacDonald, E.E. Dunn, and J.D. Trevenen, "The H.K. Ferguson Company," Proceedings of the Ninth Annual Seminar/Symposium on Project Management, Chicago, Illinois, October 22–26, 1977; reprinted by permission of the Project Management Institute.)

96 ORGANIZING, PLANNING, AND CONTROL

Sometimes, customers seek out individuals to act as project sponsors with very little regard for the project itself, or so it seems. In Figure 23, a government agency awarded a company the prime contractor's position for a $25 million effort. The project manager in the prime contractor's house earned a salary of $70,000 per year but reported to an Air Force colonel who earned substantially less. The prime contractor awarded a $2 million subcontract to a small company. The project manager in the small company earned $35,000 per year. The project manager in the prime contractor literally forced the director of engineering to act as the project sponsor because the salary structure appeared more equitable at this level. The project manager in the small company found it almost impossible to communicate directly with the project manager of the prime contractor and was forced to communicate through the director of engineering or the assistant project managers in the customer's project office. The Air Force colonel, on the other hand, looked more toward status than money, and considered the

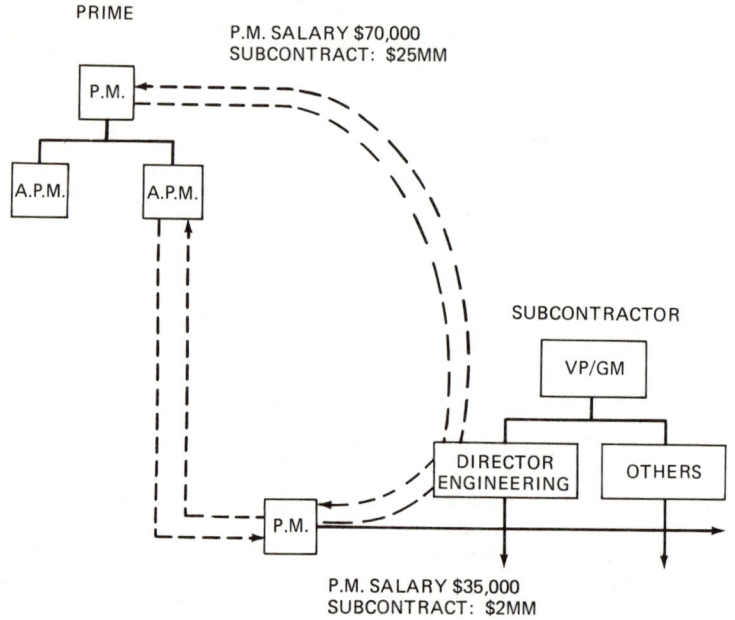

Figure 23. Forcing a project sponsor.

Table 15. What Does Project Management Expect from Top Management?

1. Clearly defined decision channels
2. Action on requests
3. Facilitation of interfacing with support areas
4. Assistance in conflict resolution
5. Resources/charter
6. Strategic/long-range information
7. Feedback
8. Advice and stage-setting support
9. Clear expectations
10. Protection from political infighting
11. Opportunity for personal and professional growth

vice-president/general manager his equal. Thus, in one company, it may be necessary for more than one executive to act in a project sponsor role depending upon the relationship desired by the customers.

Executives are usually pretty quick to accept the new role and responsibilities associated with that of a project sponsor. Unfortunately, the role of an executive in a project management environment may require a radical change in managerial style from a traditional structure. Tables 15 and 16 show the new role of an executive in a project management organization. Obviously, the new role requires change. Many executives refuse to accept change because

- They are unfamiliar with their new role and responsibilities.
- They do not understand project management or the project management environment.
- They are afraid of change.

These three items are particularly important for executives whose growth was in small organizations. The remainder of this chapter deals with the processes of convincing executives of the importance of project management and their new roles. We shall begin by discussing questions commonly asked by executives. For the most part, the questions were asked by executives in a closed session with the authors because quite often the executives do not wish functional

Table 16. What Does Top Management Expect From Project Managers?

1. Results/accountability
2. Effective reports and information
3. Minimum organizational interruption
4. Present recommendations — not alternatives
5. Capacity to handle most interpersonal problems
6. Self-starting capacity
7. Growth with the assignment

employees to hear either the question or the answer. The answers to the following questions are based upon the fact that, in each case, the executives were contemplating a change to matrix organizational structure. When reading the questions, it is important to understand that executives of the 1980s were operating under greater pressure and more risk and uncertainty than the executives of either the 1960s or 1970s, and therefore had to be "sold" on the project management approach.[34]

- *Can our people be part-time project managers?* The nature of the question suggests that the executives wanted to manage the projects within the existing resource base of the company. The answer to the question depends, of course, upon the size, nature, and complexity of the project. It is generally better to have full-time project manager responsible for several small projects than to have many part-time project managers. Executives, as well as functional personnel, will never be convinced that the matrix will work until they see it in action. Therefore, it is strongly recommended that the first few projects be "breakthrough" projects with full-time project managers. This implies that, initially, these project managers will be staff to a top-level manager rather than within a newly developed line group for project managers. Many small companies today are hoarding one or two good project managers, waiting for those one or two

---

[34] It should be noted that the conceptual phase of project management implementation begins with the functional managers who identify the need for project management because of their problems with resource control. The next step is usually best accomplished through outside consultants whom executives trust to give an impartial view.

THE EXECUTIVE'S ROLE IN PROJECT MANAGEMENT   99

big projects that will eventually come along. Small companies are generally more afraid of being caught unprepared than are large companies. In addition, it is not uncommon in small companies for an experienced project manager to be drawing a larger salary than the company president.

- *If we go to project matrix management, must we increase resources, especially the number of project managers?* The reason for this question is obvious, namely that the executives do not wish to increase the manpower base or overhead rate. Matrix management is designed to provide better control of functional resources such that more work can be completed in less time, with less money and with potentially fewer people. Unfortunately, these results may not become evident for a year or two.

Initially, executives prefer to select project managers from within the organization with the argument that project managers must know the people and the operation of the organization. Even today, some companies require that all project managers first spend at least 18 months in the functional areas prior to becoming project managers. However, there are also good reasons for filling project management positions from outside the company. Sometimes newly transferred project managers still maintain loyal ties to their functional departments and impartial project decision-making is not possible.

- *Let's assume that we set up a separate staff function called project administration which is staff to one of our executives. Can we then use our functional people as part-time project managers who report vertically to a line manager and horizontally to project administration?* With proper preparation and training, most employees can learn how to report effectively to multiple managers. However, the process is more complicated in small companies if the employee acts as a project manager and functional employee at the same time. When a conflict occurs over what is best for the horizontal or vertical line, the employee will usually bend in the direction that will put more pay into his pocket. In other words, if the part-time (or perhaps even full-time) project manager always makes decisions in the best interest of his line manager, the project will suffer. The most practical method to solve this problem is to let the functional employee act as a part-time, assistant project manager rather than as a part-time project manager because now the functional employee has someone else to plead his case for him, and he is no longer caught in the middle.

This question has serious impact on how employees are treated. If an employee reports to multiple managers and some managers treat him as though he is theory Y while others treat him as theory X, decisions will almost always be made in favor of the theory Y managers. People who report to multiple managers must understand that, even if they are theory Y employees, in time of crisis, they will be treated as though they are theory X. This type of understanding and training must be given to all employees who perform in a project environment.

- *Which vice-president should be responsible for the project administration function?* Assuming that the company does not want to create a separate position for the vice-president of projects, we must find out whether or not there exists a dominant percentage of people (on all projects) who come from one major functional group. If say 60 to 70 percent of all project employees come from engineering, then the vice-president for engineering should also control the project administration function because there now exists a common superior for the resolution of the majority of project conflicts. Having to go up two or three levels of management to find a common superior for conflict resolution can create a self-defeating attitude within the matrix.

The assignment will become more difficult if functional dominance does not exist. We must now decide upon who dominates the decision-making process of the company (i.e., is the company marketing-driven, engineering-driven, etc.?). The project administrative function will then fall under the control of this line function. Without either of these degrees of dominance, and assuming a project-driven organization, it is not uncommon to find all project managers reporting under marketing with the vice-president for marketing acting as the project sponsor.

- *Is it true that most project managers consider their next step to be that of a vice-president?* Most project managers view the organization of the company with the project managers on top and executives performing horizontally (i.e., rotate Figure 14 to the right by 90 degrees). Therefore, project managers already consider themselves executives on the project and naturally expect their next step to be executives in the total company.

However, we should mention that many project managers are so in love with their jobs that money is not an important factor, and they may wish to remain in project management. Project managers are motivated by work challenge and therefore many have refused top-level promotions because they did not consider the work to be as challenging at this level as at the project management level.

- *Can we give our employees (especially engineers) a rotation period of six to eighteen months in the project office and then return them to the functional departments where they should be more well-rounded individuals with a better appreciation and understanding of project management?* On paper, this technique looks good and may have some merit. But in the real world, the results may be disastrous. There are four detrimental effects of this arrangement. First, employees who know that they will be returning to their line function will not be as dedicated to project management as they should be and will still try to maintain a strong allegiance to their line function. The result, of course, will be that the project will suffer. Second, when the employee knows that his assignment is temporary and brief, he usually walks the straight and narrow path and avoids risk whenever possible. Risky decisions are left to other project office personnel or even his replacement. Third, depending upon the rate at which technology changes, the employee may find himself technically obsolete when he returns to his functional group. The fourth and last point is the most serious. The employee may find himself so attracted to the project management function that he would want to stay. If the company forces him to return to his functional department, there is always the risk that the employee will update his resume and begin reading the job market section of the Tuesday *Wall Street Journal.* Simply stated, a company should not place people into project management unless the company is willing to offer these people a career path there.

- *How much control should a project manager have over costs and budgets?* Executives in the areas of accounting and finance are very reluctant to delegate total cost control to the project managers. Project managers cannot be effective unless they have the right to control costs by opening and closing work orders in accordance with the established project plan. However, if the project manager redirects the project activities in a manner that causes a major deviation in the cash flow position of the project, then he must coordinate his activities with top management in order to prevent a potential company cash flow problem.

- *What role should a project manager have in strategic and operational planning?* First of all, project managers are concerned primarily with the immediate execution of an operational plan. Therefore, they are operational planners. However, because of the company-wide knowledge that the project manager obtains on functional operations and work integration, they become an invaluable asset to the executives during strategic planning, but primarily as resource people. Project managers are not known for their corporate strategic planning posture, but for their strategic project planning capability.
- *How much authority should an executive delegate to a project manager?* Generally speaking, project managers should be given as much authority as they actually need (or perhaps slightly more) to get the job accomplished. Unfortunately, this is often not the case in small companies. The key factors that management considers in the delegation of authority include:

- The maturity of the project management function
- The size, nature, and business base of the company
- The size and nature of the project
- The life cycle of the project
- The capabilities of management at all levels

The first item indicates that during matrix implementation the project manager may have less authority than he would expect to have because the executive is reluctant to give up total control. This is to be expected. The last four items indicate that even after the matrix becomes mature, not all project managers are equal when it comes to authority. The following list identifies the types of authority that can be delegated or withheld from the project manager:

- Focal position
- Conflict resolution between the project manager and functional managers
- Influence to cut across functional and organizational lines
- Participation in major management and technical decisions

THE EXECUTIVE'S ROLE IN PROJECT MANAGEMENT   103

- Collaboration in staffing the project
- Control over allocation and expenditure of funds
- Selection of subcontractors
- Rights in resolving conflicts
- Voice in maintaining integrity of project team
- Establishment of project plans
- Providing of a cost-effective information system for control
- Providing of leadership in the preparation of operational requirements
- Maintenance of prime customer liaison and contact
- Promotion of technological and managerial improvements
- Establishment of the project organization for the duration
- Cutting of red tape

The exact amount and type of authority depends upon the mood of the executive. On high-risk projects, the project manager expects to have more authority but usually has less because the executive (i.e., project sponsor) appears to be calling the shots.

• *What working relationship should exist between executives and the project manager?* The answer to this question involves two parts: internal meddling and customer communications. Executives are expected to work closely with the project manager and take an active role during the conceptual and planning stages of a project. However, after the project begins the implementation phase, active participation by executives equates to executive meddling and can do more harm than good. After planning is completed, executives should step back and let the project manager run the show. There will still be structured feedback from the project office to the executive, and the executive will still be actively involved in priority setting and conflict resolution. The exception to this would be when the executive is required to act as the project sponsor as was shown in Figure 19. In this case, the client wants to be sure that his project is receiving executive attention and feels confident when he sees one of the contractor's executives looking over the project. The project sponsor exists primarily as the executive-client contact link but can also serve as an invaluable staff resource.

Executives must not be blinded by the partial success they may achieve with executive meddling during the early days of matrix implementation. The overall, long-term effect to the company can be disastrous if executives feel that they can effectively control vertical and horizontal resources at the same time.

• *Where do we find good project managers?* First of all, project management is both an art and a science. The science aspect includes the quantitative tools and techniques for planning, scheduling, and controlling. The art aspect involves dealing with a wide variety of people. The science portion can be learned in the classroom, whereas the art portion generally comes only from on-the-job experience. Perhaps the most important characteristics are interpersonal skills and communicative skills.

Experience is usually the best teacher in project management. Figure 24, for example, shows the job description of a construction project manager. This implies that construction project managers will probably be much older than their MIS project management counterparts. In project management, experience rather than gray hair or baldness equates to maturity.

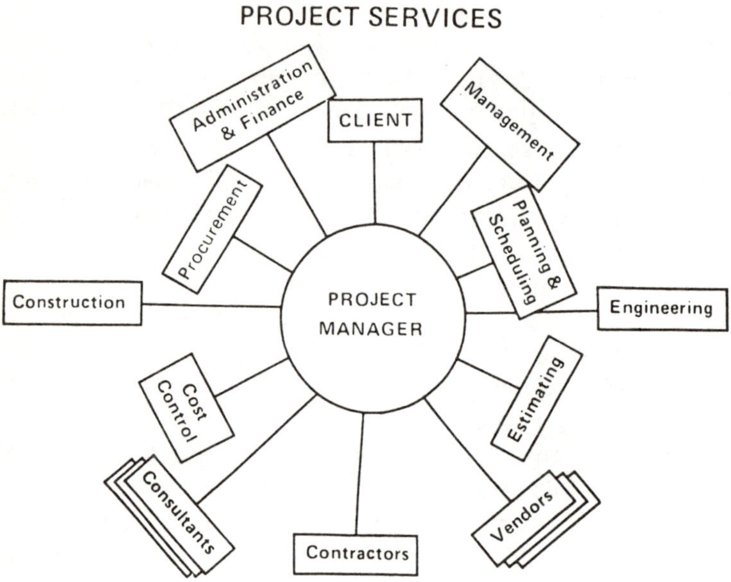

PROJECT SERVICES

Figure 24. Project Services. (From L.J. Weber, W. Riethmeier, A.F. Westergard, and K.O. Hartley, "The Project Sponsor's View," Proceedings of the Ninth Annual Seminar/Symposium, October 22-26, 1977, Chicago, Illinois, reprinted by permission of the Project Management Institute. Pp. 67-81.)

Most companies have such qualified people internally and often produce disastrous results by forcing such people to unwillingly accept a project management assignment. Project management generally works best if it is a voluntary assignment. This usually brings with it loyalty and dedication. Unfortunately, many people enter project management without fully understanding the job description of the project manager. If the employees are promoted into project management and then want out or fail, the company may have no place for them at their new salary. Sometimes it is better to laterally transfer employees to project management under the stipulation that rewards will follow if they produce.

- *What percentage of a total project budget should be available for project management and administrative support?* The answer to this question depends upon the nature of the project. Management support may run from a low of 2 percent to a high of 15 percent.
- *My company had 50 projects going on at once. The project managers handle multiple projects, each with a different priority, and can report to anyone in the company. Will a matrix give better control?* The matrix will alleviate a lot of these problems provided that all of the project managers report to one line group or if the company has only a few project managers. This will give uniform control of projects and will make it easier to establish priorities. If it becomes necessary to get better control over the project managers, then the projects should be grouped according to the customer or to similar technologies, not necessarily dollar value.
- *In a matrix, people are often assigned full-time to a project. What happens if a functional manager complains that pulling a good employee out of his department will leave a large gap?* In a matrix, the employee is still physically and administratively attached to his functional group. And even with a full-time project assignment, the employee will probably still find sufficient slack time to assist other projects, even if only in a consultant capacity.
- *On some of our projects the first step is a cost-benefit analysis to see if the project is a feasible undertaking. Who will do this in a matrix?* On some projects, the job-related characteristics are more important than the project manager's personal characteristics. In this case, it may be better to have project managers who are trained in this area rather than having the cost-benefit analysis performed by

another group. Project managers should be actively involved in any planning or decision-making that may be bottom-line oriented.

• *How do we make sure that everyone in the company knows what the priorities are?* Priorities should be transmitted to both the project and functional departments through the traditional structure within the matrix. Even with the establishment of priorities, project managers will still fight for what they believe to be in the best interest of their project. This is to be expected. Initially, during the implementation of the matrix, it may be necessary to have all priorities documented.

There is a risk within the matrix that the slippage of as little as one project could cause reestablishment of all other project priorities. Even though some project managers may control their projects so closely that they can obtain daily status, the continuous changing of priorities on a daily or even weekly basis can destroy the functioning of the matrix, because the functional managers may now be forced to continuously shift resources from project to project.

• *We have had an explosion of Operations Support Systems (the mini-computer era). How do we manage these projects? Can we use matrix management?* Matrix management works best for projects that cut across more than one functional group. Multifunctional MIS and data base packages can be very effectively managed using a matrix. Banks are a prime example of an industry where matrix management may exist primarily for such projects.

There is one major risk that should be considered. There is always the controversy over whether the programmers or the users should be the project managers. The usual arguments are that the programmers do not understand why it takes so long to write a program. Many companies have established a project management group to handle such conflicts. Each project is headed up by a project manager and two assistant project managers, one from programming and one to represent the users. Conflicts and problems are now resolved horizontally rather than vertically. In this situation, it is possible for one project manager to handle several projects at once.

• *How does top management control the responsibilities that each person will have on a project?* Neither top management nor project management controls the responsibilities. The functional managers still control their own people. Project managers can fill out a linear responsibility chart (LRC) as shown in Figure 25 in order to make sure that every work breakdown structure element is accounted for. However, the functional managers should still approve the amount of authority and responsibility that the project manager wishes to delegate to functional employees. The reason for this is that the project manager should not be able to upgrade functional employees without the consent of the functional manager. The exception would be the project office personnel who may report full-time to the project manager and also be evaluated by him. During the implementation phase of a matrix, the executives may wish to be actively involved in the LRC establishment since, in fact, it is part of the planning process and executives are expected to be closely associated with the project at this time.

• *How do we ensure effective and timely communications to all levels?* The project manager, being the focal point for all project

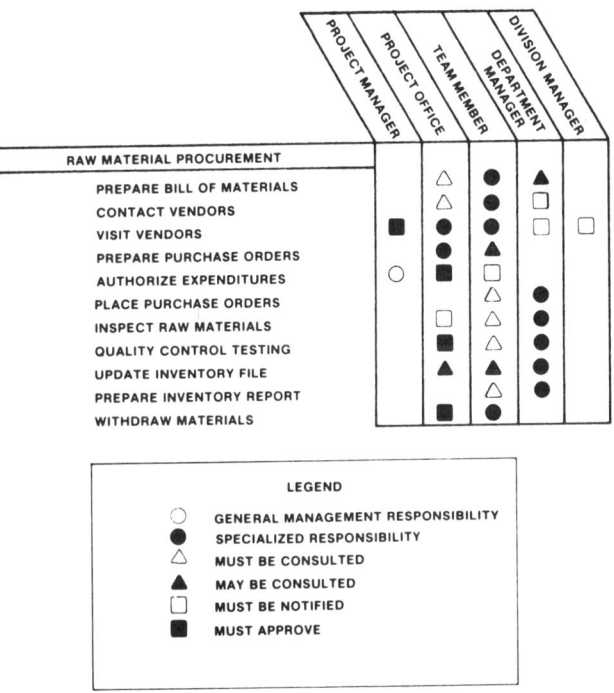

Figure 25. Linear responsibility chart.

activities, should be able to provide timely project information to everyone, including executives, at a faster rate than within the traditional structure. The ability to provide effective and timely communications should be part of every project manager's job description.

• *How do we get top management committed to project management?* Regardless of how much literature exists in the area of effective project management, executives will not become committed until they see the system operating effectively and producing the expected dollar value of profit on the bottom line of the project. In order to effectively observe and comprehend the problems, executives must understand their new role in a project management environment and should attend the same "therapy" training sessions as middle management.

• *We need an awful lot of front-end work (i.e., planning) on projects. We are living in a world of limited resources. We need commitments from our people, not just promises. How do we get that?* When the functional managers realize that project management is designed for them, and not for executives or project managers, then the functional managers will start giving commitments that they will live up to. The functional managers must be convinced that the matrix is not simply an attempt on the part of the project manager to control the functional manager's empire, but that in fact the project manager and matrix exist to support the functional managers in getting better control over their own resources such that future commitments can be kept.

• *How do we resolve problems in which there is a lack of knowledge of project team members concerning their own roles?* The responsibility here rests on the shoulders of both the project and functional managers. Planning tools, such as the linear responsibility charts, can be used, but the bottom line is still effective communications. This is why one of the major prerequisites for a project manager is to be an effective communicator and integrator.

• *How do we convince people to escalate problems and not bury them?* In a matrix organization, the critical point is the project/functional interface. Both the project and functional managers must be willing to escalate problems and ask for help, especially on the horizontal line. When the project manager gets into trouble, he goes first to the functional manager to discuss project resources. When the functional manager gets into trouble, he goes to the project manager to seek additional time, additional funding, or a change in specifications. Project personnel must realize that the project is a team effort and everyone should pitch in when problems occur.

Many people refuse to escalate problems for fear that the identification of the problem will reflect in their evaluation for promotion. The matrix structure is designed not only to put forth the best team for accomplishing the objectives, but also to resolve problems. Because the matrix approach encourages the sharing of key people, employees may find that the best corporate resources may now be available to assist them temporarily.

Executives and functional managers must encourage people to bring forth problems, especially during matrix implementation. This encouragement should probably be done verbally, with personal contact, rather than through memos.

- *Is it true that if we go to a matrix, many of our functional people will start communicating directly with our customers?* When you have a matrix structure, customers are very reluctant to have all information flow from your project offices to their project office for fear that your project office is filtering the information. Therefore, the customer may request (or even demand) that his technical people be permitted to talk to your technical people on a one-on-one basis. This should be permitted as long as the customer fully understands that

  - Functional employees reflect their own personal opinion. Official company position can come only through the project office or through the project sponsor.
  - Functional employees cannot commit to additional work that may be beyond the scope of the contract. Any changes in work must be approved by the project office.

Functionally, employees should contact the project office after each communication and relate to the project office what was discussed. The project office will then consider whether or not a memo should be written to document the results of the discussion. This memo may have to be "signed off" by both the customer and contractor.

The purpose of the question-answer session is to convince the executives that a change might be for the better. Unfortunately, with matrix management, the executives themselves may have to change their own management styles. The following are the most common arguments that executives give for avoiding change:[35]

- Why Change?
  - I must be doing something right to get where I am. I may have to start working differently. Can I succeed?
- Balance of Power
  - I understand the balance of power and my role within top management. Why change it? I might lose my present power.
- Loss of Control
  - I presently generate change on projects and in policy areas. Why change it? I won't be able to control recommended changes.
- Need for Contact with Projects
  - I will lose my ability to perceive appropriate adjustments in organization policies when I lose detail involvement in projects. Why change it?
- Excessive Delegation
  - It is not good practice to have key decisions delegated below the top men. Why change?
- Coordination
  - Coordination responsibility is a key management job. Why delegate it to project managers?

If the executives are willing to accept change, then the next step is to discuss the methods for implementation. The executives must understand the following strategies and tactics for implementation to be effective:

- Top management must delegate authority and responsibility to the project manager.

---

[35] Adapted from John M. Tettemer, "Keeping Your Boss Happy While Implementing Project Management – A Management View," *Proceedings of the Tenth Annual Seminar/Symposium of the Project Management Institute,* October 8-11, 1978, Los Angeles, pp. Ia-1 through IA-4; reproduced by permission of the Project Management Institute.

- Top management must delegate total cost control to the project manager.
- Top management must rely upon the project manager for total project planning and scheduling.
- Only the project managers must fully understand such advanced scheduling techniques as PERT/CPM. This may require additional training. Functional managers may use other scheduling techniques for resource control.
- Top management must encourage functional managers to resolve problems and conflicts at the lowest organizational levels and not always run "upstairs."
- Top management must not consider functional departments merely support groups for a project. Functional departments still control the company resources, and contrary to popular belief, the project managers actually work for the functional managers, not vice versa.
- Top management must provide sufficient training for functional employees on how to report to and interact with multiple project managers.
- Top management must take an interest in how project management should work.
- Top management must not fight among themselves as to who should control the project management function.

The project manager also has strategies and tactics that should be understood during implementation. The following key points should be carefully considered by the project manager:[36]

- Breakthrough Project
  - Start with a "breakthrough project" that the administration can keep pace with in the new project management format.
- Traditional Information for Top Management
  - The new project manager must be sure that traditional types of functional and project information are available to top management for traditional problem solving. He should take

---

[36] Adapted from John M. Tettemer, "Keeping Your Boss Happy While Implementing Project Management – A Management View," *Proceedings of the Tenth Annual Seminar/Symposium of the Project Management Institute,* October 8-11, 1978, Los Angeles, pp. IA-1 through IA-4; reproduced by permission of the Project Management Institute.

this information forward voluntarily, ahead of top management's knowledge of the problem, preferably more quickly than the traditional line of communication.
- Retention of Power
  - Every administrator should be allowed to retain his traditional power within the hierarchy during the implementation phase.
- Policy Recommendations
  - Project managers should carefully and thoughtfully develop only policy recommendations that can be easily accepted by the administration as being in concert with the organization's goals and objectives and that are easy to implement and readily accepted by those outside the organization.
- Pace
  - It is necessary for project managers to push for change, but not at a rate that in itself builds opposition.
- Schedules
  - Project managers should keep schedules and other tools in the background of their involvement with top management. (The tools of project management are of far less interest to top management than the results obtained through them.)
- Decoding of Information
  - It is extremely important that project managers decode all their reporting documents to meet the style of the executive with whom they are trying to communicate.
- Broad Perspective
  - Project managers should be sure to recommend as general policy changes only those items that are applicable to a broad range of projects. Exceptions should clearly be indicated as exceptions to meet clearly defined project objectives.

It should be readily apparent from these key points that during implementation the project managers could easily frighten executives to such a degree that all thoughts of matrix implementation will be forgotten.

The last points that should be described to executives are the "blockages" that some executives face even after the implementation phase is completed. These executive blockages include:

- Top management directly interfaces a project only during the idea development and planning phases of a project. Once the project is initiated, the executives should maintain a monitoring perspective via structured feedback from the project manager.
- Top management still establishes corporate direction and must make sure that the project managers fully understand the meaning.
- Top management must try to control those environmental factors that may be beyond the control of the project manager. These factors include such items as external communications, joint venture relationships, the provision of internal support, and the provision of environmental ongoing intelligence.
- Top management must have confidence in the project managers and must be willing to give them projects that are both difficult as well as projects that are easy to perform.
- Top management must understand that in order for work to flow horizontally in a company, a "dynamic" organizational structure is necessary. Not all activities can flow in parallel with the main activities of the company.
- Upper-level management must not want to take an active role in this "new" concept called project management.
- Upper-level management must be familiar with the new responsibilities and interface relationships in a project environment.

There is no sure-fire method today for the successful acceptance and implementation of matrix management. The best approach appears to be an early education process (including questions and answers) whereby executives, project managers, and functional personnel will be willing to at least give the system a chance. This type of early educational approach should be acceptable to all types of companies and in all industries where the matrix is applicable.

8
General Planning

The most important responsibilities of a project manager are planning, and integrating and executing plans. Almost all projects, because of their relatively short duration and often prioritized control of resources, require formal, detailed planning. The integration of the planning activities is necessary because each functional unit may develop its own planning documentation with little regard for other functional units.

Planning, in general, can best be described as the function of selecting the enterprise objectives and establishing the policies, procedures, and programs necessary for achieving them. Planning in a project environment may be described as establishing a predetermined course of action within a forecasted environment. The project sets the major milestones and the line managers hope that they can meet them. If the line manager cannot commit because the milestones are perceived as unrealistic, the project manager may have to develop alternatives, one of which may be to move the milestones. Upper-level management must become involved in the selection of alternatives during the planning stage. Planning is, of course, decision-making since it involves choosing among alternatives. Planning is a required management function to facilitate the comprehension of complex problems involving interacting factors.

One of the objectives of project planning is to completely define all work required (possibly through the development of a documented project plan) so that it will be readily indentifiable to each project participant. This is a necessity in a project environment because:

- If the task is well understood prior to being performed, much of the work can be preplanned.
- If the task is not understood, then during the actual task execution more knowledge is learned which, in turn, leads to changes in resource allocations, schedules, and priorities.
- The more uncertain the task, the greater the amount of information that must be processed in order to insure effective performance.

These three facets are important in a project environment because each project can be different, requiring a variety of different resources that has to be performed under time, cost, and performance constraints with little margin for error. Figure 26 identifies the type of project planning required to establish an effective monitoring and control system. The boxes in the upper portion of the figure represent the planning activities, and the lower portion identifies the "tracking" or monitoring of the planned activities.

Without proper planning, programs and project can start off behind the eight ball because of poorly defined requirements during the initial planning phase. Below is a list of the typical consequences of poor planning:

- Project initiation
- Wild enthusiasm
- Disillusionment
- Chaos
- Search for the guilty
- Punishment of the innocent
- Promotion of the nonparticipants
- Definition of the requirements

Obviously, the definition of the requirements should have been the first step. There are four basic reasons for project planning:

116 ORGANIZING, PLANNING, AND CONTROL

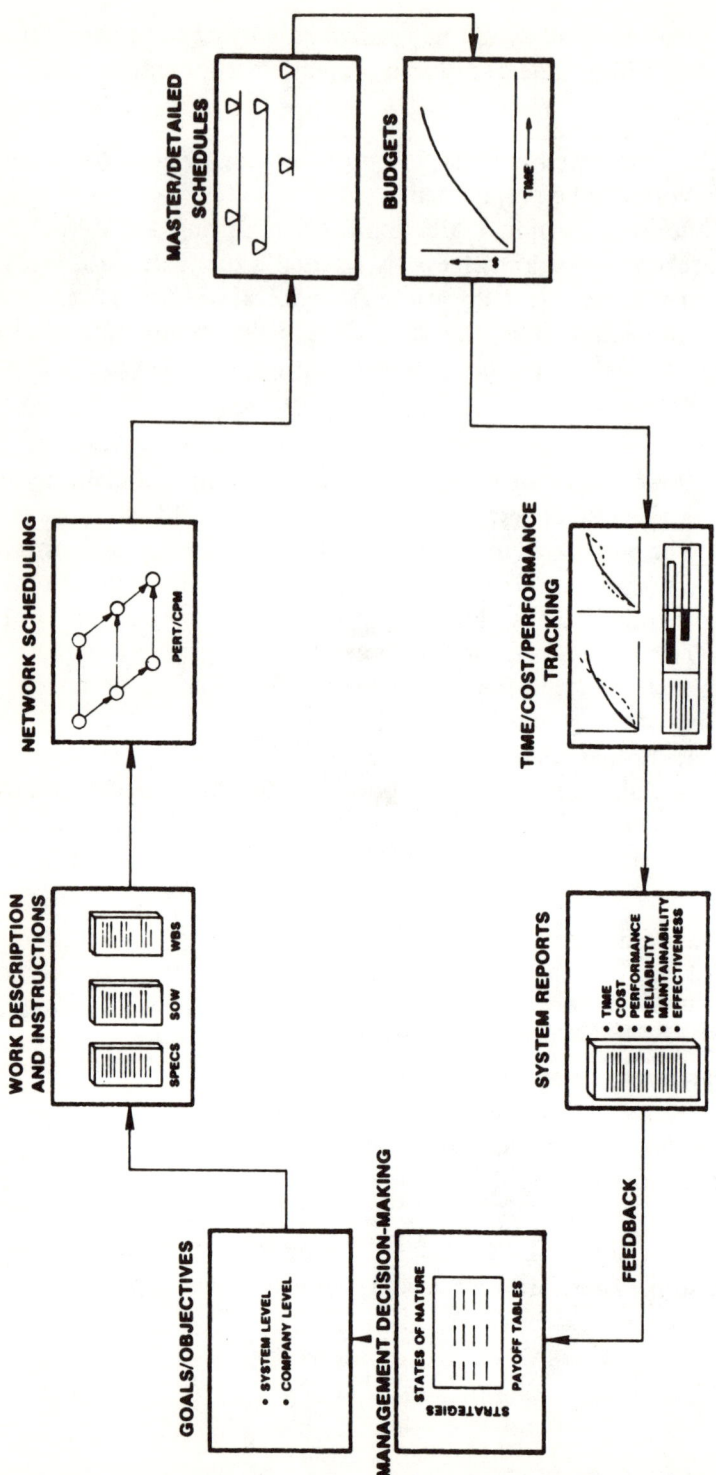

Figure 26. The project planning and control system.

- Eliminate or reduce uncertainty
- Improve efficiency of the operation
- Obtain a better understanding of the objectives
- Provide a basis for monitoring and controlling work

There are involuntary and voluntary reasons for planning. Involuntary reasons can be internal mandatory functions of the organizational complexity and organizational lag in response time, or externally, can be correlated to environmental fluctuations, uncertainty, and discontinuity. The voluntary reasons for planning are attempts to secure efficient and effective operations.

Planning is decision-making based upon futurity. It is a continuous process of making entrepreneurial decisions with an eye to the future, and methodically organizing the effort needed to carry out these decisions. Furthermore, systematic planning allows an organization to set goals. The alternative to systematic planning is decision-making based upon history. This generally results in reactive management leading to crisis management, conflict management, and fire fighting.

Planning is determining what needs to be done, by whom, and by when, in order to fulfill one's assigned responsibility. There are nine major steps that must be developed during the planning phase:

- Objective: a goal, target, or quota to be achieved by a certain time
- Program: the strategy to be followed and major actions to be taken in order to achieve or exceed objectives
- Schedule: a plan showing when individual or group activities or accomplishments will be started and/or completed
- Budget: planned expenditures required to achieve or exceed objectives
- Forecast: a projection of what will happen by a certain time
- Organization: design of the number and kinds of positions, along with corresponding duties and responsibilities, required to achieve or exceed objectives
- Policy: a general guide for decision-making and individual actions

- Procedure: a detailed method for carrying out a policy
- Standard: a level of individual or group performance defined as adequate or acceptable

Several of these steps require additional comments. Forecasting what will happen may not be easy, especially if predictions of environmental reactions are required. For example, planning is customarily defined as either strategic, tactical, or operational. Strategic planning is generally five years or more, tactical can be one to five years, and operational is the here and now of six months to one year. Although most projects are operational, they can be considered strategic especially if spin-offs or follow-up work is promising. Forecasting also requires an understanding of strengths and weaknesses, as:

- Competitive situation
- Marketing
- Research and development
- Production
- Finance
- Personnel
- Management structure

If project planning is strictly operational, then these factors may be clearly definable. However, if strategic or long-range planning is necessary, then the future economic outlook can vary, say year to year, and replanning must be accomplished at regular intervals because the goals and objectives can change (the procedure for this can be seen in Figure 26).

The last three factors, policies, procedures, and standards, can vary from project to project because of their uniqueness. Each project manager can establish project policies provided that they fall within the broad limits set forth by top management. Policies are predetermined general courses or guides based upon the following principles:[37]

---

[37] Edwin Flippo and Gary Munsinger, *Management,* 3rd ed., Boston: Allyn and Bacon, 1975, p. 83.

- Subordinate policies are supplementary to superior policies.
- Policies are based upon known principles in the operative areas.
- Policies should be complementary for coordination.
- Policies should be definable, understandable, and preferably in writing.
- Policies should be both flexible and stable.
- Policies should be reasonably comprehensive in scope.

Project policies must often conform closely to company policies, and are usually similar in nature from project to project. Procedures, on the other hand, can be drastically different from project to project, even if the same activity is performed. For example, the signing off of manufacturing plans may require different signatures in two selected projects even though the same end item is being produced.

Planning varies at each level of the organization. At the individual level, planning is required so that cognitive simulation can be established before irrevocable actions are taken. At the working group or functional level, planning must include:

- Agreement on purpose
- Assignment and acceptance of individual responsibilities
- Coordination of work activities
- Increased commitment to group goals
- Lateral communications

At the organizational or project level, planning must include:

- Recognition and resolution of group conflict of goals
- Assignment and acceptance of group responsibilities
- Increased motivation and commitment to organizational goals
- Vertical and lateral communications
- Coordination of activities between groups

The logic of planning requires answers to several questions in order for the alternatives and constraints to be fully understood. A partial list of questions would include:

- Analyze Environment
  - Where are we?
  - How and why did we get here?
- Set Objectives
  - Is this where we want to be?
  - Where would we like to be? In a year? In five years?
- List Alternative Strategies
  - Where will we go if we continue as before?
  - Is that where we want to go?
  - How could we get to where we want to go?
- List Threats and Opportunities
  - What might prevent us from getting there?
  - What might help us to get there?
- Prepare Forecasts
  - Where are we capable of going?
  - What do we need to take us where we want to go?
- Select Strategy Portfolio
  - What is the best course for us to take?
  - What are the potential benefits?
  - What are the risks?
- Prepare Action Programs
  - What do we need to do?
  - When do we need to do it?
  - How will we do it?
  - Who will do it?
- Monitor and Control
  - Are we on course? If not, why?
  - What do we need to do to be on course?
  - Can we do it?

One of the most difficult activities in the project environment is to keep the planning on target. Below are typical procedures that can assist project managers during planning activities:

- Let functional managers do their own planning. Too often operators are operators, planners are planners, and never the twain shall meet.
- Establish goals before you plan. Otherwise short-term thinking takes over.

- Set goals for the planners. This will guard against the nonessential and places your effort where there is pay off.
- Stay flexible. Use people-to-people contact and stress fast response.
- Keep a balanced outlook. Don't overreact and position yourself for an upturn.
- Welcome top management participation. Top management has the capability to make or break a plan, and may just well be the single most important variable.
- Beware of future spending plans. This may eliminate the tendency to underestimate.
- Test the assumptions behind the forecasts. This is necessary because professionals are generally too optimistic. Do not depend solely upon one set of data.
- Don't focus on today's problems. Try to get away from crisis management and fire-fighting.
- Reward those who dispell illusions. Avoid the Persian messenger syndrome (i.e. behead the bearer of bad tidings.) Reward the first to come forth with bad news.

For long-range or strategic projects, the project manager must continuously monitor the external environment in order to develop a well-structured program that can stand up under pressure. These external factors play an integral part in the planning. The project manager must be able to identify and evaluate these strategic variables in terms of the future posture of the organization with regard to constraints on existing resources.

In the project environment, strategic project planning is performed at the horizontal hierarchy level, with final approval by upper-level management. There are three basic guidelines for strategic project planning:

- Strategic project planning is a job that should be performed by managers, not for them.
- It is extremely important that upper-level management maintain a close involvement with project teams, especially during the planning phase.
- Successful strategic planning must define the authority, responsibility, and roles of the strategic planning personnel.

For the project to be successful, all members of the horizontal team must be aware of those strategic variables that can influence the success or failure of the project plan. The analysis begins with the environment, subdivided as internal, external, and competitive, as shown below:

- Internal Environment
  - Management Skills
  - Resources
  - Wage and salary levels
  - Government freeze on jobs
  - Minority groups
  - Layoffs
  - Sales Forecasts
- External Environment
  - Legal
  - Political
  - Social
  - Economic
  - Technological
- Competitive Environment
  - Industry characteristics
  - Company requirements and goals
  - Competitive history
  - Present competitive activity
  - Competitive planning
    - Return on investment
    - Market share
    - Size and variety of product lines
  - Competitive resources

Once the environmental variables are defined, the planning process continues with the following:

- Identification of company strengths and weaknesses
- Understanding of personal values of top management
- Identification of opportunities
- Definition of product market

- Identification of competitive edge
- Establishment of goals, objectives, and standards
- Identification of resource deployment

Complete identification of all strategic variables is not easily obtainable at the program level. Internal or operating variables are readily available to program personnel by virtue of the structure of the organization. The external variables are normally tracked under the perceptive eyes of top management. This presents a challenge for the organization of system. In most cases, those in the horizontal hierarchy of a program are more interested in the current operational plan and tend to become isolated from the environment after the program begins, losing insight into factors influencing the rapidly changing external variables in the process. Proper identification of these strategic variables requires that communication channels be established between top management and the project office.

Top-management support must be available for strategic planning variable identification such that effective decision-making can occur at the program level. The participation of top management in this regard has not been easy to implement. Many top-level officers consider this process a relinquishment of some of their powers and choose to retain strategic variable identification for the top levels of management.

The system approach to management does not attempt to decrease top management's role in strategic decision-making. The maturity, intellect, and wisdom of top management cannot be replaced. Ultimately, decision-making will always rest at the upper levels of management, regardless of the organizational structure.

The identification and classification of the strategic variables are necessary to establish relative emphasis, priorities, and selectivity among the alternatives, to anticipate the unexpected, and to determine the restraints and limitations of the programs. Universal classification systems are nonexistent because of the varied nature of organizations and projects. However, variables can be roughly categorized as internal and external, as shown in Table 17.

A survey of 50 companies was conducted to determine if lower-level and middle management, as well as project managers, knew what

Table 17. Strategic Planning Variables in the Tire Industry.

INTERNAL	EXTERNAL
• Operating	• Operating
• Product changes	• Customer requirements
• Volume (economies of scale)	• Capacity of plants
• Wages vs. automation	• Borrowing expenses
• R&D	• Technological advances
• Legal	• Legal
• Product quality	• OSHA noise levels
• Union and safety considerations	• DOT requirements
• Economic	• Economic
• Market indicators	• Forecast of industry
• Division of market	• Inventory (on-hand/dealers)
• Production runs (timing)	• Steel and chemical output
• Pricing/promotion policy	• Competition
• Sociopolitical	• Sociopolitical
• Allocation of resources	• Produce what is profitable
• Raw material price/availability	• Primarily third world
• Feasibility of exporting	• Threat of imports
• Productivity levels	• Stability of free market

variables in their own industry were considered by top management as important planning variables. The following results were obtained.[38]

- Top management considered fewer variables as being strategic than did middle managers.
- Middle management and top management in systems-oriented companies had better agreement on strategic variable identification than did managers in nonsystems-oriented companies.
- Top executives within the same industry differed as to the identification of strategic variables, even within companies having almost identical business bases.
- Very little attempt was made by top management to quantify the risks involved with each strategic variable.

---

[38] Harold Kerzner, "Survey of Strategic Planning Variables," unpublished report, Project/Systems Management Research Institute, Baldwin-Wallace College, 1977.

As an example of the differences between the project manager and upper-level management, consider the six strategic variables listed below that are characteristic of the machine tool industry.

- Business markets and business cycles
- Product characteristics
- Pricing and promotion policies
- Technology changes
- Labor force and available skills
- Customer organization restructuring

Both project managers and upper-level management agreed upon the first four variables. The last two were identified by upper-level management. Since many products are now made of material other than steel, the question arises as to the availability of qualified workers. This poses a problem in that many customers perform a make-or-buy analysis before contracting with machine tool companies. The machine tool companies surveyed felt that it was the responsibility of upper-level management to continuously communicate with all customers to ascertain if they are contemplating developing or enlarging their machine tool capabilities. Obviously, the decision of a prime customer to develop their own machine shop capabilities could have a severe impact on the contractor's growth potential, business base, and strategic planning philosophy.

Many project managers view the first critical step in planning as obtaining the support of top management, because once it becomes obvious to the functional managers that top management is expressing an interest in the project, they (the functional managers) are more likely to respond favorably to the project team's request for support partly to protect themselves.

Executives are also responsible for selecting the project manager, and the person chosen should have planning expertise. Not all technical specialists are good planners. As Rogers points out:[39]

> The technical planners, whether they are engineers or systems analysts must be experts at designing the system, but seldom do

---

[39] Lloyd A. Rogers, "Guidelines for Project Management Teams," *Industrial Engineering* (December 12, 1974). Published and copyright 1974 by the American Institute of Industrial Engineers, Inc., Norcross, Georgia 30092.

they recognize the need to "put on another hat" when system design specifications are completed and design the project control or implementation plan. If this is not done, setting a project completion target date of a set of management checkpoint milestones is done by guesswork at best. Management will set the checkpoint milestones, and the technical planners will hope they can meet the schedule.

Executives must not arbitrarily set unrealistic milestones and then force line managers to fulfill them. Both project and line managers should try to adhere to unrealistic milestones, but if a line manager says he cannot, executives should comply because the line manager is supposedly the expert. Sometimes, executives lose sight of what they are doing. As an example, a bank executive took the six-month completion milestone and made it three months. The project and line managers rescheduled all of the other projects to reach this milestone. The executive then did the same thing on three other projects and again the project and line managers came to his rescue. The executive began to believe that the line people did not know how to estimate and that they probably loaded up every schedule with "fat." So the executive changed the milestones on all of the other projects to what his "gut feeling" told him was realistic. The reader can imagine the chaos that followed.

Executives should interface with project and line personnel during the planning stage in order to define the requirements and establish reasonable deadlines. Executives must realize that creating an unreasonable deadline may require the reestablishment of priorities and, of course, changing priorities can push milestones forward.

No matter how hard we try, planning is not perfect and sometimes plans fail. Typical reasons why plans fail include:

- Corporate goals are not understood at the lower organizational levels.
- Plans encompass too much in too little time.
- Poor financial estimates are given.
- Plans are based upon insufficient data.
- No attempt is made to systematize the planning process.
- Planning is performed by a planning group.

- No one knows the ultimate objective.
- No one knows the staffing requirements.
- No one knows the major milestone dates, including written reports.
- Project estimates are best guesses, and are not based upon standards or history.
- Not enough time was given for proper estimating.
- No one bothered to see if there would be personnel available with the necessary skills.
- People are not working toward the same specifications.
- People are consistently shuffled in and out of the project with little regard for schedule.

Why do these situations occur, and who should be blamed? If corporate goals are not understood, it is because corporate executives were negligent in providing the necessary strategic information and feedback. If a plan fails because of severe optimism, then the responsibility lies with both the project and line managers for not assessing risk. Project managers should ask the line managers if the estimates are optimistic or pessimistic, and expect an honest answer. Erroneous financial estimates are the responsibility of the line manager. If the project fails because of a poor definition of the requirements, then the project manager is totally at fault.

Project managers must be willing to accept failure. Sometimes, a situation occurs that can lead to failure, and the problem rests with either upper-level management or some other group. As an example, consider the major utility company with a planning group that budgets (with the help of functional groups) and selects those projects to be completed within a given time period. A project manager on one of these projects discovered that the project should have started a month earlier in order to meet the completion date. It is in cases like this that project managers will not become dedicated to projects unless they are active members during the planning and know what assumptions and constraints were considered in development of the plan.

Sometimes, the project manager is part of the planning group and as part of a feasibility study is asked to prepare, with the assistance of functional managers, a schedule and cost summary for a project that will occur three years downstream, if the project is approved at all. Suppose that three years downstream the project is approved. How does the project manager get functional managers to accept the schedule and cost summary that they themselves prepared three years before? It cannot be done because technology may have changed, people may be working higher or lower on the learning curve, and salary and raw material escalation factors are inaccurate.

Sometimes project plans fail because simple details are forgotten or overlooked. Examples of this might be:

- Neglecting to tell a line manager early enough that the prototype is not ready and that rescheduling is necessary
- Neglecting to see if the line manager can provide additional employees for the next two weeks because it was possible six months ago

Sometimes plans fail because the project manager "bites off more than he can chew," and then something happens. Even if the project manager is effective at doing a lot of the work, overburdening is unnecessary. Many projects have failed because the project manager was the only one who knew what was going on, and then got sick.

There are always situations where projects have to be stopped. Below are several reasons why:

- Final achievement of the objectives
- Poor initial planning and market prognosis
- Discovery of a better alternative
- A change in the company interest and strategy
- Exceeding of allocated time
- Exceeding of budgeted costs
- Key people leaving the organization
- Personal whims of management
- Problem too complex for the resources available

Once the reasons for cancellation are defined, the next problem is how to go about stopping the projects.

GENERAL PLANNING

- Orderly planned termination
- The "hatchet" (withdrawal of funds and removal of personnel)
- Reassignment of people to higher priority
- Redirection of efforts toward different objectives
- Burying it or letting it die on the vine (i.e., not taking any official action)

There are three major problem areas to be considered in stopping projects:

- Worker morale
- Reassignment of personnel
- Adequate documentation and wrap-up

Sometimes, executives do not realize the relationship between projects, and what happens if one is cancelled prematurely. As an example, the following remarks were made by an executive concerning data processing operations:

> When 75%–80% of the resource commitment is obtained, there is the point of no return and the benefits to be obtained from the project are anticipated. However, project costs, once forecast, are seldom adjusted during the project life cycle. Adjustments, when made, are normally to increase costs prior to or during conversion. Increases in cost are always in small increments and usually occur when the corporation is "committed," i.e. 75%–80% of the actual costs are expended, however, total actual costs are not known until the project is over. . . .
>
> Projects can and sometimes should be cancelled at any point in the project life cycle. Projects are seldom cancelled because costs exceed forecasts. More often, resources are drained from successful projects. The result of the action is the corporation as a whole becomes marginally successful in bringing all identified projects on line. One might assume individual projects can be analyzed to determine which projects are successful and which are unsuccessful. However, the corporate movement of resources makes the determination difficult without elaborate computer systems. For example, as Project A appears to be successful, resources are

diverted to less successful Project B. The costs associated with Project A increase dramatically as all remaining activities become critical to Project A completion. Increasing costs for Project A are associated with overtime, traveling, etc. Costs for Project B are increasing at a straight time rate and more activities are being accomplished because more manpower can be expended. Often resources, particularly manpower working on Project B, are charged to Project A because the money is in the budget for Project A. The net result in Projects A and B overrun authorized budgets by about the same percentage. In the eyes of top corporate management, neither project team has done well nor have the teams performed poorly. This mediocrity in performance is often the goal of the corporate project management technique.

9
Project Planning

Successful project management, whether it be in response to an in-house project or a customer request, must utilize effective planning techniques. From a systems point of view, management must make effective utilization of resources. This effective utilization over several different types of projects requires a systematic plan in which the entire company is considered one large network subdivided into smaller ones.

The first step in total program scheduling is understanding the project objectives. These goals may be to develop expertise in a given area, become competitive, modify an existing facility for later use, or simply to keep key personnel employed.

The objectives are generally not independent; they are all interrelated both implicitly and explicitly. Many times it is not possible to satisfy all objectives. At this point, management must prioritize the objectives as to which are strategic and which are not.

Once the objectives are clearly defined, four questions must be considered:

- What are the major elements of the work required to satisfy the objectives and how are these elements interrelated?
- Which functional divisions will assume responsibility for accomplishment of these objectives and the major element work requirements?

- Are the required corporate and organizational resources available?
- What are the information flow requirements for the project?

At what point does upper-level management become involved? If the project is large and complex, then careful planning and analysis must be accomplished by both the direct and indirect labor-charging organizational units. The project organizational structure must be designed to fit the project; work plans and schedules must be established such that maximum allocation of resources can be made; resource costing and accounting systems must be developed; and a management information and reporting system must be established.

Effective total program planning cannot be accomplished unless all of the necessary information becomes available at project initiation. These information requirements are:

- The statement of work (SOW)
- The project specifications
- The milestone schedule
- The work breakdown structure (WBS)

The statement of work (SOW) is a narrative description of the work to be accomplished. It includes the objectives of the project, a brief description of the work, and the funding constraint if one exists. The specifications and schedule may be called out by the statement of work. The schedule is a "gross" schedule and includes such items as the

- Start date
- End date
- Major milestones
- Written reports (data items)

Written reports should always be identified so that if functional input is required, the functional manager will know to assign an individual who has writing skills. After all, it is no secret as to who would write the report if the line people did not. In addition, reports may be priced out at a cost per page of report. The current rate appears to be $10 to $12 per page.

The last major item is the work breakdown structure. The WBS is the breaking down of the statement of work into smaller elements so that better visibility and control will be obtained. In planning a project, the project manager must structure the work into small elements that are:

- Manageable, in that specific authority and responsibility can be assigned
- Independent or with minimum interfacing with and dependence on other ongoing elements
- Integratable so that the total package can be seen
- Measurable in terms of progress

The first major step in the planning process is the development of the work breakdown structure. The WBS is the single most important element because it provides a common framework from which:

- The total program can be described as a summation of subdivided elements.
- Planning can be performed.
- Costs and budgets can be established.
- Time, cost, and performance can be tracked.
- Objectives can be linked to company resources in a logical manner.
- Schedules and status reporting procedures can be established.
- Network construction and control planning can be initiated.
- The responsibility assignments for each element can be established.

The WBS acts as a vehicle for breaking the work down into smaller elements, thus providing a greater probability that every major and minor activity will be accounted for. Although a variety of work breakdown structures exist, the most common is the six-level indentured structure shown below:

Level	Description
1	Total program
2	Project
3	Task
4	Subtask
5	Work package
6	Level of effort

Level 1 is the total program and is composed of a set of projects. The summation of the activities and costs associated with each project must equal the total program. Each project, however, can be broken down into tasks, where the summation of all tasks equals the summation of all projects which, in turn, comprises the total program. The reason for this subdivision of effort is simply for ease of control. Program management therefore becomes synonymous with the integration of activities, and the project manager acts as the integrator using the WBS as the common framework.

The upper three levels of the WBS are normally specified by the customer (if part of an RFP/RFQ) as the summary levels for reporting purposes. The lower levels are generated by the contractor for in-house control. Each level serves a vital purpose; level 1 is generally used for the authorization and release of all work, budgets are prepared at level 2, and schedules are prepared at level 3. Certain characteristics can now be generalized for these levels:

- The top three levels of the WBS reflect integrated efforts and should not be related to one specific department. Effort required by departments or sections should be defined in subtasks and work packages.
- The summation of all elements in one level must be the sum of all work in the next-lower level.
- Each element of work should be assigned to one and only one level of effort. For example, the construction of the foundation of a house should be included in one project (or task), not extended over two or three.
- The WBS must be accompanied by a description of the scope of effort required or else only those individuals who issue the WBS

will have a complete understanding of what work has to be accomplished. It is common practice to reproduce the customer's statement of work as the description for the WBS.

In setting up the work breakdown structure, tasks should

- Have clearly defined start and end dates
- Be usable as a communicative tool in which results can be compared with expectations
- Be estimated on a total time duration, not when the task must start or end
- Be structured so that a minimum of project office control and documentation (i.e., forms) are necessary

Table 18 shows a simple work breakdown structure with the associate numbering system; the first number represents the total program (in this case, it is represented by 01), the second number represents the project, and the third number identifies the task. Therefore, number 01-03-00 represents project 3 of program 01 while 01-03-02 represents task 2 of project 3. This type of numbering system is not unique; each company may have its own system depending on how costs are to be controlled.

Table 18. Work Breakdown Structure for New Plant Construction and Start-up.

Program: New Plant Construction and Start-up	01-00-00
Project 1: Analytical Study	01-01-00
Task 1: Marketing/Production Study	01-01-01
Task 2: Cost Effectiveness Analysis	01-01-02
Project 2: Design Layout	01-02-00
Task 1: Product Processing Sketches	01-02-01
Task 2: Product Processing Blueprints	01-02-02
Project 3: Installation	01-03-00
Task 1: Fabrication	01-03-01
Task 2: Setup	01-03-02
Task 3: Testing and Run	01-03-03
Project 4: Program Support	01-04-00
Task 1: Management	01-04-01
Task 2: Purchase of Raw Materials	01-04-02

The preparation of the work breakdown structure is not easy. The WBS is a communications tool, providing detailed information to different levels of management. If the WBS does not contain enough levels, then the integration of activities may prove difficult. If too many levels exist, then unproductive time will be incurred along with additional costs and paperwork. No attempt should be made to have the same number of levels for all projects, tasks, etc. Each major work element should be considered by itself. Remember, the work breakdown structure establishes the number of required networks for cost control.

For many programs, the work breakdown structure is established by the customer. If the contractor is required to develop a WBS, then certain guidelines must be considered. A partial list is identified below:

- The complexity and technical requirements of the program (i.e., the statement of work)
- The program cost
- The time span of the program
- The contractor's resource requirements
- The contractor's and customer's internal structure for management control and reporting
- The number of subcontracts

Applying these guidelines serves only to identify the complexity of the program. This data must then be subdivided and released together with detailed information, to the different levels of the organization. The WBS should follow specified criteria because, although preparation of the WBS is performed by the program office, the actual work is performed by the doers, and the planners must be in agreement as to what is expected. A sample criteria listing for developing a work breakdown structure is shown below:

- The WBS and work description should be easy to understand.
- All schedules should follow the WBS.
- No attempt should be made to arbitrarily subdivide work to the lowest possible level. The lowest level of work should not end up being a ridiculous cost in comparison to other efforts.

- Since scope of effort can change during a program, every effort should be made to maintain flexibility in the WBS.

From a cost-control point of view, cost analysis down to the fifth level is advantageous. However, it should be noted that the cost required to prepare cost-analysis data to each lower level may increase exponentially, especially if the customer requires data to be presented in a specified format that is not part of the company's standard operating procedures. The level 5 work packages are normally for in-house control only.

The WBS can be subdivided into subobjectives with finer divisions of effort as we go lower into the WBS. By defining subobjectives, we add greater understanding and, it is hoped, clarity of action for those individuals who will be required to complete the objectives. Whenever work is structured, understood, and easily identifiable and within the capabilities of the individuals, there will almost always exist a high degree of confidence that the objective can be reached.

Work breakdown structures can be used to structure work for reaching such objectives as lowering costs, reducing absenteeism, improving morale, and lowering scrap factors. The lowest subdivision now becomes an end item or subobjective, not necessarily a work package as described here. However, since we are describing project management, for the remainder of the text we will consider the lowest level as the work package.

10
Program Plan

Fundamental to the success of any project is documented planning in the form of a program plan. In an ideal situation, the program office can present the functional manager with a copy of the program plan and simply say, "Accomplish it." The concept of the program plan came under severe scrutiny during the 1960s when the Department of Defense required all contractors to submit detailed planning to such extremes that many organizations were wasting talented people by having them serve as writers instead of doers. Since then, because of the complexity of large programs, requirements imposed on the program plan have been eased.

For large and often complex programs, customers may require a program plan that documents all activities within the program. The program plan then serves as a guideline for the lifetime of the program and may be revised as often as once a month, depending upon the circumstances and the type of program (i.e., research and development programs require more revisions to the program plan than do manufacturing or construction programs.) The program plan provides the following framework:

- Eliminates conflicts between functional managers
- Eliminates conflicts between functional management and program management

- Provides a standard communicative tool throughout the lifetime of the program (it should be geared to the work breakdown structure)
- Provides verification that the contractor understands the customer's objectives and requirements
- Provides a means for identifying inconsistencies in the planning phase
- Provides a means for early identification of problem areas and risks so that no surprises occur "downstream"
- Contains all of the schedules as a basis for progress analysis and reporting

Development of a program plan can be time-consuming and costly. The input requirements for the program plan depend on the size of the project and the integration of resources and activities. All levels of the organization participate. The upper levels provide summary information and the lower levels provide the details. The program plan, as with activity schedules, does not preclude departments from developing their own planning.

The program plan must identify how the company resources will be integrated. Finalization of the program is an iterative process, as shown in Figure 27. Since the program plan must explain the events in Figure 27, additional iterations are required which can cause changes in a program.

The program plan is a standard from which performance can be measured, not only by the customer, but by program and functional management as well. The plan serves as a cookbook for the duration of the program by defining for all personnel identified with the program:

- How will it be accomplished?
- What will be accomplished?
- Where will it be accomplished?
- When will it be accomplished?
- Why will it be accomplished?

140 ORGANIZING, PLANNING, AND CONTROL

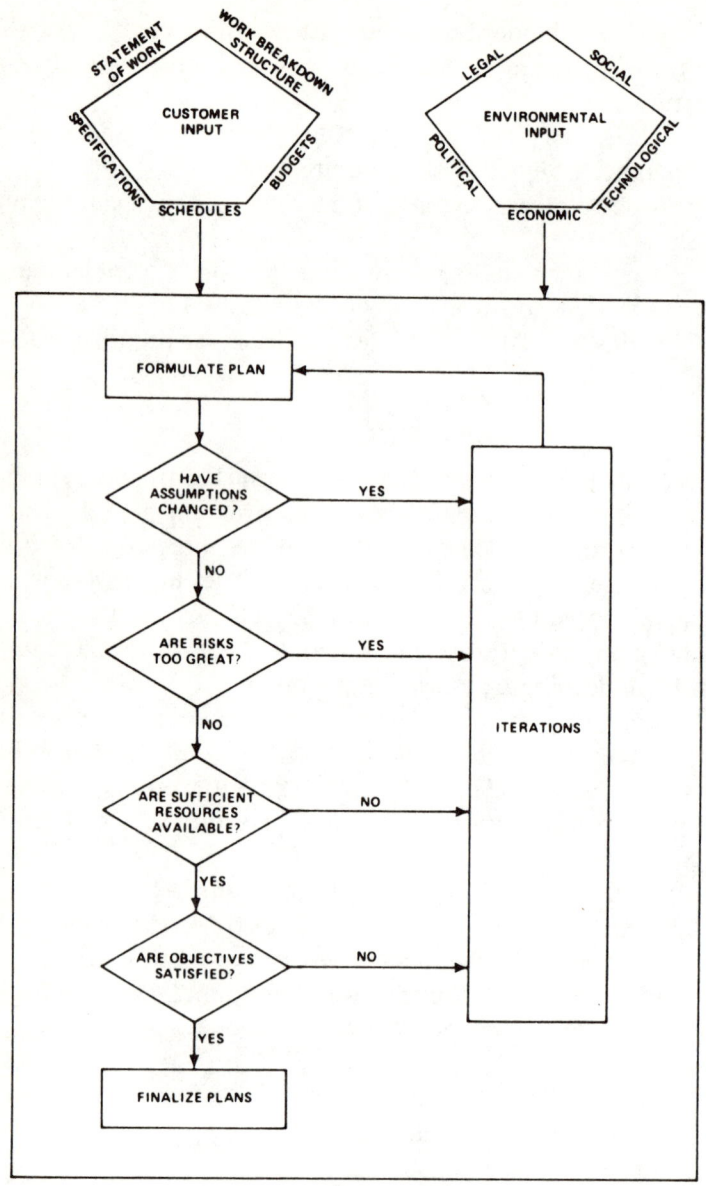

Figure 27. Iterations for the planning process.

PROGRAM PLAN   141

The answers to these questions force both the contractor and the customer to take a hard look at:

- Program requirements
- Program management
- Program schedules
- Facility requirements
- Logistic support
- Financial support
- Manpower and organization

The program plan is more than just a set of instructions. It is an attempt to eliminate crisis by preventing anything from "falling through the crack." The plan is documented and approved by both the customer and the contractor to determine what data, if any, is missing and the probable resulting effect. As the program matures, the program plan is revised to account for new or missing data. The most common reasons for revising a plan are:

- "Crashing" activities to meet end dates
- Trade-off decisions involving manpower, scheduling, and performance
- Adjusting and leveling manpower requests

Maturity of a program usually implies that crisis will decrease. Unfortunately, this is not always the case.

The makeup of the program plan may vary from contractor to contractor.[40] Most program plans can be subdivided into four main sections: introduction, summary and conclusions, management, and technical. The complexity of the information is usually up to the discretion of the contractor provided that customer requirements, as may be specified in the statement of work, are satisfied.

The introductory section contains the definition of the program and the major parts involved. If the program follows another, or is

---

[40]Cleland and King define 14 subsections for a program plan. This detail appears more applicable to the technical and management volumes of a proposal. They do, however, provide a more detailed picture than presented here. See Cleland and King, *System Analysis and Project Management*, New York: McGraw-Hill, 1975, pp. 371-380.

an outgrowth of similar activities, this is identified together with a brief summary of the background and history behind the project.

The summary and conclusion section identifies the targets and objectives of the program and includes the necessary "lip service" on how successful the program will be and how all problems can be overcome. This section must also include the program master schedule showing how all projects and activities are related. The total program master schedule should include the following:

- An appropriate scheduling system (bar charts, milestone charts, network, etc.)
- A listing of activities at the project level or lower
- The possible interrelationships between activities. This can be accomplished by logic networks, critical path networks, or PERT networks.
- Activity time estimates (this is a natural result of the item above)

The summary and conclusion chapter is usually the second section in the program plan so that upper-level customer management can have a complete overview of the program without having to search through the technical information.

The management section of the program plan contains procedures, charts, and schedules for the following:

- The assignment of key personnel to the program. This usually refers only to the program office personnel and team members, since under normal operations these will be the only individuals interfacing with customers.
- Manpower, planning, and training will be discussed to assure customers that qualified people will be available from the functional units.
- A linear responsibility chart might also be included to identify to customers the authority relationships that will exist in the program.

Situations exist where the management section may be omitted from the proposal. For a follow-up program, the customer may not require this section if management's positions are unchanged. Management sections are also not required if the management information was previously provided in the proposal or if the customer and contractor have continuous business dealings.

The technical section may include as much as 75 to 90 percent of the program plan, especially if the effort includes research and development. The technical section may require constant updating as the program matures. The following items can be included as part of the technical section:

- A detailed breakdown of the charts and schedules used in the program master schedule, possibly including schedule/cost estimates.
- A listing of the testing to be accomplished for each activity. (It is best to include the exact testing matrices.)
- Procedures for accomplishment of the testing. This might also include a description of the key elements in the operations or manufacturing plans as well as a listing of the facility and logistic requirements.

Table 19. Types of Plans.

TYPE OF PLAN	DESCRIPTION
• Budget	How much money is allocated to each event?
• Configuration management	How are technical changes made?
• Facilities	What facilities resources are available?
• Logistics support	How will replacements be handled?
• Management	How is the program office organized?
• Manufacturing	What are the time-phased manufacturing events?
• Procurement	What are my resources? Should I make or buy? If vendors are not qualified, how shall I qualify them?
• Quality assurance	How will I guarantee specifications will be met?
• Research/development	What are the technical activities?
• Scheduling	Are all critical dates accounted for?
• Tooling	What are my time-phased tooling requirements?
• Training	How will I manage qualified personnel?
• Transportation	How will goods and service by shipped?

144 ORGANIZING, PLANNING, AND CONTROL

- Identification of materials and material specifications. (This might also include system specifications.)
- Although uncommon, some program plans attempt to identify the risks associated with specific technical requirements. This has the tendency to scare management personnel who are unfamiliar with the technical procedures and should therefore be omitted if at all possible.

The program plan, as used here, contains a description of all phases of the program. For many programs, especially large ones,

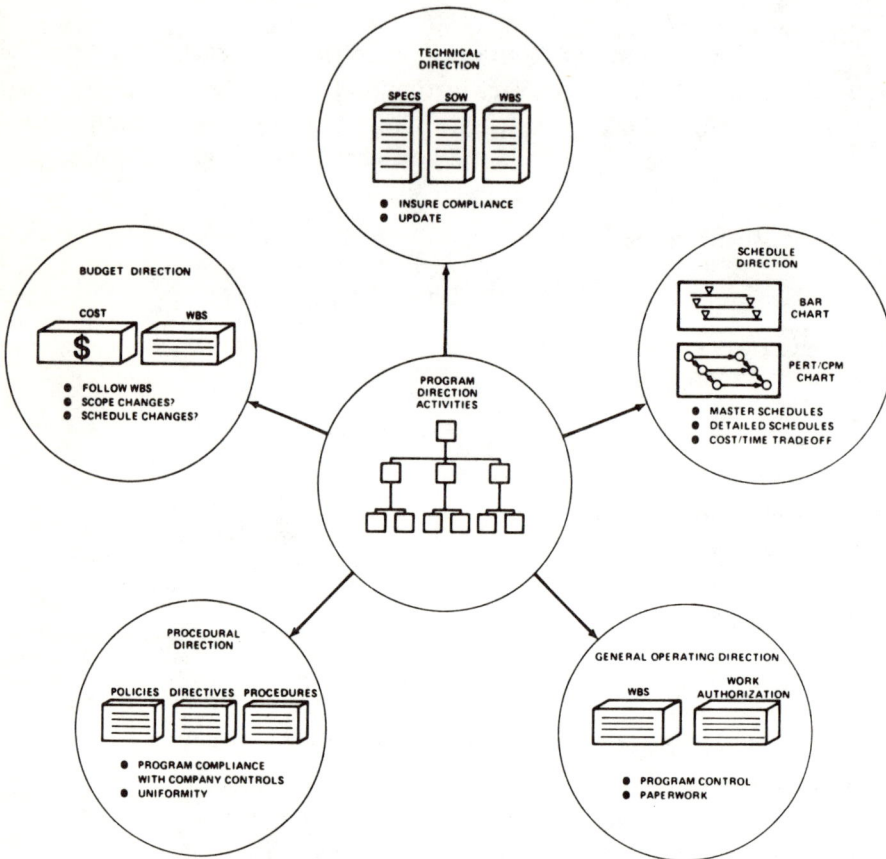

Figure 28. Program direction activities.

detailed planning is required for all major events and activities. Table 19 identifies the type of individual plans that may be required in place of a (total) program plan. However, care must be taken in that too much paperwork can easily inhibit successful management of a program.

The program plan, once agreed upon by the contractor and customer, is then used to provide program direction. This is shown in Figure 28. If the program plan is written clearly, then any functional manager or supervisor should be able to identify what is expected of him.

The program plan should be distributed to each member of the program team, all functional managers and supervisors interfacing with the program, and all key functional personnel. The program plan does not contain all of the answers, for if it did, there would be no need for a program office. The plan serves merely as a guide.

One final note must be mentioned concerning the legality of the program plan. The program plan may be specified contractually to satisfy certain requirements as identified in the customer's statement of work. The contractor retains the right as to how to accomplish this, unless of course, this is also identified in the SOW. If the statement of work specifies that quality assurance testing be accomplished on 15 end items off of the product on line, then 15 is the minimum number that must be tested. The program plan may show that 25 items are to be tested. If the contractor develops cost overrun problems, he may wish to revert to the SOW and test only 15 items. Contractually, he may do this without informing the customer. In most cases, however, the customer is notified and the program is revised.

11
Detailed Schedules and Charts

The detailed scheduling of activities is the first major requirement of the program office after program go-ahead. The program office normally assumes full responsibility for activity scheduling if the activity is not too complex. For large programs, functional management input is required before scheduling can be completed. Depending on program size and contractual requirements, it is not unusual for the program office to maintain, at all times, a program staff member whose responsibility is that of a scheduler. This individual continuously develops and updates activity schedules to provide a means of tracking program work. The resulting information is then supplied to the program office personnel, functional management, team members, and last but not least, the customer.

Activity schedules are invaluable for projecting the single most important tool for determining how company resources should be integrated such that synergy will be produced. Activity schedules are invaluable for projecting time-phased resource utilization requirements as well as for providing a basis for visually tracking performance. Most programs begin with the development of the schedules so that accurate cost estimates can be made. The schedules serve as master plans from which both the customer and management have an up-to-date picture of operations.

Certain guidelines should be followed in preparation of schedules, regardless of the projected use or complexity:

- All major events and dates must be clearly identified. If a statement of work is supplied by the customer, then those dates shown on the accompanying schedules must be included. If for any reason the customer's milestone dates cannot be met, then the customer should be notified immediately.
- The exact sequence of work should be defined through a network in which interrelationships between events can be identified.
- Schedules should be directly relatable to the work breakdown structure. If the WBS is developed according to a specific sequence of work, then it becomes an easy task to identify work sequences in schedules using the same numbering system as in the WBS. The minimum requirement should be to show where and when all tasks start and finish.
- All schedules must identify the time constraints and, if possible, should identify those resources required for each event.

Although these four guidelines serve as reference for schedule preparation, they do not define how complex the schedules should be. Before the schedules are prepared, three questions should be considered:

- How many events or activities should each network have?
- How much of a detailed technical breakdown should be included?
- Who is the intended audience for this schedule?

Most organizations develop multiple schedules: summary schedules for management and planners, and detailed schedules for the doers and lower-level control. The detailed schedules may be strictly for interdepartmental activities. Program management must approve all schedules down through the first three levels of the work breakdown structure. For lower-level schedules (i.e., detailed interdepartmental) program management may or may not request sign of approval.

The necessity for two schedules is clear. According to Martin,[41]

> In larger complicated projects, planning and status review by different echelons are facilitated by the use of detailed and summary

---

[41] Charles Martin, *Project Management: How to Make It Work*, New York: Amacom, a division of American Management Associations, 1976, p. 137.

networks. Higher levels of management can view the entire project and the interrelationships of major tasks without looking into the detail of the individual subtasks. Lower levels of management and supervision can examine their parts of the project in fine detail without being distracted by those parts of the project with which they have no interface.

One of the most difficult problems to identify in schedules is a hedge position. A hedge position is a situation in which the contractor may not be able to meet a customer's milestone date without incurring a risk, or may not be able to meet activity requirements following a milestone date because of contractual requirements. To illustrate a common hedge position, consider the example below:

Example: Condor Corporation is currently working on a project that includes three phases: design, development, and qualification of a certain component. Contractual requirements with the customer specify that no components will be fabricated for the development phase until the design review meeting is held following the design phase. Condor has determined that if they do not begin component fabrication prior to the design review meeting, then the second and third phases will slip. Condor is willing to accept risk that should specifications be unacceptable during the design review meeting, the costs associated with preauthorization of fabrication will be incurred. How should this be shown on a schedule? (The problems associated with performing unauthorized work are not being considered here.)

The solution to this example is not an easy one. Condor must play an honest game and identify on the master production schedule that component fabrication will begin early, at the contractor's risk. This should be followed up by a contractual letter in which both the customer and contractor understand the risks and implications.

The above example also brings up the question as to whether this hedge position could have been eliminated with proper planning. Hedge positions are notorious for occurring in research and development or design phases of a program. Condor's technical community, for example, may have anticipated that each component could be fabricated in one week based on certain raw materials. If new raw materials were required or a new fabrication process had to be developed, it is then possible that the new component fabrication time could increase from one week to two or three, thus creating an unanticipated hedge position.

Detailed schedules are prepared for almost every activity. It is the responsibility of the program office to marry all of the detailed schedules into one master schedule to verify that all activities can be completed as planned. The preparation sequence of schedules (and also for program plans) is shown in Figure 29. The program office submits a request for detailed schedules to the functional managers. The request may be in the form of a planning work authorization document. The functional managers then prepare summary schedules, detailed schedules, and if time permits, interdepartmental schedules. Each functional manager then reviews his schedules with the program team members, who integrate all of the plans and schedules and verify that all contractual dates can be met.

Before submitting the schedules to publication, rough drafts of each schedule and plan should be reviewed with the customer. This procedure accomplishes the following:

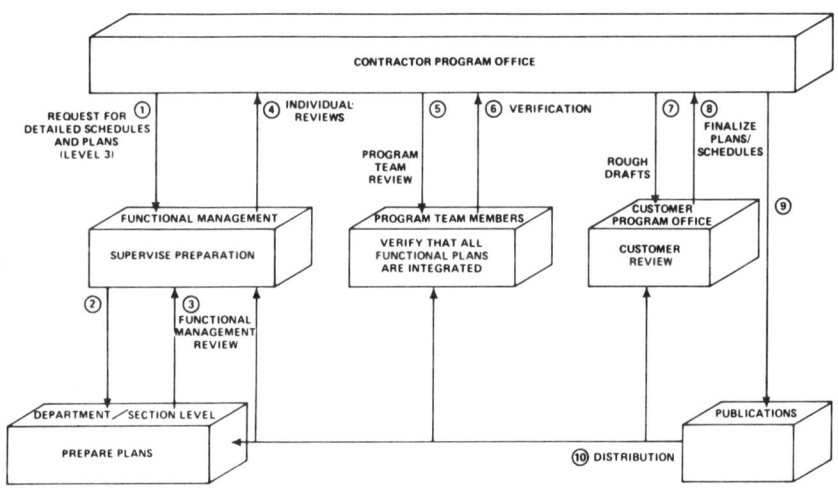

Figure 29. Preparation sequence for schedules and program plans.

- Verifies that nothing has fallen through the crack
- Prevents immediate revisions to a published document and can prevent embarrassing moments
- Minimizes production costs by reducing the number of early revisions
- Shows customers early in the program that you welcome their help and input into the planning phase

After the document is published, it should be distributed to all program office personnel, functional team members, functional management, and the customer.

The exact method of preparing the schedules is usually up to the individual performing the activity. All schedules, however, must be approved by the program office. The schedules are normally prepared in a manner that is suitable to both the customer and contractor in a manner that is easily understood by all. The schedules may then be used for in-house use as well as customer review meetings, in which case the contractor can kill two birds with one stone by tracking cost and performance on the original schedules.

In addition to the detailed schedules, the program office, with input provided by functional management, must develop organizational charts. The organizational charts provide information to all active participants of the project as to who has responsibility for each activity. The organizational charts display the formal (and often informal) lines of communication.

The program office may also establish linear responsibility charts (LRCs). Regardless of the best attempts by management, many functions in an organization can overlap between more than one functional unit. Also, management might wish to have the responsibility for a certain activity given to a functional unit that normally would not have this responsibility. This is a common occurrence on short-duration programs where management desires to cut costs and red tape.

Care must be taken that project personnel do not forget the reason why the schedule was developed. The primary objective of detailed schedules is usually to coordinate activities into a master plan in order to complete the project with the:

- Best time
- Least cost
- Least risk

Of course, the objective can be constrained by:

- Calendar completion dates
- Cash or cash flow restrictions
- Limited resources
- Approvals

There are also secondary objectives of scheduling:

- Studying alternatives
- Developing an optimal
- Using resources effectively
- Communicating
- Refining the estimating criteria
- Obtaining good project control
- Providing for easy revisions

12
Cost Control

Cost control is equally if not more important to small companies as large companies. Small companies generally have tighter monetary controls, mainly because of the risk associated with the failure of as little as one project, but have less sophisticated control techniques. Large companies may have the luxury to spread project losses over several projects whereas the small company may have few projects.

Too many people have a poor definition of cost control. Cost control is not only monitoring of costs and recording perhaps massive quantities of data, but also analyzing the data in order to take corrective action before it is too late. Cost control should be performed by all personnel who incur costs, not merely the project office.

Cost control implies good cost management, which must include:

- Cost estimating
- Cost accounting
- Project cash flow
- Company cash flow
- Direct labor costing
- Overhead rate costing
- Others, such as incentives, penalties, and profit sharing

Cost control is actually a subsystem of the *management cost and control system* (MCCS) rather than a complete system per se. This is shown in Figure 30, where the MCCS is represented as a two-cycle

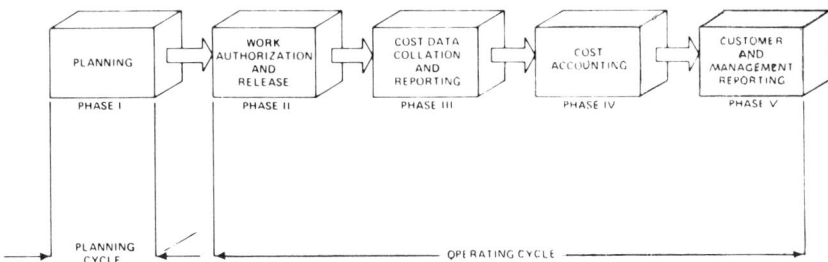

Figure 30. Phases of a management cost and control system.

process: a planning cycle and an operating cycle. The operating cycle is what is commonly referred to as the cost-control system. Failure of a cost-control system to accurately describe the true status of a project does not necessarily imply that the cost-control system is at fault. Any cost-control system is only as good as the original plan against which performance will be measured. It is more common for the plan to be at fault rather than the control system. Therefore, the designing of a company's planning system must take into account the cost-control system as well. For this reason, it is common for the planning cycle to be referred to as planning and control, whereas the operating cycle is referred to as cost and control.

The planning and control system selected must be able to satisfy management's needs and requirements in order that they can accurately project the status toward objective completion. The planning and control system must, therefore, provide information that

- Gives a picture of true work progress
- Will relate cost and schedule performance
- Identifies potential problems as to their sources
- Provides information to project managers with a practical level of summarization
- Demonstrates that the milestones are valid, timely, and auditable

The planning and control system, in addition to being a tool by which objectives can be defined (i.e., hierarchy of objectives and organization accountability), exists as a tool to develop planning, measure progress, and control change. As a tool for planning, the system must be able to be used to:

- Plan and schedule work
- Identify those indicators that will be used for measurement
- Establish direct labor budgets
- Establish overhead budgets
- Identify management reserve

Establishing budgets requires that the planner fully understand the meaning of standards. There are two categories of standards. Performance results standards are quantitative measurements and include such items as quality of work, quantity of work, cost of work, and time to complete. Process standards are qualitative and include personal, functional, and physical factors relationships. Standards are advantageous in that they provide a means for unity, a basis for effective control, and an incentive for others. The disadvantage of standards is that performance is often frozen and employees are quite often unable to adjust to the differences.

As a tool for measuring progress and controlling change, the systems must be able to

- Measure resources consumed
- Measure status and accomplishments
- Compare measurements to projections and standards
- Provide the basis for diagnosis and replanning

Almost all project planning and control systems have identifiable design requirements. These include:

- A common framework from which to integrate time, cost, and technical performance
- Ability to track progress of significant parameters
- Quick response
- Capability for end-value prediction
- Accurate and appropriate data for decision-making by each level of management
- Full exception reporting with problem analysis capability
- Immediate quantitative evaluation of alternative solutions

Even with a fully developed planning and control system, there are numerous benefits and costs. The appropriate system must consider a cost-benefit analysis, and include such items as:

- Project Benefits
  - Planning and control techniques facilitate:
    - Derivation of output specifications (project objectives)
    - Delineation of required activities (work)
    - Coordination and communication between organizational units
    - Determination of type, amount, and timing of necessary resources
    - Recognition of high-risk elements and assessment of uncertainties
    - Suggestions of alternative courses of action
    - Realization of effect of resource level changes on schedule and output performance
    - Measurement and reporting of genuine progress
    - Identification of potential problems
    - Basis for problem-solving, decision-making, and corrective action
    - Assurance of coupling between planning and control
- Project Cost
  - Planning and control techniques require:
    - New forms (new systems) of information from additional sources and incremental processing (managerial time, computer expense, etc.)
    - Additional personnel or smaller span of control to free managerial time for planning and control tasks (increased overhead)
    - Training in use of techniques (time and materials)

Two new programs are currently being used by the government and industry in conjunction with MCCS as an attempt to improve effectiveness in cost control. The zero-base budgeting program was established to provide better estimating techniques for the verification portion of control. The design-to-cost program assists the decision-making part of the control process by identifying a decision-making framework from which replanning can take place.

Effective management of a program during the operating cycle requires that a well-organized cost and control system be designed, developed, and implemented to provide immediate feedback so that the up-to-date usage of resources can be compared to the target objectives established during the planning cycle. The requirements for an effective control system (for both cost and schedule/performance) should include:[42]

- Thorough planning of the work to be performed to complete the project
- Good estimating of time, labor, and costs
- Clear communication of scope of required tasks
- Disciplined budget and authorization of expenditures
- Timely accounting of physical progress and cost expenditures
- Periodic reestimation of time and cost to complete remaining work
- Frequent, periodic comparison of actual progress and expenditures to schedules and budgets, both at the time of comparison and at project completion

Management must compare the time, cost, and performance of the program to the budgeted time, cost, and performance not independently, but in an integrated manner. Being within one's budget at the proper time serves no useful purpose if performance is only 75 percent. Likewise, having a production line turn out exactly 200 items, when planned, loses its significance if a 50 percent cost overrun was incurred. All three resource parameters (time, cost, and performance) must be analyzed as a group or else we might win the battle but lose the war. Because of this, the use of the expression "management cost and control system" is vague in that it implies that only costs are controlled. This is not true. An effective control system monitors schedule and performance as well as costs by setting budgets,

---

[42] Russell, Archibald, *Managing High-Technology Programs and Projects,* New York: Wiley, 1976, p. 191.

measuring expenditures against budgets and identifying variances, assuring that the expenditures are proper, and taking corrective action when required.

Previously we defined the work breakdown structure as being that element which acts as the source from which all costs and controls must emanate. The work breakdown structure therefore serves as the tool from which performance can be subdivided into objectives and subobjectives. As work progresses, the WBS provides the framework from which costs, time, and schedule/performance can be compared against the budget for each level of the WBS.

The first purpose of control therefore becomes a verification process accomplished by the comparison of actual performance to date with the predetermined plans and standards set forth in the planning phase. The comparison serves to verify that:

- The objectives have been successfully translated into performance standards.
- The performance standards are, in fact, a reliable representation of program activities and events.
- Meaningful budgets are established such that actual versus planned comparisons can be made.

In other words, the comparison verifies that the corrective standards were selected and that they are properly used.

The second purpose of control is that of decision-making. Three useful reports are required by management to make effective and timely decisions. These are:

- The project plan, schedule, and budget prepared during the planning phase.
- A detailed comparison between resources expended to date and those predetermined. This includes an estimate of the work remaining and the impact on activity completion.
- A projection of resources to be expended out through program completion.

These reports are then supplied to both the managers and doers. Three useful results arise through the use of these three reports generated by a thorough decision-making stage of control:

158 ORGANIZING, PLANNING, AND CONTROL

- Feedback to management, the planners, and the doers
- Identification of any major deviations from the current program plan, schedule, or budget
- The opportunity to initiate contingency planning early enough so that cost, performance, and time requirements can undergo corrective action without loss of resources

These reports, if properly prepared, provide management with the opportunity to minimize downstream changes by making proper corrections here and now. As shown in Figure 31, possible cost reductions are usually available more readily in the early project phases, but are reduced as we go further into the project life cycle phases. Downstream, the cost for changes could easily exceed the original cost of the project.

The management cost and control system (MCCS) takes on paramount importance during the operating cycle of the project. The operating cycle is composed of four phases:

- Work authorization and release (phase II)
- Cost data collection and reporting (phase III)
- Cost analysis (phase IV)
- Reporting: customer and management (phase V)

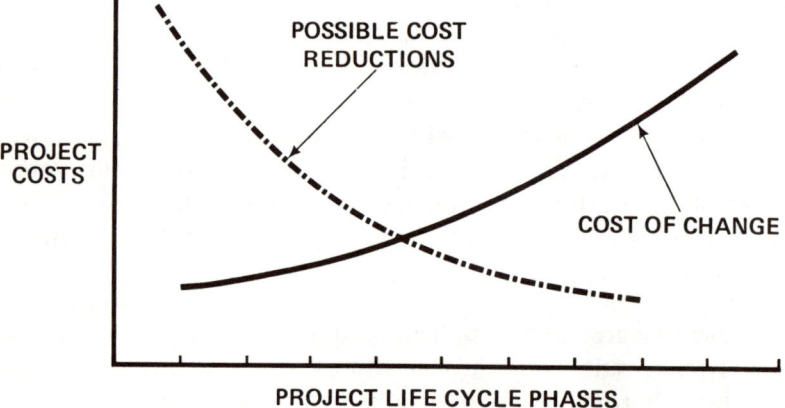

Figure 31. Cost reductions.

These four phases, when combined with the planning cycle (phase I) constitute a closed network that forms the basis for the management cost and control system.

Phase II is considered a work release. After planning is completed and a contract is received, work is authorized via a work description document. This multipurpose form is used to release the contract, authorize planning, record detail description of the work outlined in the work breakdown structure, and release work.

Contract services may require a work description form to release the contract. The contractual work description form sets forth general contractual requirements and authorizes program management to proceed.

Program management may then issue a subdivided work description form to the functional units so that work can begin. This form sets forth contractual requirements and planning guidelines for the applicable performing organizations. The subdivided work description package established during the proposal and updated after negotiations by the program team is incrementally released by program management to the work control centers in manufacturing, engineering, publications, and program management as the authority for release of work orders to the performing organizations. The subdivided work description specifies how contractual requirements are to be accomplished, the functional organizations involved, and their specific responsibilities, and authorizes the expenditure of resources within a particular time frame.

The work control center assigns a work order number to the subdivided work description form, if no additional instructions are required, and releases the documents to the performing organizations. If additional instructions are required, the work control center can prepare a more detailed work release document (shop traveler, tool order, work order release), assign applicable work order numbers, and release the documents to the performing organizations.

A work order number is required for all in-house direct and indirect charging. The work order number also serves as a cross-reference number for automatic assignment of the indentured work breakdown structure number to labor and material data records in the computer.

Small companies can avoid this additional paperwork cost by going directly from an awarded contract to a single work order which may be the only work order needed for the entire contract.

160 ORGANIZING, PLANNING, AND CONTROL

Since project managers control resources through the line managers rather than directly, project managers end up controlling direct labor costs by opening and closing work orders. To illustrate this, consider the cost-account code breakdown shown in Figure 32 and the work authorization form shown in Figure 33. The work authorization form specifically identifies the cost centers that are open for this charge number, the man-hours available for each cost center, and the operational time period for the charge number. Because the exact dates of operation are completely defined, the charge number can be assigned perhaps as much as a year in advance of the work-begin date.

If the man-hours are assigned to Cost Center 2400, then any 24XX cost center can use this charge number. If the work authorization form specifies Cost Center 2610, then any 261X cost center can use the charge number. However, if Cost Center 2623 is specified, then no lower cost accounts exist and this is the only cost center that can use this work order charge number. In other words, if a charge number

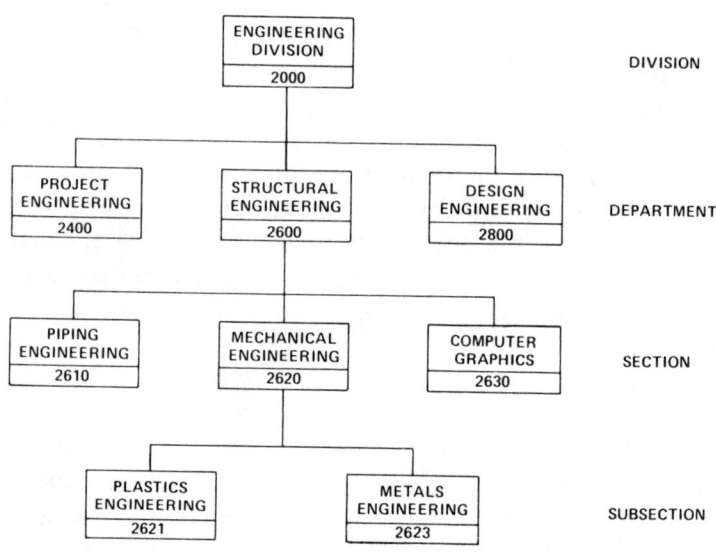

Figure 32. Cost-account code breakdown.

is opened up at the department level, then the department manger has the right to subdivide the assigned man-hours among the various sections and subsections. Company policy usually identifies the permissible cost center levels that can be assigned in the work authorization form. These permissible levels are related to the work breakdown structure level. For example, Cost Center 5000 (i.e., divisional) can be assigned at the project level of the work breakdown structure, but only departmental, sectional, or subsectional cost accounts can be assigned at the task level of the work breakdown structure.

If a cost center needs additional time or additional man-hours, then a cost-account change notice form must be initiated, usually by the requesting cost center, and approved by the project office. Figure 34 shows a typical cost-account change notice form.

Large companies have computerized cost-control and reporting systems. Small companies have manual or partially computerized systems. The major difficulty in using Figures 32 and 33 depends upon whether or not the employee fills out time cards and upon the frequency with which the time cards are filled out. Project-driven organizations fill out time cards at least once a week and are inputted

WORK AUTHORIZATION FORM

WBS NO: 31-03-02   WORK ORDER NO: D1385

DATE OF ORIGINAL RELEASE: 3 FEB 80

DATE OF REVISION   :   18 MAR 80

REVISION NUMBER   :   C

DESCRIPTION	COST CENTERS	HOURS	WORK BEGINS	WORK ENDS
TEST MATERIAL VB–2 IN ACCORDANCE WITH THE PROGRAM PLAN AND MIL STANDARD G1483-52. THIS TASK INCLUDES A WRITTEN REPORT.	2400 2610 2621 2623 5000*	150 160 140 46 600	1 AUG 80	15 SEPT. 80

PROJECT OFFICE AUTHORIZATION SIGNATURE _____

*NOTE: SOME COMPANIES DO NOT PERMIT DIVISION COST CENTERS TO CHARGE AT LEVEL 3 OF THE WBS

Figure 33. Work authorization form. (*Note:* Some companies do not permit division cost centers to charge at level 3 of the WBS.)

162 ORGANIZING, PLANNING, AND CONTROL

CACN No. _____ Revision to Cost Account No. _____ Date _____

DESCRIPTION OF CHANGE:

_____
_____
_____
_____
_____
_____

REASON FOR CHANGE:

_____
_____
_____
_____
_____
_____

	Requested Budget	Authorized Budget	
Labor Hours	_____	_____	Period of Performance:
Material $	_____	_____	From _____
Indirect $	_____	_____	To _____

BUDGET SOURCE:
☐ Funded Contract Change
☐ Management Reserve
☐ Undistributed Budget
☐ Other _____

INITIATED BY: _____

APPROVALS: Program Mgr. _____
Prog. Control _____

Figure 34. Cost-account change notice (CACN).

to a computerized system. Nonproject-driven organizations fill out time cards on a monthly basis with computerization dependent upon the size of the company.

Cost data collection and reporting is the second phase of the operating cycle of the MCCS. Actual cost and the budgeted cost of work performed for each contract or in-house project are accumulated in detailed cost accounts by cost center and cost element, and reported in accordance with the flowcharts shown in Figure 35. These detailed elements, for both actual costs incurred and the budgeted cost of work performed, are usually printed out monthly for all levels of the

COST CONTROL

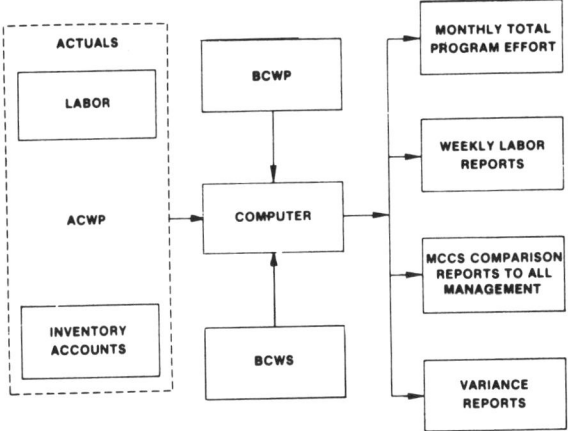

Figure 35. Cost data collection and reporting flowchart.

work breakdown structure. In addition, weekly supplemental direct labor reports can be printed which show the actual labor charges incurred and compared to the predicted efforts.

Table 20 shows a typical weekly labor report. The first column identifies the WBS number.[43] If more than one work order were assigned to this WBS element, then the work order number would appear under the WBS number. This procedure would be repeated for all work orders under the same WBS number. The second column contains the cost centers charging to this WBS element (and possibly work order numbers). Cost Center 41XX represents department 41 and is a roll up of Cost Centers 4110, 4115, and 4118. Cost Center 4XXX represents the entire division and is a roll up of all 4000-level departments. Cost Center XXXX represents the total for all divisions charging to this WBS element. The weekly labor reports must list all cost centers authorized to charge to this WBS element regardless of whether or not they have incurred any costs over the last reporting period.

---

[43] Only three levels of cost reporting are assumed here. If work packages were used, then the WBS number would identify all five levels of control.

164 ORGANIZING, PLANNING, AND CONTROL

Table 20. Weekly Labor Report.

WBS NO.	COST CENTER	H $	WEEKLY ACTUAL	CURRENT MONTH SUBTOTAL	PREVIOUS MONTH			YEAR TO DATE			TOTAL EAC	WORK ORDER RELEASE
					ACWP	BCWP	ACWP	BCWP	BCWS			
01-03-06	4110	H $	200 1000	300 1500	300 1500	300 1500	1000 5000	1000 5000	1000 5000	1000 5000	1000
	4115	H $	200 1000	300 1500	300 1500	300 1500	1000 5000	1000 5000	1000 5000	2000 10000	2000
	4118	H $	200 1000	300 1500	300 1500	300 1500	1000 5000	1000 5000	1000 5000	2000 10000	1800
	41XX	H $	600 3000	900 4500	900 4500	900 4500	900 4500	900 4500	900 4500	5000 25000	4800
	4443	H $	100 600	200 1200	400 2400	360 2260	800 4800	700 4200	1400 8400	2000 12000	1800
	4446	H $	200 800	400 1600	1000 4000	1200 4800	2000 8000	2000 8000	2300 9200	3000 12000	2500
	4448	H $	300 1500	600 3000	1000 5000	1200 6000	2000 10000	2000 10000	2300 11500	3000 15000	3000
	44XX	H $	600 2900	1200 5800	2400 11400	2760 13060	4800 22800	4700 22200	6000 29100	8000 39000	7300
	4XXXX	H $	1200 5900	2100 10300	3300 15900	3660 17560	5700 27300	5600 26700	6900 33600	13000 64000	12100
	XXXX	H $	8000 56000	18000 126000	20000 140000	19000 133000	50000 350000	48000 336000	47000 329000	61000 427000	58000

Most weekly labor reports provide current month subtotals and previous month totals. Although these also appear on the detailed monthly report, they are included in the weekly report for a quick comparison. Year-to-date totals are usually not on the weekly report unless the users request it for an immediate comparison to the estimate at completion (EAC) and the work order release.

Weekly labor output is a vital tool for members of the program office in that these reports can indicate trends in cost and performance in sufficient time that contingency plans can be established and implemented. If these reports were not available, then cost and labor overruns would not be apparent until the following month when the detailed monthly labor, cost, and materials output is obtained.

In Table 20, Cost Center 4110 has spent their entire budget. The work appears to be completed on schedule. The responsible program office team may wish to eliminate this cost center's authority to continue charging to this WBS element by issuing a new SWD or work order canceling this department's efforts. Cost Center 4115 appears to be only halfway through. If time is becoming short, then Cost Center 4115 must add resources in order to meet requirements. Cost Center 4443 appears to be heading for an overrun. This could also indicate a management reserve. In this case the responsible program team member feels that the work can be accomplished in fewer hours.

Work order releases are used to authorize certain cost centers to begin charging their time to a specific cost reporting element. Work orders specify hours, not dollars. The hours indicate the targets that the program office would like to have the departments shoot for. If the program office wished to be more specific and compel the departments to live within these hours, then the budgeted cost for work scheduled (BCWS) should be changed to reflect the reduced hours.

There are four categories of cost data that are normally accumulated. They are:

- Labor
- Material
- Other direct charges
- Overhead

Project managers can maintain reasonable control over labor, material, and other direct charges. Overhead costs, on the other hand, are calculated yearly or monthly and applied retroactively to all applicable programs. Management reserves are often used to counterbalance the effects of adverse changes in overhead rates.

LABOR

Direct labor is that labor which is readily, economically, and consistently identifiable to a specific contract or program. Actual direct labor hours are reported by time cards which show section organization and work order number. These cards are mechanically processed by the computer. The computer sums up and prints out these actual hours at each level of the organization and work breakdown structure.

The budgeted cost of work performed is determined by adding the budgets for completed work packages and completed portions of open work packages together with the budgets for level of effort work. The reporting of accomplishments is the responsibility of the cognizant program team member. At the end of each accounting period, this program team member receives a computer status completion report listing all work packages planned for the contract except those dealing with the passage of time (level of effort) which are earned by computer.

The report shows what work packages have been reported as complete in prior accounting periods. The program team member, with the assistance of the operating organizations, adds work package accomplishment for the current period, or verifies work package accomplishment for the current reporting period already entered on the report by the computer from the daily time card status system, signs the report, and forwards the report to program management. After approval of the report, it is processed by the computer. The budgeted cost of work performed for each element of the work breakdown structure is computed for the department, division, and directorate levels of the organization. The accumulated actuals and budgeted cost of work performed are then printed out by current period together with cumulatives-to-date.

MATERIAL

The major portion of components and raw materials used on a program are procured under an inventory account and issued to the using cost account by stores requisition when they are withdrawn from controlled stores. The actual current inventory unit price of these items is stored in the computer bank by component part or raw material lot number and updated as required to reflect actual price. This price may include a percentage for scrap (as noted on the material list) for establishment of budgeted cost of work scheduled. When these components or raw materials are withdrawn from inventory through stores requisition by the using organization, the actual price and the planned (budgeted cost of work performed) price are charged to the using cost account. These are accumulated and applied to the actual and BCWP columns on the monthly MCCS reports, operating cost report, and critical variance report, if applicable.

In some cases when material cannot be identified as to its exact specification, a dollar value for the work package may be estimated by cost element and earned via the status completion report.

Some materials, such as support hardware, x-ray film, carbon dioxide, and miscellaneous tooling materials may be procured and maintained under overhead accounts. Usage reports or overhead stores requisitions on these items are submitted by the using organization to cost accounting, who relieve the overhead account and charge this material directly to the using cost account in accordance with cost accounting procedures. These materials are earned on the basis of actual usage and are reported by cost accounting.

In some instances, components, materials, or fabricated parts may be transferred to or from a program. These transfers are accomplished through use of a material transfer form in accordance with standard management procedures. Where the transfer is accomplished on components or materials within the stores or substores task, no effect on material usage is reflected.

Materials used in laboratory-type investigations to solve manufacturing or engineering problems and planned as level of effort are charged directly to the using cost account through the applicable cost element. The budgeted cost of work performed for these materials is earned through the passage of time as previously planned.

OTHER DIRECT CHARGES

Other direct charges are items such as travel, vendor rework, or freight charges that are specifically incurred in performance of contractual work. Purchase order contracts and travel authorizations are coded to the applicable cost accounts.

OVERHEAD

Overhead (and G&A and corporate costs, if applicable) is applied monthly as a percentage of direct costs. Reimbursable overhead expenses are recorded and accumulated into various expense accounts within the major overhead pools. Overhead costs are allocated monthly by applying booking rates to applicable direct costs. At the end of the year (or in some cases, monthly) these rates are adjusted to actual cost.

For extremely small organizations, small cost accounts may not be acceptable or even cost effective. However, as a bare minimum, the following accounting criteria should be used when project costs are recorded and summarized, regardless of company size:

- Direct costs must be recorded on a consistent basis.
- Material accounting must be related to performance measurement.
- Costs must be summarized according to the WBS.
- Costs must be summarized according to functional units.
- Indirect costs must be recorded.

13
Variances and Earned Value

A variance is defined as any schedule, technical performance, or cost deviation from a specific plan. Variances are used by all levels of management to verify the budgeting system and the scheduling system. Both the budgeting and scheduling system variances must be compared together because:

- The cost variance compares deviations only from the budget and does not provide a measure of comparison between work scheduled and work accomplished.
- The scheduling variance provides a comparison between planned and actual performance but does not include costs.

In order to calculate variances we must define the three basic variances for budgeting and actual costs for work scheduled and performed. Archibald defines these variables as:[44]

- Budgeted cost for work scheduled (BCWS) is the budgeted amount of cost for work scheduled to be accomplished plus the amount of level of effort or apportioned effort scheduled to be accomplished in a given time period.
- Budgeted cost for work performed (BCWP) is the budgeted amount of cost for completed work, plus budgeted for level of

---

[44] Russell D. Archibald, *Managing High-Technology Programs and Projects,* New York: Wiley, 1976, p. 176.

effort or apportioned effort activity completed within a given time period. This is sometimes referred to as *earned value*.
- Actual cost for work performed (ACWP) is the amount reported as actually expended in completing the work accomplished within a given time period.

These costs can then be applied to any level of the work breakdown structure (i.e., program, project, task, subtask, work package) for work that is completed, in-program, or anticipated. Using these definitions, we can obtain the following variance definitions:

- Cost variance (CV) calculation:
$$CV = BCWP - ACWP$$
A negative variance indicates a cost overrun condition.
- Schedule variance (SV) calculation:
$$SV = BCWP - BCWS$$
A negative variance indicates a behind schedule condition.

In the analysis of both cost and schedule, costs are used as the lowest common denominator. In other words, the schedule variance is given as a function of cost. To alleviate this problem, the variances are usually converted to percentages.

- Cost variance percentage (CVP):
$$CVP = \frac{CV}{BCWP}$$
- Schedule variance percentage (SVP):
$$SVP = \frac{SV}{BCWS}$$

The schedule variance may be represented by hours, days, weeks, or even dollars.

Variances are almost always identified as critical items and are reported to all organizational levels. Critical variances are established for each level of the organization in accordance with management policies.

Not all companies have a uniform methodology for variance thresholds. Permitted variances may be dependent upon such factors as

VARIANCES AND EARNED VALUE 171

- Life cycle phase
- Length of life cycle phase
- Length of project
- Type of estimate
- Accuracy of estimate

Variance controls may be different from program to program. Table identifies a sample variance criteria for Program X.

For many programs and projects variances are permitted to change over the duration of the program. For strict manufacturing programs (product management), variances may be fixed over the program time span using criteria as in Table 21. For programs that include research and development, larger deviations may be permitted during the earlier phases than during the later phases. Figure 36 shows time-phased cost variances for a program requiring research and development, qualification, and production phases. Since the risk should decrease as time goes on, the variance boundaries are reduced.

Table 21. Variance Control For Program X.

ORGANIZATIONAL LEVEL	VARIANCE THRESHOLDS[a]
Section	Variances greater than $750 and exceed 25% of costs
Section	Variances greater than $2500 and exceed 10% of costs
Section	Variances greater than $20,000
Department	Variances greater than $2000 that exceed 25% of costs
Department	Variances greater than $7500 that exceed 10% of costs
Department	Variances greater than $40,000
Division	Variances greater than $10,000 that exceed 10% of costs

[a] Thresholds are usually tighter within company reporting system than required external to government. Thresholds for external reporting are usually adjusted during various phases of program (percent lower at end).

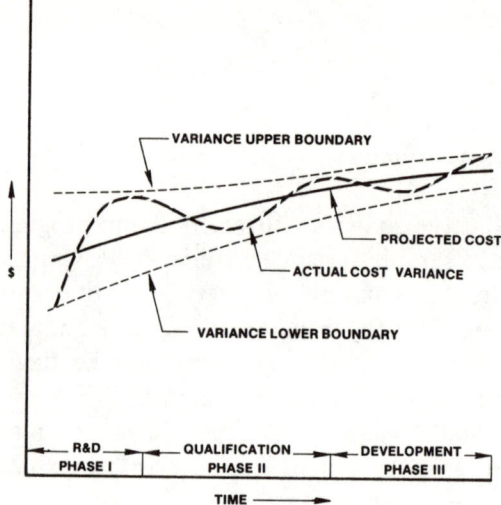

Figure 36. Project variance projections.

By using both cost and schedule variances we can develop an integrated cost/schedule reporting system that provides the basis for variance analysis by measuring cost performance in relation to work accomplished. This system insures that both cost budgeting and performance scheduling are constructed upon the same data base.

Figure 37 shows an integrated cost/schedule system. The figure identifies a performance slippage to date. This might not be a bad situation if the costs are proportionately underrun. However, from the upper portion of Figure 37, we find that costs are overrun (in comparison to budgeted costs), thus adding to the severity of the situation.

Also shown in Figure 37 is the management reserve. This is identified as the difference between the contracted cost for projected performance to date and the budgeted cost. Management reserves are contingency funds established by the program manager to counteract unavoidable delays that can affect the project's critical path. It is a natural tendency for a functional manager (and some project managers) to substantially inflate estimates so as to protect the

VARIANCES AND EARNED VALUE   173

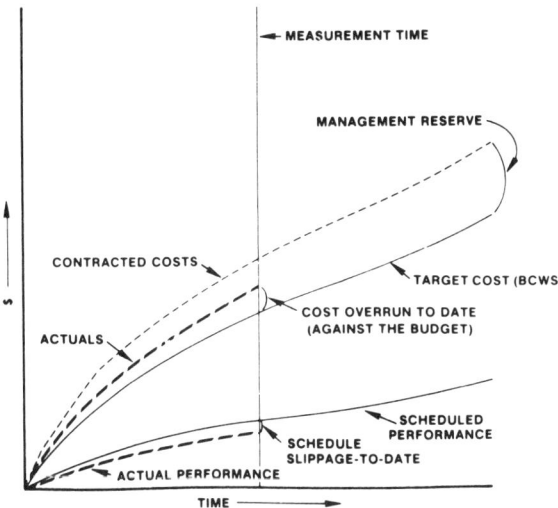

Figure 37. Integrated cost/schedule system.

particular organization and provide a certain amount of cushion. Furthermore, if the inflated budget is approved, managers will undoubtedly use up all of the allocated funds, including reserves. According to Parkinson:[45]

- The work at hand expands to fill the time available.
- Expenditures rise to meet budget.

Managers must identify all such reserves for contingency plans, in time, cost, and performance (i.e., PERT slack time).

The line indicated as actual in Figure 37 shows a cost overrun compared to the budget. However, costs are still within the contractual requirement if we consider the management reserve. Therefore, things may not be as bad as they seem.

---

[45] C.N. Parkinson, *Parkinson's Law,* Boston: Houghton Mifflin, 1957.

Government subcontractors are required to have a government-approved cost/schedule control system. The information requirements that must be demonstrated by such a system include

- Budgeted cost for work scheduled (BCWS)
- Budgeted cost for work performed (BCWP)
- Actual cost for work performed (ACWP)
- Estimated cost at completion
- Budgeted cost at completion
- Cost and schedule variances/explanations
- Traceability

The last two items imply that standardized policies and procedures should exist for reporting and controlling variances.

When permitted variances are exceeded, cost account variance analysis reports as shown in Figure 38 are required. Signature approval of these reports may be required by

- The functional employees responsible for the work
- The functional managers responsible for the work
- The cost accountant and/or the assistant project manager for cost control
- The project manager, work breakdown structure element manager, or someone with signature authority from the project office

One of the key parameters used in variance analysis is the *earned value* concept, which is the same as BCWP. Earned value, or whatever other name might be used in the literature, is a forecasting variable used to predict whether the project will finish over or under the budget. As an example, on June 1, the budget showed that 800 hours should have been expended for a given task. However, only 600 hours appeared on the labor report. Therefore, the performance is (800/600) × 100, or 133 percent, and the task is underrunning in performance. If the actual hours were 1000, then performance would be 80 percent and an overrun would be occurring.

The difficulty in performing variance analysis is in the calculation of BCWP because it is necessary to predict the percent complete. To

COST ACCOUNT VARIANCE ANALYSIS REPORT

COST ACCOUNT NO/CAM						REPORTING LEVEL		
WBS/DESCRIPTION						AS OF		
COST PERF. DATA				VARIANCE		AT COMPLETION		
	BCWS	BCWP	ACWP	SCH	COST	BUDGET	EAC	VAR.
MONTH TO DATE ($)						/////	/////	/////
CONTRACT TO DATE ($K)								

PROBLEM CAUSE AND IMPACT

CORRECTIVE ACTION (INCLUDE EXPECTED RECOVERY DATE)

COST ACCOUNT MANAGER	DATE	COST CENTER MGR.	DATE	WBS ELEMENT MANAGER	DATE		DATE

Figure 38. Cost account variance analysis report.

eliminate this problem, many companies use standard dollar expenditures for the project, regardless of percent complete. For example, we could say that 10 percent of the costs are to be "booked" for each 10 percent of the time interval. Another technique, and perhaps the most common, is the 50/50 rule:

- Half of the budget for each element is recorded at the time that the work is scheduled to begin and the other half at the time

176 ORGANIZING, PLANNING, AND CONTROL

that the work is scheduled to be completed. For a project with a large number of elements, the amount of distortion from such a procedure is minimal.

One of the advantages of using the 50/50 rule is that it eliminates the necessity for the continuous determination of the percent complete. However, if percent complete can be determined, then percent complete can be plotted against time expended as shown in Figure 39.

Generally speaking, the concept of earned value may not be an effective control tool if used in the lower levels of the WBS. Task levels and above are normally worth the effort for the calculations of

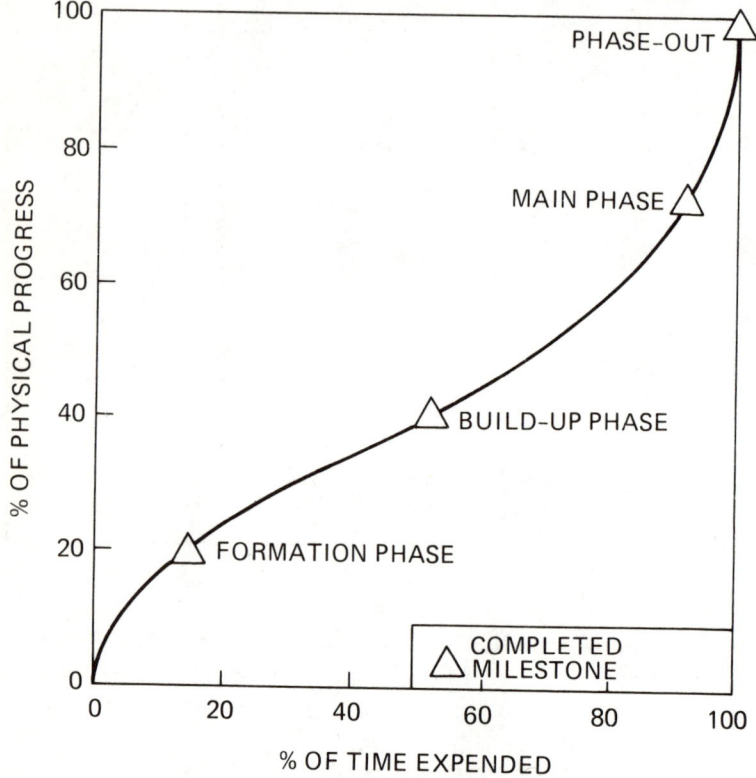

Figure 39. Physical progress versus time expended.

VARIANCES AND EARNED VALUE 177

earned value. As an example, consider Figure 40, which shows the contractual cost data for task 3 of Project Z, and Table 22, which shows the cost data status at the end of the fourth month. The following is a brief summary of the cost data for each subtask:

Subtask 1: All contractual funds were budgeted. Cost/performance was on time as indicated by the milestone position. Subtask is completed.

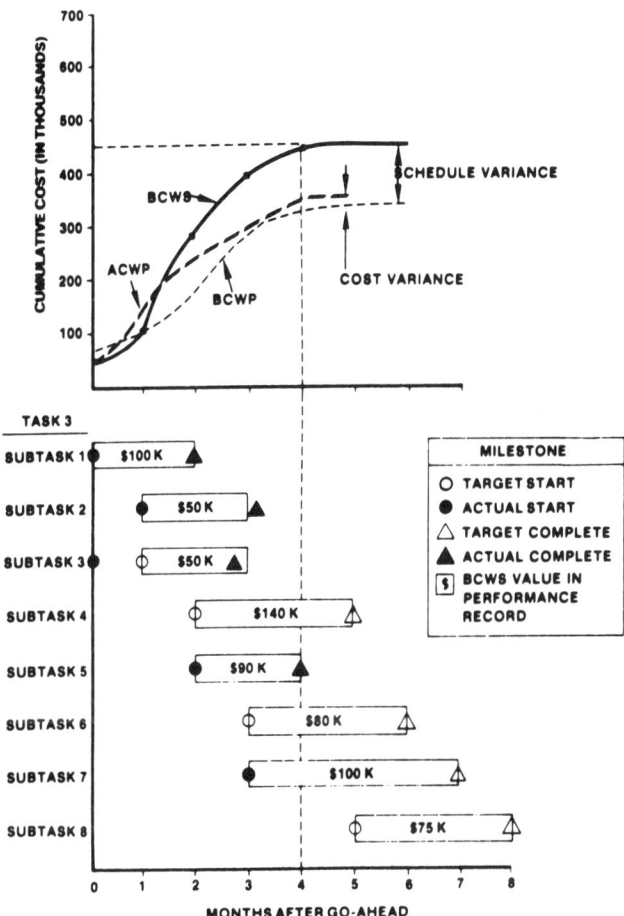

Figure 40. Project Z task 3 cost data (contractual).

Subtask 2: All contractual funds were budgeted. A cost overrun of $5000 was incurred, and milestone was completed later than expected. Subtask is completed.

Subtask 3: Subtask is completed. Costs were underrun by $10,000 probably due to early start.

Subtask 4: Work is behind schedule. Actually, work has not yet begun.

Subtask 5: Work is completed on schedule, but with a $50,000 cost overrun.

Subtask 6: Work has not yet started. Effort is behind schedule.

Subtask 7: Work has begun and appears to be 25 percent complete.

Subtask 8: Not yet started.

Using the data in Table 22 we can calculate the estimate at completion (EAC) by the expression

$$\begin{aligned} EAC &= (ACWP/BCWP) \times \text{total budget} \\ &= (360/340) \times 579{,}000 \\ &= \$613{,}059 \end{aligned}$$

Table 22. Project Z Task 3 Cost Summary for Work Completed or in Progress (cost in thousands).[a]

	CONTRACTUAL	BCWS	BCWP	ACWP	COST VARIANCE[b]	SCHEDULE VARIANCE
Direct labor hours[c]	25,000	21,400	15,300	14,000	(1300)	
Direct labor dollars	200	150	125	131	6	25
Labor overhead	200	150	125	131	6	25
Material dollars	70	66	26	30	4	40
Subtotal	470	366	276	292	16	90
G&A (10%)	47	36	28	29	1	8
Subtotal	517	402	304	321	17	98
Fee (12%)	62	48	36	39	3	12
Total	579	450	340	360	20	110

[a] This page assumes a 50/50 ratio for planned and earned values of budget.

[b] Favorable variances are in parentheses.

[c] Direct labor hours are normally not shown in the cost package summaries but are included here for simplicity.

VARIANCE AND EARNED VALUE 179

This implies that we are overrunning our costs by 5.88 percent and the final cost will exceed the budget by $34,059. However, we have not considered management reserve. The management reserve will reduce this overrun. The final analysis is that the work is being accomplished almost on schedule but costs are being overrun.

The question that remains to be answered is, "Where is the cost overrun occurring?" To answer this question, we must analyze the cost summary sheet for Project Z, task 3. Table 22 represents a hypothetical case for the cost elements of Project Z, task 3. From Table 22 we see that positive (overrun) variances exist for labor dollars, overhead dollars, and material costs. Because labor overhead is measured as a percentage of direct labor dollars, the problem appears to be in the direct labor dollars.

From the contractual column in Table 22 the project was estimated at $8.00 per hour direct labor (= $200,000/25 hours) but actuals to date are $131,000/14,000 hours, or $9.36 per hour. Therefore, we are employing more higher-salaried people than anticipated. This salary increase is partially offset by the fact that there exists a negative variance of 1300 direct labor hours indicating that these higher-salaried employees are performing at a more favorable position on the learning curve. Since the milestones (from Figure 40) appear to be on target, work is progressing as planned.

The labor overhead rate has not changed. The contractual, BCWS, and BCWP overhead rates were estimated at 100 percent. The actuals, obtained from month-end reports, indicate that the true overhead rate is as predicted.

The following conclusions can be drawn:

- Work is being performed as planned (almost on schedule, although at a more favorable position on the learning curve.)
- Direct labor costs are increasing through the use of higher-salaried employees.
- Overhead rates are as anticipated.
- Direct labor hours must be reduced even further to compensate for increased costs or else profits will be drastically reduced.

This type of analysis could have been carried out to one more level by identifying exactly which departments were using the more expensive employees. This step should probably be completed anyway to see if lower-paid employees are available and can work at this required position on the learning curves. Had the labor costs been a result of increased labor hours, this step would have definitely been necessary to identify the reason for the overrun in house. Perhaps poor estimating was the cause.

In Table 22, there also appears a positive variance in materials. This should likewise require further analysis. The cause may be the result of improperly identified hardware, material escalation costs increasing beyond what was planned, increased scrap factors, or a change in subcontractors.

It should be obvious from the above analysis that a detailed investigation into the cause of variances appears to be the best method for identifying causes. The concept of earned value, although a crude estimate, identifies trends concerning the status of specific WBS elements. Using this concept, the budgeted cost for work scheduled (BCWS) may be called planned earned value (PEV) and the budgeted cost for work performed (BCWP) may be referred to as actual earned value (AEV). Earned values are used to determine whether costs are being incurred faster or slower than planned. However, cost overruns do not necessarily mean that there will be an eventual overrun, because the work may be getting done faster than planned.

There exist 13 cases for comparing planned versus actual performance. These 13 cases are shown in Table 23. Each case is described below using the relationships:

- Cost variance = planned earned value − actuals
- Schedule/performance variances = actual earned value − planned earned value

Case 1: This is the ideal planning situation where everything goes according to schedule.

Case 2: Costs are behind schedule and program appears to be underrunning. Work is being accomplished at less than 100 percent since actuals exceed AEV (or BCWP). This indicates that a cost overrun can be anticipated. This situation grows even worse when we see that we are 50 percent behind schedule also. This is one of the worst possible cases.

Case 3: In this case we have good news and bad news. The good news is that we are performing the work efficiently (efficiency exceeds 100 percent). The bad news is that we are behind schedule.

Case 4: The work is not being accomplished according to schedule (i.e., it is behind schedule), but the costs are being maintained for what has been accomplished.

Case 5: The costs are on target with the schedule, but the work is 25 percent behind schedule because the work is being performed at 75 percent efficiency.

Case 6: Because we are operating at 125 percent efficiency, work is ahead of schedule by 25 percent but within scheduled costs. We are performing at a more favorable position on the learning curve.

Case 7: We are operating at a 100 percent efficiency and work is being accomplished ahead of schedule. Costs are being maintained according to budget.

Case 8: Work is being accomplished properly and costs are being underrun.

Case 9: Work is being accomplished properly, but costs are being overrun.

Case 10: Costs are being overrun while under-accomplishing the plan. Work is being accomplished inefficiently. This situation is very bad.

Table 23. Variance Analysis Case Studies.

CASE	PLANNED EARNED VALUE (BCWS)	ACTUALS (ACWP)	ACTUAL EARNED VALUE (BCWP)
1	800	800	800
2	800	600	400
3	800	400	600
4	800	600	600
5	800	800	600
6	800	800	1000
7	800	1000	1000
8	800	600	800
9	800	1000	800
10	800	1000	600
11	800	600	1000
12	800	1200	1000
13	800	1000	1200

Case 11: Performance is ahead of schedule and the costs are lower than planned. This situation results in a big Christmas bonus.

Case 12: Work is being done inefficiently and a possible cost overrun can occur. However, performance is ahead of schedule. The overall result may be either an overrun in cost or underrun in schedule.

Case 13: Although costs are greater than those budgeted, performance is ahead of schedule and work is being accomplished very efficiently. This is also a good situation.

In each of these cases, the concept of earned value was used to predict trends in cost and variance analysis. The usefulness of this method has both pros and cons. According to Martin:[46]

> The usefulness of earned value measurements in project management is controversial. The most enthusiastic managers regard it as the best way to prevent surprises and as a most workable tool. Others consider the information helpful in managing the project but not worth the cost of obtaining it. Still others say the information becomes available too late or there are better ways to obtain it. The most critical managers view it as a complete waste of time.

Each of the critical variances (or earned values) identified usually requires a formal analysis to determine the cause of the variance, the corrective action to be taken, and the effect on the estimate to completion. These analyses are performed by the organizations that were assigned the budget (BCWS) at the level of accumulation directed by program management.

ORGANIZATION-LEVEL ANALYSIS

Each critical variance identified on the organizational MCCS reports may require the completion of MCCS variance procedures by the supervisor of the cost center involved. Analyzing both the work breakdown and organizational structure, the supervisor systematically

---

[46] Charles C. Martin, *Project Management: How to Make It Work,* New York: Amacom, a division of American Management Associations, 1976, p. 203.

concentrates his efforts on cost and schedule problems appearing within his organization.

Analysis begins at the lowest organizational level by the supervisor involved. Critical variances are noted at the cost account on the MCCS report. If a schedule variance is involved and the subtask consists of a number of work packages, the supervisor may refer to a separate report which breaks down each cost account into the various work packages that are ahead of or behind schedule. The supervisor can then analyze the variance on the basis of the work package involved and determine with the aid of supporting organizations the cause of the variance, the corrective action that can be taken, or the possible effect on associated or future planned effort.

Cost variances involving labor are analyzed by the supervisor on the basis of the performance of his organization in accomplishing the work assigned within the budgeted man-hours and planned labor rate. The cause of any variance to this performance is determined and corrective action is then implemented.

Cost variances on nonlabor effort are analyzed by the supervisor with the aid of the program team member and other supporting organizations.

All material variance analyses are normally initiated by cost accounting as a service to the using organization These variance analyses are completed, including cause and corrective action, to the extent that can be explained by cost accounting. They are then sent to the using organization which reviews the analyses and completes those resulting from schedule performance or usage. If a variance is recognized as a change in the material acquisition price, this information is supplied by cost accounting to the responsible organization and a change to the estimate to complete is initiated by the using organization.

The supervisor should forward copies of each completed MCCS variance analysis/EAC change form to his higher-level manager and the program team member.

PROGRAM TEAM ANALYSIS

The program team member may receive a team critical variance report which lists variances in his organization at the lowest level of the work breakdown structure at the division cost center level by cost element. Upon request of the program manager, analyses of variances contributing to the variances on the team critical variance report are summarized by the responsible program team member and reviewed with the program manager.

The program manager uses this information to review the program status with upper-level management. This review is normally on a monthly basis. In addition, the results of these analyses are used to explain variances in the contractually required reports to the customer.

After the analyses of the variances have been made, reports must be developed for both the customer and in-house (upper-level) management. Customer reporting procedures and specifications can be more detailed than in-house reporting and are often governed by the contract. Contractual requirements specify the reports required, the frequency of submission and distribution, and the customer regulation that specifies the preparation instructions for the report.

The types of reports required by the customer and management depend upon the size of the program and the magnitude of the variance. Most reports usually contain the tracking of the vital technical parameters. These might include:

- The major milestones necessary for project success
- Comparison to specifications
- Types or conditions of testing
- Correlation of technical performance to the activity network and the work breakdown structure

One final note must be mentioned concerning reports. To facilitate time and money, each of these reports might be no more than one or two pages. In many cases, the reports are merely fill-in-the-blank type. When necessary, explanations can be provided by additional pages.

One of the best ways of reducing or even eliminating executive meddling on projects is to provide executives with frequent, meaningful status reports so that the executive can accurately realize the true status of the project. Figure 41 shows a relatively simple status report. These types of status reports should be short, concise, and with pertinent information only.

BLUE SPIDER PROJECT
MONTHLY PROJECT REPORT #4

June 1, 1982

1. *VARIANCE ANALYSIS* (Cost in Thousands)

Subtask	Milestone Status	Budgeted Cost Work Scheduled	Budget Cost Work Performed	Actual Cost	Variance (%) Schedule	Variance (%) Cost
1	Completed	100	100	100	0	0
2	Completed	50	50	50	0	-10
3	Completed	50	50	40	0	20
4	Not started	70	0	0	-100	—
5	Completed	90	90	140	0	-55.5
6	Not started	40	0	0	-100	—
7	Started	50	50	25	0	50
8	Not started	0	0	0	—	—
Total		450	340	360	-24.4	-5.9

2. *ESTIMATE AT COMPLETION (EAC)*
   EAC   = (360/340) × $579,000 = $613,059
   Overrun = 613,059 − 579,000 = $34,059

3. *COST SUMMARY*
   Costs are running approximately 5.9% over budget due to higher-salaried labor.

4. *SCHEDULE SUMMARY*
   The 24.4% behind schedule condition is due to subtasks 4 and 6 which have not yet begun due to lack of raw materials and the 50/50 method for booking costs. Overtime will get us back on schedule but at an additional cost of 2.5% of direct labor costs.

5. *MILESTONE REPORT*

Milestone/Subtask	Scheduled Completion	Projected Completion	Actual Completion
1	4/1/82		4/1/82
2	5/1/82		5/8/82
3	5/1/82		4/23/82
4	7/1/82	7/1/82	
5	6/1/82		6/1/82
6	8/1/82	8/1/82	
7	9/1/82	9/1/82	
8	10/1/82	10/1/82	

6. *EVENT REPORT*

Current Problem	Potential Impact	Corrective Action
a. Lack of raw materials	Cost overrun and behind schedule condition	Overtime is scheduled. We will try to use lower-salaried people. Raw materials are expected to be on dock next week.
b. Customer unhappy with test results, and wants additional work	May need additional planning	Customer will provide us with revised statement of work on 6/15/82.

Gary Anderson, Project Manager

Figure 41.

Reporting procedures for variance analysis should be as brief as possible. The reason for this is simple: the shorter and more concise the report, the faster feedback can be generated and responses developed. The time parameter becomes critical if rescheduling must be accomplished with limited resources. The two most common situations that provide constraints on resource rescheduling are:

- The end date is fixed.
- The resources available are constant (or limited).

With a fixed end date, program rescheduling generally requires that additional resources be supplied. In the second situation, program slippage may be the only alternative unless a constant sum of resources can be redistributed so as to shorten the length of the critical path.

Once the variance analysis is completed, both project and functional management must diagnose the problem and search for corrective actions. This includes:

- Finding the cure for the problem
- Developing a plan to recover the position

This by no means implies that all variances require corrective action. There are four major responses to a variance report:

- Ignoring
- Functional modification
- Replanning
- System redesign

There exist permissible variances for all levels of the organization. If the variance is within these permitted deviations, then there will be no response and the variance might be ignored. There are situations where the variance might be marginal (or even within limits) and corrective action is required. This would normally occur at the functional level and might simply involve using another test procedure or possibly considering some other alternative not delineated in the program plan.

If major variances occur, then either replanning or system redesign must take place. The replanning process requires the redefining and reestablishing of project goals as work progresses, but always within system specifications. This might include making trade-offs in time, cost, and performance or defining new project activities and methods of pursuing the project, such as new PERT networks. If resources are limited, then a proper redistribution or reallocation must be made. If resources are not limited, then additional personnel, financing, equipment, facilities, or information may be required.

If replanning cannot be accomplished without system redesign, then system specifications may have to be changed.[47] This is the worst possible case because performance may have to be sacrificed to satisfy the constraints of time and money.

Whenever companies operate on a matrix structure, job descriptions, responsibilities, and management directives must be carefully prepared and distributed to all key individuals in the organization. This is an absolute necessity when a multitude of people must interact to control company resources. Management policies must establish the decision-making policies associated with management cost and control systems. Otherwise, dual standards can occur within the same organization and the decision-making process becomes a tedious flow of red tape. The following might be a management policy guide for a program or project manager:

- Approving all estimates and negotiating all estimates and the definition of work requirements with the respective organizations.
- Approving the budget and directing distribution and budgeting of available funds to all organizational levels by program element.
- Defining the work required and the schedule.
- Authorizing work release. He may not, however, authorize work beyond the scope of the contract.
- Approving the program bill of materials, detailed plans, and program schedules for need and compliance with program requirements.
- Approving the procuring work statement, the schedules, the source selection, the negotiated price, and the type of contract on major procurement.

---

[47] Here we are discussing system specifications. Functional modification responses can also require specification changes, but not on the system level. Examples of function modifications might be a change in tolerances for testing or for purchasing raw materials.

- Monitoring the functional organization's performance against released budgets, schedules, and program requirements.
- When cost performance is unacceptable, taking appropriate action with the affected organization to modify the work requirements or to stimulate corrective action within the functional organization so as to reduce cost without changing the contracted scope of work.
- Being responsible for all communications and policy matters on contracted programs such that no communicative directive will be issued without the signature or concurrence of the program manager.

Describing the responsibilities of a manager is only a portion of the management policy or management guideline package. Because the program manager must cross over functional boundaries to accomplish all of the above, it is also necessary to describe the role and responsibility of the functional manager as well as the relationship between functional and program management for major program activities. Table 24 defines the responsibilities for the program manager, the functional manager, and their relationship (i.e., interaction) for development and implementation of a management cost and control system. Similar tables can be developed for planning and scheduling, communications, customer relations, and contract administration.

No matter how good the cost and control system is, problems can occur. Below are common causes of cost problems:

- Poor estimating techniques and/or standards resulting in unrealistic budgets
- Out-of-sequence starting and completion of activities and events
- Inadequate work breakdown structure
- No management policy on reporting and control practices
- Poor work definition at the lower levels of the organization
- Management reduction of budgets or bids to be competitive or to eliminate "fat"
- Inadequate formal planning which results in unnoticed or often uncontrolled increase in scope of effort
- Poor comparison of actual and planned costs

- Comparison of actual and planned costs at the wrong level of management
- Unforeseen technical problems
- Schedule delays which require overtime or idle time costing
- Unrealistic material escalation factors

Cost overruns can occur in any phase of project development. Below are the most common causes for cost overruns:

- Proposal Phase
  - Failure to understand customer requirements
  - Unrealistic appraisal of in-house capabilities
  - Underestimation of time requirement
- Planning Phase
  - Omissions
  - Accuracy of the work breakdown structure
  - Misinterpretation of information
  - Use of wrong estimating techniques
  - Failure to identify and concentrate on major cost elements
  - Failure to assess and provide for risks
- Negotiation Phase
  - Forcing of a speedy compromise
  - Procurement ceiling costs
  - Idea that negotiation team must "win this one"
- Contractual Phase
  - Contractual discrepancies
  - SOW different from RFP requirements
  - Proposal team different from project team
- Design Phase
  - Acceptance of customer requests without management approval
  - Customer communications channels and data items
  - Design review meetings
- Production Phase
  - Excessive material costs
  - Unacceptable specifications
  - Manufacturing and engineering disagreement

Table 24. Program Controls Interrelationships.

PROGRAM MANAGER	FUNCTIONAL MANAGER	RELATIONSHIP
Program Controls: Makes or approves all decisions that affect the contractually committed target time, cost, and performance requirements or objectives of the program.	*Program Controls:* Assembles and furnishes the information needed to assist the program manager in making decisions. Submits to the program manager all proposed changes that affect program cost, schedule targets, and technical requirements and objectives through the program team member.	*Program Controls:* Management controls, contract administration, budgeting, estimating, and financial controls are a functional specialty. The program manager utilizes the services of the specialist organizations. The specialists retain their own channels to the general manager but must keep the program manager informed through the program team member.
Approves all engineering change control decisions that affect the contractually committed target time, cost, and performance requirements or objectives of the program.	Implements engineering change decisions approved by the program manager. Advises him of any resulting programming impasses and negotiates adjustments through the program team member.	
Establishes program budgets in conjunction with the cognizant program team members; monitors and negotiates changes.		In all matters pertaining to budget and cost control, the program manager utilizes the services of the program team member representing the cognizant financial control organization.
Authorizes release of the budget and work authorization for the performance of approved work, and negotiates any intra-directorate reallocation above section level with the affected functional organizations through the program team members.	Within the allocated budget, provides manpower skills, facilities, and other resources pertaining to his functional specialty to the degree and level necessary to meet program schedule, cost, and technical performance requirements of the contract.	

Table 24. Program Controls Interrelationships. (continued)

Requests the assignment of a program team member to the program, and approves the release of the team member from the program.	Coordinates with the program manager in the selection and assignment of a program team member to the program or release of the program team member from the program.	Program manager does not hire or fire functional personnel. Program team members should not be removed from the program without the concurrence of the program manager.
Establishes report requirements and controls necessary for evaluation of all phases of program performance consistent with effective policies and procedures.	Works in concert with other functional organizations to ensure that he and they are proceeding satisfactorily in the completion of mutually interdependent program tasks and events.	Insofar as possible, program controls must be satisfied from existing data and controls as defined by division policies and procedures.
Measures and evaluates performance of tasks against the established plan. Identifies current and potential problems. Decides upon and authorizes corrective action.	Follows up all activities of his organization to ensure satisfactory performance to program requirements. Detects actual or potential problems. Takes timely corrective action in his organization, and when such problems involve interface with other functional organizations, notifies them and coordinates the initiation of mutually satisfactory remedial action. Keeps the program manager advised (through the program team member) of conditions affecting the program, existing or expected problems, problems solved, and corrective action required or performed.	The program manager directs or redirects activities of functional organizations only through the cognizant program team member. Functional managers are responsible for the performance of their organizations. Functional managers do not implement decisions involving increased total program costs, changes in schedule, or changes in technical performance without prior approval of the program team member and the program manager.
	Appraises the program team members and/or functional organizations of program changes affecting their function.	
	Assures the establishment, coordination, and execution of support programs to the extent required or permitted by the contract.	This includes such programs as value engineering, data management, and configuration management.

PART III
NEW BUSINESS DEVELOPMENT

14
New Contracts:
The Lifeblood for Project Management

MARKETING A PROJECT

To the realistic manager, winning new contracts is the lifeblood of any project-oriented business. Its practices are, however, substantially different from traditional product businesses and require highly specialized and disciplined team efforts among marketing, technical, and operating personnel, plus significant customer involvement.

What Characterizes Project Marketing?

Projects are different from products in many respects. Marketing projects requires the ability to identify, pursue, and capture one-of-a-kind business opportunities characterized by:

- *A systematic effort* is usually required to develop a new program lead into an actual contract. The program acquisition effort is often highly integrated with ongoing programs and involves key personnel from both the potential customer and the performing organization.
- *Custom design:* While traditional businesses provide standard products and services for a variety of applications and customers, projects are custom-designed items to fit specific requirements of a single customer community.

- *Project life cycle:* Project-oriented businesses have a beginning and an end and are not self-perpetuating. Business must be generated on a project-by-project basis rather than by creating demand for a standard product or service.
- *Marketing phase:* Long lead times often exist between project definition, start-up, and completion.
- *Risks:* Risks are present especially in the research, design, and production of programs. The program manager not only has to integrate the multidisciplinary tasks and program elements within budget and schedule constraints, but also has to manage inventions and technology.
- *The technical capability to perform* is critical to the successful pursuit and acquisition of a new project or program.

Projects Are Good Business

In spite of the risks and problems, profits on projects are usually very low in comparison with commercial business practices. One may wonder why companies pursue project businesses. Clearly there are many reasons why projects and programs are good business:

- Although immediate profits, as a percentage of sales, are usually small, the return on capital investment is often very attractive. Progress payment practices keep inventories and receivables to a minimum and enable companies to undertake programs many times larger in value than the assets of the total company.
- Once a contract has been secured and is being managed properly, the program is of relatively low financial risk to the company. The company has little additional selling expenditure and has a predictable market over the life cycle of the program.
- Program business must be viewed from a broader perspective than motivation for immediate profits. It provides an opportunity to develop the company's technical capabilities and build an experience base for future business growth.
- Winning one program contract often provides attractive growth potential such as: (1) growth with the program via additions and changes; (2) follow-on work; (3) spare parts, maintenance, and training; and (4) being able to compete effectively in the

next program phase, such as nurturing a study program into a development and finally a production contract.

In summary, new business is the lifeblood of an organization. It is especially crucial in project-oriented businesses which lack the ongoing nature of conventional markets.

New business developments are complex undertakings. The management of a new program acquisition is different from commercial marketing practices. It requires special skills, tools, techniques, and most importantly, competent, experienced people from all parts of the organization, to carry the effort successfully through the various stages of acquisition planning, marketing, proposal development, and contract negotiation. It is this fundamental set of management techniques that will be discussed in this section. But first, let us define the markets of project-oriented businesses and their acquisition planning.

15
Planning for Growth

DEFINING THE MARKET

Customers come in various forms and sizes. For small and medium-sized businesses, particularly, it seems to be a true challenge to compete for contracts from large industrial or governmental organizations. Although the contract received by a firm may be relatively small, it is often subcontracted via a larger organization. Selling to such a diversified heterogeneous customer is a true marketing challenge which requires a highly sophisticated and disciplined approach.

The first step in a new business development effort is to define the market to be pursued. The market segment for a new program opportunity is normally in an area of relevant past experience, technical capability, and customer involvement. Good marketeers in the program business have to think as product line managers. They have to understand all dimensions of the business and be able to define and pursue market objectives consistent with the capabilities of their organizations.

Market Predictability

Program businesses operate in an opportunity-driven market. It is a mistaken belief, however, that these markets are unpredictable and unmanageable. Market planning and strategizing is important. New program opportunities develop over periods of time, sometimes years for larger programs. These developments must be properly tracked and cultivated to form the bases for management actions such as (1) bid decisions, (2) resource commitment, (3) technical readiness, and (4) effective customer liaison.

The strategy of winning new business is supported by systematic, disciplined approaches, which are illustrated in Figure 42 and discussed in five basic steps:

1. Identifying new business opportunities
2. Planning the business acquisition
3. Developing the new contract opportunity
4. Creating a winning proposal
5. Negotiating the contract

IDENTIFYING NEW BUSINESS OPPORTUNITIES

Identifying a new program opportunity is a marketing job. During the initial stages one does not evaluate or pursue the opportunity — that comes later. Furthermore, identifying new opportunities should be an ongoing activity. It involves the scanning of the relevant market sector for new business. It is a function that should be performed by all members of the project team in addition to marketing support groups. There are many sources for identifying new business leads such as:

- Customer meetings on ongoing program
- Professional meetings and conventions
- Trade shows
- Trade journals
- Customer service
- Advertising your capabilities
- Personal contacts

All one can expect, at this point, is to learn of an established or potential customer requirement in one of the following categories:

- Follow-on to previous or current program
- Next phase program
- Additions or changes to ongoing programs

200 NEW BUSINESS DEVELOPMENT

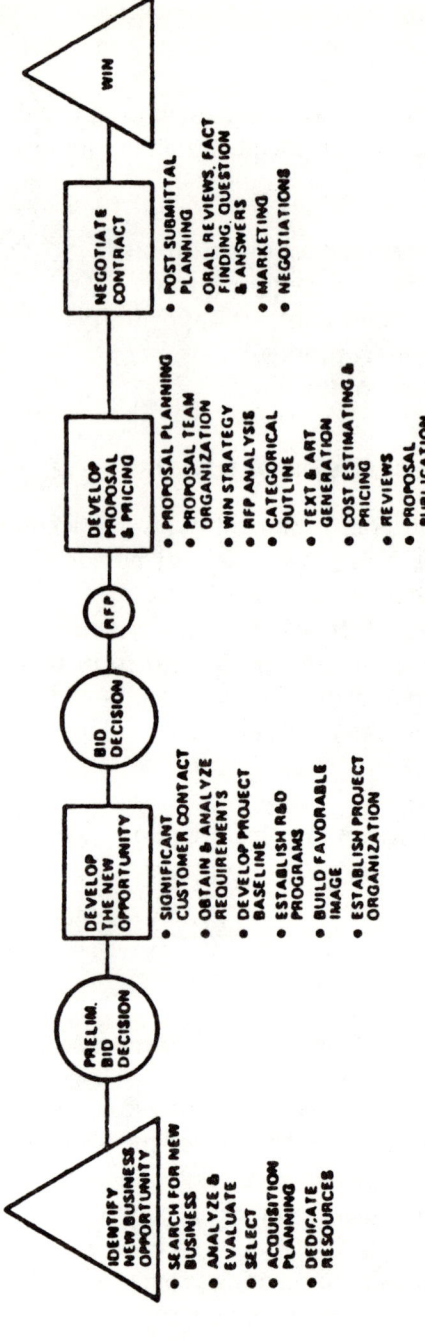

Figure 42. The phases of winning new contracts in project-oriented businesses.

- New programs in your established market sector or area of technological strength
- New programs in related markets
- Related programs, such as training, maintenance, or spares

For most businesses, ongoing program activities are the best source of new opportunities. Not only are the lines of customer communication better than in a new market but, more importantly, the image as an experienced, reliable contractor has been established giving a clear competitive advantage in any future business pursuit.

The target result of this analysis is an acquisition plan and bid decision. Analyzing the new opportunitity and preparing the acquisition plan is an interactive effort. Often many meetings are needed between the customer and the performing organization before a clear picture emerges of the customer requirements and the contractor's capabilities. A major fringe benefit of proper customer contact is the potential for building confidence and credibility with the customer. It shows that your organization understands their requirements and has the capability to fulfill them. This is a necessary prerequisite for eventually negotiating the contract. The new business identification phase concludes with a formal analysis of the new project opportunity, which is summarized in the following section.

THE ACQUISITION PLAN

The acquisition plan provides the basis for the formal bid decision and a detailed plan for the acquisition of the new business. The plan is an important management tool which provides:

- An assessment of the new program opportunity as a basis for appropriating resources for developing and bidding the new business
- A road map of the total acquisition effort with specific milestones against which progress can be measured and controlled

Typically, the new business acquisition plan should include the following elements:

1. *Brief description of new business opportunity* — starting the requirements, specifications, scope, schedule, budget, customer organization, and key decision-makers.

2. *Why should we bid?* — a perspective regarding establishing business plans and desirable results such as profits, markets, growth, and technology.

3. *Competitive assessment* — description of each competing firm regarding their past activities in the subject area, including (a) related experiences; (b) current contract; (c) customer interfaces; (d) specific strengths and weaknesses; and (e) potential baseline approach.

4. *Critical win factors* — listing of specific factors important to winning the new program, including their rationale. (Example: low implementation risk and short schedule important to customer because of need for equipment in two years.)

5. *Ability to write a winning proposal* — addresses the specifics needed to prepare a winning proposal. This includes (a) availability of the right proposal personnel, (b) understanding of customer problems, (c) unique competitive advantage, (d) expected bid cost to be under customer budget, (e) special arrangements (e.g., teaming, license model), (f) engineering readiness to write proposal, and (g) ability to price competitively.

6. *Win strategy* — chronological listing of critical milestones guiding the acquisition effort from its present position to winning the new program. It should show those activities critical for positioning yourself uniquely in the competitive field. Includes timing and responsible individuals for each milestone.

For example, if low implementation risk and short schedules are important to the customer, the summary of the win strategy may state:

"Build credibility with the customer by introducing key personnel and discussing baseline prior to RFP."

"Stress related experience on ABC Program."

"Guarantee 100 percent dedicated personnel and list program personnel by name."

"Submit detailed schedule with measurable milestones and specific reviews."

"Submit XYZ module with proposal for evaluation."

7. *Capture plan* — a detailed action plan in support of the win strategy and all business plans. This should integrate the critical win

factors and the specific action plan. All activities such as timing, budgets, and responsible individuals identified should have measurable milestones. The capture plan is a working document to map out and guide the overall acquisition effort. It is a living document that should be revised and refined as the acquisition effort progresses.

8. *Ability to perform under contract* — this is often a separate document but a summary should be included in the acquisition plan stating (a) technical requirements, (b) manpower, (c) facilities, (d) teaming and subcontracting; and (e) program schedules.

9. *Problems and risks* — list of problems critical to the implementation of the capture plan, such as (a) risks to techniques, staffing, facilities, schedules, or procurement; (b) customer-orientated risks; (c) licenses/patents/rights/ and (d) contingency plan.

10. *Resource plan* — summarizes the key personnel, support services, and other resources needed for capturing the new business. The bottom line of this plan is the total acquisition cost.

There are many ways to present the acquisition plan. However, an established format which is accepted as a standard throughout the organization, has several advantages. It provides a unified, standard format for quickly finding information during a review or analysis. Standard forms also serve as check lists. They force the planner to include not only information conveniently obtainable but also to seek out the other data necessary for winning new business. Finally, a standard format provides a quick and easy assessment of the new opportunity for key decision-makers.

THE BID BOARD

Few decisions are more fundamental to new business than the bid decision. Resources for the pursuit of new business come from operating profits. These resources are scarce and should be carefully controlled. Bid boards serve as management gates for release and control of these resources. The bid board is an expert panel usually convened by the general manager that analyzes the acquisition activities to determine status, and also to assess the investment versus opportunity in acquiring new business. An acquisition plan provides the major framework for the meeting of such bid boards.

Major acquisitions require a series of bid board sessions, starting as early as 12 to 18 months prior to the request for proposal (RFP). Subsequent bid boards reaffirm the bid decision and update the acquisition plans. It is the responsibility of the proposal manager to gather and present pertinent information in a manner that provides the bid board with complete information for analysis and decision. This requires significant preparation and customer contact. A team presentation is effective as all disciplines should be involved.

16
Types of Solicitations and Contracts

One major area of confusion faced by the small-business entrepreneur is the variety of solicitations and contract types that are part of the new project acquisition. Many contractors are under the impression that they have little or no choice in the selection of the contract type. It is true that most solicitations specify the type of contract to be procured, yet the prospective contractor can often negotiate the contract type that meets the overall requirements of the contract best for all contracting parties.

To lay the foundation for responding properly to a given solicitation, a brief review of the principal contract types, solicitations, and corresponding types of procurement is provided here. The terminology and the processes described are those observed in U.S. government procurement practices. However, most private firms have adopted identical or nearly identical processes that rely on standard disciplined methods of proposal solicitation, evaluation, and contract negotiations.

ADVERTISED AND NEGOTIATED PROCUREMENT

Basically, there are two major methods for initiating new contract procurement: formal advertising or negotiation. An overview of these methods is provided in Table 25.

Table 25. Major Procurement Types.

TYPE OF PROCUREMENT	TYPICAL PROGRAM	TYPICAL CONTRACT TYPE[a]
Advertised Procurement:		
IFB – Invitation for Bids. Response to the IFB is by formal proposal. Award is made to the lowest bidder with a fully complaint proposal.	Off-the-shelf type products, services, or simple well-defined projects: • Integrated circuits • Fibers • Snow removal service • Art exhibition program	FPP
Negotiated Procurement:		
RFP – Request for Proposal. Response to the RFP is by formal aid proposal, evaluated by the contracting organization against specific selection criteria. The contracting organization usually starts negotiating with the party that submitted the *best* overall proposal, considering all technical, managerial, and price factors. Alternative proposals are possible.	Most common type of solicitation used when advertised procurement is inappropriate: • Professional services • Development programs • Research studies • Production programs	CPFF CPIF CPAF FFP
RFQ – Request for Quotation. Similar to the RFP, but mostly used to obtain prices and performance data for products or services without specific and detailed customer requirements.	Program is a standard off-the-shelf service or development • Specialty tested components • Consulting service • Product modification • Training program	FFP CPFF
Sole-Source Procurement. Contracting organization selects single firm for solicitation and negotiation. Unsolicited proposals are a major source leading to sole-source procurements.	Specialty programs with one firm uniquely qualified or programs that should have limited exposure to the public • Specialty programs • "Secret mission" programs • Follow-on programs • Spares and logistics programs	CPFF CPIF CPAF FFP

[a] For contract type definitions see Table 26.

Advertised Procurement

The basic tool for "formal advertising" is the *invitation for bid (IFB)*, which lists all customer requirements. Prospective contractors can obtain the IFB notices through various channels. Two methods are most common: (1) filing a formal application with the contracting organization to be included on the bidder's list in the area of your interest and (2) scanning appropriate advertising media, such as newspapers, trade journals or the *Commerce Business Daily,* for government contract opportunities. For most of these advertised opportunities you can request the IFB directly from the contracting organization. Prospective contractors submit proposals which should be fully responsive to the customer requirements. On the bid-opening date all proposals and supporting bids are opened and the contract is awarded to the lowest fully responsive bidder. No advantage is gained by a firm whose proposal exceeds the customer requirements. However, if two competitors submit responsive proposals with identical price tags, the contract will often be awarded to the bidder with the more attractive proposal.

The criteria often used by the contracting organization for initiating the solicitation by formal advertising are that (1) the procurement can be completely described in terms of specifications and requirements; (2) there is an adequate number of potential qualified bidders; and (3) sufficient time is available to procure the contract via formal advertisement.

Negotiated Procurement

The most common vehicle for initiating a negotiated procurement is the *request for proposal (RFP)*. Firms interested in competing for the contract submit a formal bid proposal that describes the work, approaches, expected results, and cost. Each proposal is then evaluated by the contracting organization. The proposal evaluation is often a very complex formal process that considers many factors such as responsiveness to the RFP, soundness of approach, features, results, risks, prior experience, credibility, resource availability, and cost. The contracting organization usually starts negotiating with the bidder who first submits the "best" overall proposal as determined against the preestablished criteria. Significant customer contact is often necessary to interpret the customer requirements properly and consequently to submit a responsible winning proposal.

The major difference between an IFB and RFP is the negotiation that usually follows the bid evaluation in response to a RFP. The negotiations can include any facet of the contract, including technical factors, management, and cost.

Another common vehicle for initiating a solicitation is the *request for quotation (RFQ),* which leads to a procurement process similar to the RFP but is often used only to obtain prices and performance data on certain products and services. Often the buyer has not worked out the detailed requirements necessary for issuing a proper RFP. Thus, the RFQ usually leads to a simpler, less costly response and evaluation. In addition, the RFP is frequently used to obtain budgetary data or purchase established products and services.

Unless a sole-source procurement is the method chosen by the customer, the process for obtaining an RFP or an FRQ is similar to that of obtaining an IFB. It is solicited either through bidder's list or through the pertinent advertising media.

TWO PRINCIPAL TYPES OF CONTRACTS

The term *type of contract* has many meanings and covers a broad spectrum of legal aspects. However, in the discussion in this chapter this term is defined as the method of payment referred to when speaking about a *contract type*.

There are basically two contract types: *fixed price* and *cost*. For fixed price contracts the financial obligation rests with the contractor, who must deliver the agreed-upon contractual items at a fixed price, or be subjected to penalties specified in the default clause. The most common variations of fixed price contracts are described in Table 26: (1) firm fixed price (FFP), (2) fixed price with escalation (FPE), and (3) fixed price plus incentive fee (FPIF).

For cost-type contracts the contractor is reimbursed the cost of materials, labor, travel, overhead, and other items — including profit — according to negotiated agreements. The contractor makes the *best effort* to fulfill the specific technical requirements, usually set forth in the proposal, statement of work, and specifications, but

Table 26. Major Contract Types.

CONTRACT TYPES AND CHARACTERISTICS	TYPICAL PROGRAMS
Fixed Price Contracts:	
FFP — Firm Fixed Price. A definite price is agreed on for specific results prior to contract award. The contractor bears full profit and loss responsibility. FFPs impose a minimum administrative burden on both the contractor and the customer regarding cost reporting and tracking. Contract changes often soften the FFP.	Well-defined programs with predictable cost and low implementation risks: • Production to specs • Training program • Banquet
FPE — Fixed Price with Escalation. The contract provides for upward or downward adjustment of the fixed price according to an agreed-on index.	Well-defined programs with predictable effort but with uncertain stability of market and labor conditions: • Long-range programs
FPIF — Fixed Price Plus Incentive Fee. In addition to the fixed price, the contract provides an agreed-on incentive fee for certain performance-cost trade-offs, schedule advances, or the exceeding of particular contractual requirements.	Variation of FFP type used in situations where cost information or performance requirements are not sufficiently developed to permit negotiations of firm targets: • Development program
Cost-Type Contracts:	
CPFF — Cost Plus Fixed Fee. The contract provides for the payment of a fixed fee to to the contractor in addition to the cost incurred, which is also fully reimbursable.	Exploratory or developmental types of programs with uncertain level of effort and cost: • Research programs • Study programs • Advanced developments • Consulting
CPIF — Cost Plus Incentive Fee. This cost-reimbursable contract provides for an adjustable fee depending on cost or technical contract performance. Usually five factors are negotiated at the outset of the contract: (1) target cost, (2) target fee, (3) maximum fee, (4) minimum fee, and (5) sharing formula.	Especially development and test programs: • Equipment developments • Prototype developments • Proposal developments
CPAF — Cost Plus Award Fee. The contract is similar to CPFF contract with the addition of an award fee subjectively determined by the contracting organization based on the proposal evaluation or negotiated contract performance factors. This contract type is used in U.S. government contracting.	Complex programs with difficult-to-measure contract performance: • Development programs • Research programs • Studies

cannot be held liable if, in spite of his best effort, the desired results are not produced within the estimated cost or time frame. The most common cost-type contracts are summarized in Table 26. They are (1) Cost Plus Fixed Fee (CPFF), (2) Cost Plus Incentive Fee (CPIF) and (3) Cost Plus Award Fee (CPAF).

Which Type of Contract Is Right for You?

The prime consideration for selecting a contract type is related to the quality of program definition. This includes technical feasibility, risks, uncertainties, degree of detail of program plan, and experience factors. All of these factors translate into the degree of predictability for contract cost and timing. The responsibility for determining the proper contract type rests primarily with the contracting organization, as they have the power to initiate the type of solicitation that is most suitable to them. It should be recognized, however, that insensitivity to the performance criteria of a particular contract situation invariably leads to serious contractual problems and often to default. This caution is directed toward contracting organizations that, for reasons of limiting resource commitment and simplicity of cost tracking, often put pressure on their source selection authorities to lean toward fixed-price procurements. Today, fixed-price procurements are a fact of life in contracting with either industry or government.

Clearly, the fixed price procurement has many advantages to both contracting parties. It is advantageous if the project or program is sufficiently defined with clearly described expected results, predictable cost, and low implementation risks. On the other hand, if the new program is associated with technical risks, uncertainties, or calls for state-of-the-art advances, a cost-type contract is more appropriate. Typically, such cost-type programs include research, studies, exploratory work, consulting, advanced developments, and prototyping. A forced fit of fixed price contract to a cost-plus situation usually leads to major conflicts over cost, schedules, and technical performance among the contracting parties. In such a situation, the advantage of fixed resource commitment is lost very quickly. The contract is often too vague for holding the contractor legally accountable to specific deliverable items. Also, other complications may arise because the fixed price contract, by its nature, does not foster among

Table 27. Contracting Information Sources.

HANDBOOK AND REFERENCE BOOKS	*Anatomy of a Win,* by Jim M. Beveridge, J. M. Beveridge Associates, 8448 Wagner Creek Road, Talent, Ore. 97540, 1978. *Business Guide to Dealing with the Federal Government,* Drake Publishers Incorporated, 381 Park Avenue South, New York, N.Y. 10016, 1973 ($3.95). *Contract Planning and Organization,* United Nations Publications, United Nations, LX2300, New York, N.Y. 10017, 1974 ($2.50). *Creating Superior Proposals,* by Jim M. Beveridge and E. J. Velton, J. M. Beveridge Associates, 8448 Wagner Creek Road, Talent, Ore. 97540, 1978. *Gordon's Modern Annotated Forms of Agreement,* by S. Gordon and S. Kuzman, Prentice-Hall, Englewood Cliffs, N.J. 07632, 1969. *Guide for Drawing Up Contracts for Large Industrial Works,* United Nations Publications, United Nations, LX2300, New York, N.Y. 10017, 1972 (1.50). *A Handbook for Proposal Preparation and Management* by Roy Loring and Harold Kerzner, Van Nostrand Reinhold, New York, 1982. *How to Create a Winning Proposal,* by J. Ammon-Wexler and Catherine ap Carmel, Mercury Communications, 730 Mission Street, Santa Cruz, Calif. 95060, 1977. *Selling to United States Govenment,* United States Small Business Administration, Washington, D.C. 20416, 1973 (free). *What You Should Know About Contracts,* by Robert A. Farmer, Arco Publishing Company, 219 Park Avenue South, New York, N.Y. 10003, 1969 ($4.95).
PERIODICALS AND NEWSPAPERS	*Briefing Papers,* Federal Publications, 1725 K Street NW, Washington, D.C. 20006, bimonthly ($68.00 per year). *Commerce Business Daily,* U.S. Department of Commerce, Office of Field Services, U.S. Government Printing Office, Washington, D.C. 20402 ($80.00 per year). *Forms of Business Agreement,* Institute of Business Planning, IPB Plaza, Englewood Cliffs, N.J. 07632, monthly ($198.00 per year). *Government Contractor,* Federal Publications, 1725 K Street NW, Washington, D.C. 20006, biweekly ($156.00). *Government Contracts Reports,* Commerce Clearance House, 4025 West Peterson Avenue, Chicago, Ill. 60646, weekly ($4.00 per year). *NCMA Newsletter,* National Contract Management Association, 675 East Wardlow Road, Long Beach, Calif. 90807, monthly.
DIRECTORIES	*Government Contracts Directory,* Government Data Publications, 422 Washington Building, Washington, D.C. 20005, annual ($100.00). *Government Contracts Guide,* Commerce Clearing House, 4025 West Peterson Avenue, Chicago, Ill. 60646 ($17.50)

Table 27. Contracting Information Sources. (continued)

DIRECTORIES (continued)	*Selling to NASA*, U.S. Government Printing Office, Washington, D.C. 20502 (free).
	Selling to Navy Prime Contractors, U.S. Government Printing Office, Washington, D.C. 20502 ($1.00).
	United States Government Purchasing and Sales Directory, U.S. Small Business Administration, U.S. Government Printing Office, Washington, D.C. 20402, 1972 ($2.35).
ON-LINE DATA BASES	*Defense Market Measurement System*, Frost and Sullivan, 109 Fulton Street, New York, N.Y. 10038.
	Federal Register, Capital Services, 511 Second Street NE, Washington, D.C. 20002.
ASSOCIATIONS AND SOCIETIES	Electronic Industries Association, EIA, 2001 Eye Street, NE, Washington, D.C. 20006
	National Contract Management Association, 2001 Jefferson Davis Highway, Arlington, Va. 22202.
	National Institute of Government Purchasing, 1001 Connecticut Avenue NW, Washington, D.C. 20036.

the contracting parties a great deal of the teamwork that may be needed to work out the program details and specific customer requirements.

To resolve this dilemma it may be desirable to divide a project into major phases and design individual contracts for each phase. For example, the ultimate objective of a new program may be mass-producing low-cost data modems. The total program could be broken down into:

Phase 1	Requirements Analysis	CPFF
Phase 2	Feasibility Study	CPFF
Phase 3	Procurement Plan and RFP	CPFF
Phase 4	Program Development Plan	CPAF
Phase 5	Prototype Design and Development	CPIF
Phase 6	Production Engineering/DTUPC	CPIF
Phase 7	Volume Production	FFP
Phase 8	Spare Parts Program	FPE

The initial program phase often is to develop a detailed plan and the specific requirements for the advanced phases. For major programs, contractors usually have the opportunity to discuss the procurement with the contracting organization prior to formalizing the solicitation. This is the time to assess the pros and cons of the particular contract type under consideration and to influence the customer community to select the type that is appropriate for the upcoming procurement.

Identifying and pursuing new program business often involves very specialized procedures and services, especially when contracting with a government agency. Table 27 lists some of the key sources available. These reference documents can provide guidance and checklists on identifying, pursuing, and capturing new contract business.

UNSOLICITED PROCUREMENTS

While most contracts are negotiated in response to a specific formal solicitation, millions of dollars in project opportunities are procured each year without formal solicitation.

Unsolicited proposals are effective vehicles to win new business, especially for smaller firms, which often do not have the resources or multidisciplines to meet specific requirements of a formal request for proposal (RFP). Most importantly, unsolicited proposals put your firm in the unique position of being the only bidder. But even if the customer opts for a negotiated or advertised procurement, the solicitation will be structured around your proposal thus uniquely positioning your response relative to potential competitors.

Unsolicited proposals differ from solicited proposals primarily in the degree of formality and detail in the proposed program. To be successful, the unsolicited proposal should be supported by oral presentations to the customer community.

17
Developing the New Contract Opportunity

We live in a competitive world. Winning new business requires significant homework in preparation for the bid proposal. Selling a new program is unique and different from selling in other markets. It often requires selling an organization capability for a customer development — something that has not been done before. This is different from selling an off-the-shelf product that can be examined prior to contract. It requires establishing your credibility and building confidence in the customer's mind so that your organization is selected as the best candidate for the new program. Such a "can-do" image usually has four facets.

FIRST: SIGNIFICANT CUSTOMER CONTACT

Early customer liaison is vital in learning about the customer requirements and needs. It is necessary to define the project baseline, the potential problem areas, and the risks involved.

Establishing meaningful customer contact is no simple task. Today's structured customer organizations involve many key decision-making personnel, conflicting requirements and needs, and biases. There rarely is only one person responsible for signing-off on a major procurement. Technical and marketing involvement at all levels is necessary to reach all decision-making parties in the customer community.

Your new business acquisition plan will be the road map for your marketing efforts. The benefits of this customer contact are that you:

- Learn about the specific customer requirements
- Obtain information for refining baseline prior to proposal
- Can participate in customer problem-solving
- Build a favorable image as a competent, credible contractor
- Check out your baseline approach and its acceptability prior to proposal
- Develop rapport and a good working relationship with the customer

SECOND: PRIOR RELEVANT EXPERIENCE

Nothing is more convincing to the customer than demonstrated prior performance in the same or related area of the new program. It shows the customer that you have produced on a similar task. This reduces the perceived technical risks and associated budget and schedule uncertainties. Therefore, it is of vital importance to demonstrate to the customer that your organization (a) understands their new requirements and (b) has performed satisfactorily on similar programs. This image of an experienced contractor can be communicated in many ways:

- Field demonstration of working systems and equipment
- Listing of previous or current customers, their equipment and applications
- Model demonstrations
- Technical status presentations
- Product promotional folders
- Technical papers and articles
- Trade show demonstrations and displays
- Slide or video presentation of equipment in operation
- Simulation of the system, equipment, or services
- Printed specs, photos, or input/output of the proposed equipment or its parts
- Advertisements

Demonstrating prior experience is integrated and interactive with the customer liaison activities. To be successful, particularly on larger programs, requires both leadership and discipline. Start with a well-defined customer contact plan as part of your overall acquisition plan. This requires well-planned involvement at all levels in order to make these contacts with relevant personnel in the customer community. One major benefit derived from these intensive marketing efforts is that you create an image, with the customer, as an experienced, sound contractor. Secondly, you are learning more about the new program, its specific requirements, and the risks involved as well as the concerns and biases of the customer. This information will make it easier to respond effectively to a formal or informal request for proposal.

THIRD: READINESS TO PERFORM

Once the basic requirements and specifications of the new program are known, it is often necessary to mount a substantial technical preproposal effort to advance the baseline design to a point that permits a clear definition of the new program. These efforts may be funded by the customer or may be borne by the contractor. Typical efforts include (1) feasibility studies, (2) system designs, (3) simulation, (4) design and testing of certain critical elements in the new equipment or the new process, (5) prototype models, or (6) any developments necessary to bid the new job within the desired scope of technical and financial risks.

Development prior to contract is expensive, has no guarantee of return, and precludes the company from pursuing other activities. Then why do organizations spend their resources for such development? It is often an absolutely necessary cost for winning new business. These early developments reduce the implementation risks to an acceptable level for both the customer and the contractor. Further, these developments might be necessary to catch up with a competitor or to convince the customer that certain alternative approaches are preferable.

Clearly, preproposal developments are costly. Therefore, they should be thorough and well detailed and approved as part of the overall acquisition plan. The plans and specific results should be accurately communicated to the customer. This will help to build a quality image for your firm while giving the potential contractor additional insight into the detailed program requirements. Finally, one should not overlook two sources of funding for these activities: (1) customer funding for these advanced programs prior to contract — often the customer is willing to fund contract-definition activities because it may reduce the risks and the uncertainties of contractual performance; (2) inclusion with other ongoing developments. The program manager might find that a similar effort is under way in a corporate research department or even within the customer's organization.

FOURTH: ESTABLISHING THE ORGANIZATION

Another element of credibility is the contractor's organizational readiness to perform under contract. This includes facilities, key personnel, support groups, and management structure. Reliability in this area is particularly critical in winning a program that is large relative to your company size. Often a contractor goes out on a limb and establishes a new program organization to satisfy specific program or customer requirements. This may require major organizational changes.

Few companies go into reorganization lightly, especially prior to contract. However, in most cases it is possible to establish all the elements of the new program organization without physically moving people or facilities, and without erecting new buildings. What is needed is an organization plan exactly detailing the procedures to be followed as soon as the contract is awarded. Further, the new program organization can be defined on paper together with its proper charter and all structural and authority relationships. This should be sufficient for customer discussion and will give a head start once the contract is received. Usually it is not the moving of partitions, people, or facilities that takes time, but the determination of where to move them and how to establish the necessary working relationships.

As a checklist, the following organizational components should be defined clearly and discussed with the customer prior to a major new contract:

- Organizational structure
- Charter
- Policy-management guidelines
- Job description
- Authority and responsibility relationships
- Type and number of offices and laboratories
- Facilities listing
- Floor plans
- Staffing plan
- Milestone schedule and budget for reorganization

A company seldom needs to reorganize completely to accommodate a new program. It requires resources and risks for both the contractor and the customer. Most likely the customer and program requirements can be accommodated within the existing organization by redefining organizational relationships, authority and responsibility structures, without physically moving people and facilities. Matrix organizations, in particular, have the flexibility and capacity to handle large additional program business with only minor organizational changes.

18
Creating Winning Proposals

Bid proposals are payoff vehicles. They are one of the final products of your marketing effort. Whether you are bidding on a service contract or an engineering development, a government contract or a commercial program, the process is the same and, in the end, you must submit a proposal.

Yet, with all due respect to the importance of the bid proposal as a marketing tool, many senior managers point out that the proposal is only one part of the total marketing effort. The proposal is usually not the vehicle that sells your program — the proposal stage may be too late. The program concept and the soundness of its approach, the alternatives, your credibility, etc., must be established during the face-to-face discussions with the customer. So, why this fuss about writing a superior proposal? Because we still live in a competitive world. Your competition is working toward the same goal of winning this program. They, too, may have sold the customer on their approaches and capabilities. Hence, among the top contenders, the field is probably very close. More importantly, beating most of the competition is not good enough. As in a poker game, there is no second place. Therefore, while it is correct that the proposal is only part of the total marketing effort, it must be a superior proposal. Proposal development is a serious business in itself.

Most people hate to work on proposals. Proposal development requires hard work and long hours, often in a constantly changing work environment. Proposals are multidisciplinary efforts of a special kind. But, like any other multifunctional program, they require an orderly and disciplined effort that relies on many special tools to integrate the various activities of developing a high-scoring quality proposal. This is particularly true for large program proposals which require large capital commitments. Smaller proposals often can be managed with less formality. However, at a minimum, they should include the following tasks to ensure a quality bid proposal:

- Proposal team organization
- Proposal schedule
- Categorical outline with writing assignments and page allocation
- Tone and emphasis/win strategy
- RFP analysis
- Technical baseline review
- Draft writing
- Reviews
- Art/illustration development
- Cost estimating
- Proposal production
- Final management review

For each activity or milestone the plan should define the responsible individual(s) and schedules.

THE DRIVING FORCES IN THE WIN EQUATION

The driving forces of a winning bid proposal include more than just the price. They include the factors outlined in the proposal as well as the contractor image created prior to proposal submission. In fact, research shows that a low price bid is advantageous toward winning *only* in program acquisitions with low complexity, low technical risk, and high competition. In most other situations price is important only in the context of all competitive factors such as:

- Compliance with customer requirements
- Relevant past experience
- Past performance on similar programs

- Soundness of approach
- Cost credibility
- Competitive price

Another insight into pricing strategies is provided by considering the effects of the business environment. Profits are squeezed out by aggressive pricing among competitors. Therefore, the need for aggressive pricing increases with the (1) strength of competition, (2) tightness of customer budget, (3) internal cost deficiencies, (4) program risks, and (5) desire to win.

19
Pricing Strategies

THE LOW-BIDDER DILEMMA

There is little argument about the importance of the price tag to the proposal. The question is, what price will win the job? Everyone has an answer to this question. The decision process that leads to the final price of your proposal is highly complex and has many uncertainties. Yet proposal managers, driven by the desire to win the job, may think that a very low priced proposal will help. But, hopefully, winning is only the beginning. We have short- and long-range objectives on profit, market penetration, a new product development, etc. These objectives may be incompatible or irrelevant to a low-price strategy per se, such as:

- A suspiciously low price, particularly on cost-plus type proposals, might be perceived by the customer as unrealistic, thus affecting the bidder's cost credibility or even the technical ability to perform.
- The bid price may be unnecessarily low relative to the competition and customer budget, therefore eroding profits.
- The price may be irrelevant to the bid objective, such as entering a new market. Therefore, the contractor has to sell the proposal in a credible way (e.g., using cost sharing).
- Low pricing without market information is meaningless. The price level is always relative to (1) the competitive prices, (2) the customer budget, and (3) the bidder's cost estimate.

- The bid proposal and its price may cover only part of the total program. The ability to win phase II, or follow-on business, depends on phase I performance and phase II price.
- The financial objectives of the customer may be more complex than just finding the lowest bidder. They may include cost objectives for total system life cycle cost (LCC), for design to unit production cost (DTUPC), or for specific logistic support items. To present sound approaches for attaining these system cost-performance parameters and targets may be equally, if not more, important than a low bid for its development.

Further, it is refreshing to note that in spite of customer pressures toward low cost and fixed price, the lowest bidder is certainly not an automatic winner. Both commercial and governmental customers are increasingly concerned about cost realism and the ability to perform under contract. A compliant, sound technical proposal, based on past experience with realistic, well-documented cost figures, is often chosen over the lowest bidder, who may project a risky image regarding technical performance, cost, or schedule.

THE PRICING PROCESS

With the complexities involved, it is not surprising that many business managers consider pricing an art. Having the right intelligence information on customer cost budgets and competitive pricing would certainly help. However, the reality is that whatever information is available to one bidder is generally available to the others. Even more revealing is the fact that intelligence sources are often unreliable. The only thing worse than missing information is wrong or misleading information. When it comes to competitive pricing, the old saying still applies: Those who talk don't know; and those who know don't talk! It is true, partially, that pricing remains an art. However, a disciplined approach certainly helps to develop all the input for a rational pricing recommendation. Tables 28 and 29 show the principal inputs and the decision-making process in detail, developing the rationale that leads to the final price. A side benefit of using a disciplined management process is that it leads to the documentation of the many factors and assumptions involved at a later point in

224 NEW BUSINESS DEVELOPMENT

Table 28. Inputs to Pricing Decision.

- Reliable cost estimate of proposed baseline
- Associated risks and uncertainties
- Strategic business value of program (short- and long-range): sales, profit, ROI, new market penetration, technology development, manpower utilization, etc.
- Customer budget
- Competitive scenario

time. These can be compared and analyzed, contributing to the learning experiences that make up the managerial skills needed for effective business decisions.

Two Global Pricing Strategies

Specific pricing strategies must be developed for each individual situation. Frequently, however, one of two situations prevails when project acquisitions are pursued competitively. First, the new business opportunity is a one-of-a-kind program with little or no follow-on potential; a situation classified as type I acquisition. Second, the new business opportunity is an entry point to a larger follow-on or repeat business, or represents a planned penetration into a new market. This acquisition is classified as type II.

Clearly, in each case, we have specific but different business objectives. The objective for type I acquisition is to win the program and execute it profitably and satisfactorily according to contractual agreements. The type II objective is often to win the program and perform well, thereby gaining a foothold in a new market segment or a new customer community in place of making a profit. Accordingly, each acquisition type has its own unique pricing strategy as summarized in Table 30.

Comparing the two pricing strategies for the two global situations (as shown in Table 30) reveals a great deal of similarities for the first five points. The fundamental difference is that for a profitable new business acquisition the bid price is determined according to actual cost, while in a "must-win" situation the price is determined by the market forces. It should be emphasized that one of the most crucial inputs in the pricing decision is the cost estimate of the proposed

PRICING STRATEGIES 225

Table 29. Pricing Decision Process.

STEP/ISSUE	ACTION
Cost estimate	Obtain a realistic cost estimate for the proposed baseline, scrubbed and agreed on with operating departments.
Risks	Summarize associated risks and contingencies and their impact on the program cost. Areas: technical, schedules, staffing, facilities, licenses, patent rights, customer equipment, etc.
Program budget	Update customer budget or budget estimate for the proposed program. (This information is available usually long before an RFP is issued.)
Cost realism	Assure cost realism by comparing the major cost elements to top-down estimates, customer budget bogies, and parametric ratios. Correct or justify all abnormalities.
Competitive assessment	Update. Summarize the strengths and weaknesses of major competitors against your firm, considering (1) related experience, (2) current business, (3) customer relations, (4) unique features in proposed program, etc.
Business objective	Refresh on strategic business objectives: "Why are we bidding?" • Profitable program execution • Stage-setting for follow-on business • New market penetration • Winning a new customer • New technology/capability • Other • Any combination
Customer objective	Summarize customer's key objectives: • Low cost • Low risk • New capability development • Experimental program • Other • Any combination
Base prize	Adjust the cost estimate for risks and add the desired profit margins/fees.
Pricing decision	Compare the base price to the (1) customer budget, (2) competitive assessment, (3) business objectives, and (4) customer objectives. Derive two price figures: (i) the highest price that most likely will still win the job and (ii) the lowest price your company is willing to negotiate. Hopefully, this price is below the threshold for winning. The pricing decision is made by considering all the inputs 1 through 8. The aggressiveness of the final bid price largely depends on the underlying business objectives.

Table 30. Two Global Pricing Strategies.

TYPE I ACQUISITION (ONE-OF-A-KIND PROGRAM WITH LITTLE OR NO FOLLOW-ON BUSINESS)	TYPE II ACQUISITION (NEW PROGRAM HAS POTENTIAL FOR LARGE FOLLOW-ON BUSINESS OR REPRESENTS A DESIRED PENETRATION INTO NEW MARKETS)
Pricing Strategy:	**Pricing Strategy:**
1. Develop cost model and estimating guidelines, design proposed project/program baseline for minimum cost, to minimum customer requirements.	1. Design proposed project/program baseline complaint with customer requirements, with innovative features but minimum risks.
2. Estimate cost realistically for minimum requirements.	2. Estimate cost realistically.
3. Scrub the baseline, squeeze out unnecessary costs. Trade-offs, make-buy.	3. Scrub baseline. Squeeze out unnecessary costs.
4. Determine realistic minimum cost. Obtain commitment from performing organizations.	4. Determine realistic minimum cost. Obtain commitment from performing organizations.
5. Adjust cost estimate for risks.	5. Determine "should-cost" including risk adjustments.
6. Add desired margins. Determine the price.	6. Compare your final cost estimate to customer budget and the "most likely" winning price.
7. Compare price to customer budget and competitive cost information	7. Determine the gross profit margin necessary for your winning proposal. This margin could be negative!
8. Bid only if price is within competitive range.	8. Decide whether the gross margin is acceptable according to the must-win desire.
	9. Depending on the strength of your desire to win, bid the "most likely" winning price or lower.
	10. If the bid price is below cost, it is often necessary to provide a detailed explanation to the customer of where the additional funding is coming from. The source could be company profits or sharing of related activities. In any case, a clear resource picture should be given to the customer.

baseline. The design of this baseline to the minimum requirements should be started early in accordance with well-defined ground rules, cost models, and established cost targets. Too often the baseline design is performed in parallel with the proposal development. At the proposal stage it is too late to review and fine-tune the baseline for minimum cost. Further, such a late start does not allow much of an option for a final bid decision. Even if the price appears outside the competitive range, it makes little sense to terminate the proposal development. As all the resources have been spent anyway, one might just as well submit a bid in spite of the remote chance of winning.

Clearly, effective pricing begins a long time before proposal development. It starts with preliminary customer requirements, well-understood subtasks, and a top-down estimate with should-cost targets. This allows the functional organization to design a baseline to meet the customer requirements and cost targets, and gives management the time to review and redirect the design before the proposal is submitted. It further gives management an early opportunity to assess the chances of winning during the acquisition cycle, at a point in time when additional resources can be allocated or the acquisition effort can be terminated before too many resources are committed to a hopeless effort.

The final pricing session should be an integration and review of information already well known in basic context. The process and management tools outlined here should help to provide the framework and discipline for deriving pricing decisions in an orderly and effective way.

20
Closing the Contract

Sending off the bid proposal starts the postsubmission phase. Regardless of the type of customer or the formalities involved, even for an oral proposal, the procurement will go through the following principal steps:

1. Bid proposals received
2. Proposals evaluated
3. Proposal results compared
4. Alternatives assessed
5. Clarifications and new information from bidders
6. Negotiations
7. Award

While bidders usually have no influence on proposal evaluation or source selection process, they can certainly prepare properly for the upcoming presentation opportunities to the customer. Depending on the procurement, these opportunities for improving the competitive position come in the following forms:

- Follow-up calls and visits
- Responding to formal requests for more data or clarification

- Fact finding requested by customer
- Oral presentations
- Invitations to field visits
- Sending samples or prototypes
- White paper
- Supportive advertising
- Contact via related contract work
- Plant or office visits
- Press releases
- Negotiations

The bidder's objective on all postsubmission activities should be improving competitive position. For starters, the bidder must assess his proposal relative to the customer requirements and to competing alternatives. In order to do this realistically the bidder needs customer contact. Any opportunity for customer contact should be utilized. Follow-up calls and visits are effective in less formal procurements, while fact-finding and related contact work are often used by bidders in formal buying. These are just a few methods to open officially closed doors into the customer community.

Only through active customer contact is it possible to realistically assess the competitive situation and organize for improvement and winning negotiations. Table 31 provides a listing of steps for which the bidder should organize. Customer contact and interaction are often difficult to arrange, especially in more formal procurements which may require innovative marketing approaches.

While the proposal evaluation period is being used by the customer to determine the best proposal, the bidder has the opportunity to improve his position in three principal areas: (1) clarification of proposed program scope and content; (2) image building as a sound, reliable contractor; and (3) counteracting advances made by competing bidders.

The proposal evaluation period is highly dynamic in terms of changing scores, particularly among the top contenders. The bidder who is well organized and prepared to interact with the customer community stands the best chance of being called first for negotiations, thus gaining a better basis for negotiating an equitable contract.

Table 31. Organizing the Postsubmission Effort.

1. *Reassess your proposal.* Study your proposal and reassess (1) strengths, (2) weaknesses, and (3) compliance to customer requirements.
2. *Develop an action plan.* List all weak points of your proposal, potential for improvment, and actions toward improvement.
3. *Open communications.* Establish and maintain communications with the customer during the proposal evaluation period. Determine the various roles people play in the customer community during the evaluation.
4. *Find your score.* Try to determine how you scored with your proposal. Find out what the customer liked, disliked, perceived as risks; credibility problems and standing against the competition. To determine your score realistically and objectively requires communications skills, sensitivity, and usually a great deal of prior customer contact. Determining your proposal score is an important prerequisite for being able to clarify specific items and to improve your competitive position.
5. *Seek interaction.* Seek out opportunities for interacting with the customer as early as possible. Such opportunities may be presenting additional information for clarifying or enhancing specific proposed items. The meeting or presentation should be requested by the customer; it is a great opportunity for the bidder to "sell" his proposal further. This includes clarifications, modifications, options, and image building.
6. *Prepare for formal meetings.* Be sure you are well prepared for meetings, fact-finding sessions, or presentations requested by the customer. This is your opportunity not only to clarify but also to strengthen your proposal; show additional material and introduce new personnel if needed.
7. *Reassess cost and price.* Cost and proposed effort are often fluid during the initial program phases. Many times, the discussion of the proposal narrows down the real customer requirements. This provides an opportunity to reassess and adjust the bid price.
8. *Obtain start-work order.* It is often possible to obtain a start-work order before the program is formally under contract. This provides a limited mutual commitment and saves time.
9. *Stay on top until closure.* From the time of submitting the bid to obtaining the final contract, the bidder must keep abreast with all developments in the customer community that affect the proposal. Try to help the customer justify the source selection and be responsive to customer requests for additional information and meetings. Frequent interaction with the customer is pervasive.
10. *Prepare for formal negotiations.* Negotiation comes in many forms. Program contract negotiations mostly center on the technical performance, schedule, and cost. They should be conducted among the technical and managerial personnel of the contracting parties. If in addition to the technicalities the contract covers extensive legal provisions, terms, and conditions, etc., the bidder should seek the interpretation and advice of legal counsel.

PART IV
PROGRAM MANAGEMENT LEADERSHIP

21
People Are Your Most Valuable Asset

More than in any other organizational form, leadership skills are essential for effective management of the multidisciplinary activities that come into play during the project life cycle. The ability to build project teams, motivate people, and create organizational structures conducive to innovative and effective work requires sophisticated interpersonal and organizational skills.

Personnel management is more complex in project organizations than in conventional forms of management because project managers have to deal effectively with a variety of interfaces and support personnel over whom they have little or no formal authority. In their search for solutions to complex problems, project managers often must cross functional lines within their parent organization to gain support for their projects from different disciplines. More often than not, project managers have little or no formal authority over those individuals who can provide the needed advice and assistance. Equally important is the project manager's ability to manage intense conflict situations. This ability often can mean the difference between successful and unsuccessful project performance.

There is no single magic formula for successful program management. However, most senior managers agree that effective program managers need to understand the interaction of organizational and behavioral clements in order to build an environment conducive to their teams' motivational needs.[48]

The following chapters deal with the primary issues of program leadership effectiveness especially as they relate to small and medium-sized businesses. These issues are: (1) people skills, (2) organizational structure, and (3) management style.

---

[48] For a discussion of field research data on project management leadership style see Gary R. Gemmill and Hans J. Thamhain, "Influence Styles of Project Managers," *Academy of Management Journal* (June, 1974); Hans J. Thamhain and David Wilemon, "Leadership, Conflict, and Program Management Effectiveness," *Sloan Management Review* (Fall, 1977); – and – "Team Building in Project Management," *Project Management Quarterly* (Summer, 1983).

22
The Art of Interpersonal Compliance

UNDERSTANDING PROFESSIONAL NEEDS

Understanding people is important in any management situation. It is absolutely essential, however, for the management of today's projects and programs. The breed of managers that evolved within these contemporary organizations has to confront new problems in managing their complex tasks. Company-internally they must be able to operate in a multidisciplinary environment that requires dealing effectively with a variety of interfaces and support personnel over whom they often have little or no control. Company-externally the project manager has to cope with constant and rapid change regarding the technology, markets, regulations, and socioeconomic factors. To be effective, the manager has to lead and motivate a work force toward innovative results in an often unstructured organizational environment.

Moreover, traditional methods of authority-based direction, performance measures, and control are virtually impractical in such contemporary environments. Finding ways of gaining the desired level of support is a true challenge, particularly for project managers in small and medium-sized businesses who often cannot afford the setup and overhead of formal project organizations, but have to operate in a less formalized and structured work environment. To be effective in these situations requires a large degree of interpersonal and organizational skill, plus an understanding of the motivational bases, the needs of project personnel. The ability to recognize these needs and to build a work environment conducive to their fulfillment seems to be crucial for effective teamwork and project performance.

Fifteen specific professional needs have been identified in field research of project personnel.[49] The following discussion shows how the fulfillment of these professional needs can drive project personnel to higher performance or, conversely, how the inability to fulfill these needs may become a barrier to teamwork and high project performance. This relationship was further substantiated in other research studies (263), which found a significant positive correlation between the ability of the project manager to satisfy the professional needs of his or her personnel and overall project performance.

1. *Interesting and challenging work:* Work that is interesting and challenging seems to satisfy various professional esteem needs. It appears to be oriented toward the intrinsic motivation of the individual. It further helps to integrate personal goals and interests with the objectives of the organization. Seventy percent of all project personnel perceive "interesting and challenging work" among the most important needs.

2. *Professionally stimulating work environment:* The second most frequent need expressed by project personnel is the need for a "professionally stimulating work environment." This need is very closely related to the need for interesting and challenging work. In fact many responses cross-reference it within the same scenario. Project professionals indicate that a stimulating work environment is very important for professional involvement, creativity, and interdisciplinary support. Further, follow-up interviews indicate that a stimulating work environment fosters team building; people are motivated and interested in the work itself; they are result-oriented, communicate effectively, have the capacity for conflict resolution, and are committed toward established organizational goals.[50]

---

[49] For a detailed discussion of the field research study see H.J. Thamain, "The Effective Engineering Manager," *Conference Proceedings,* 1981 IEEE Engineering Management Conference, Dayton, Ohio. While the original study was conducted in an engineering work environment, subsequent investigations validated the findings for nonengineering situations as well.
[50] The quality of this work environment is defined through its organizational structure, facilities, and management style. It includes a very complex set of variables, maybe closest resembled by Ouchi's Theory Z Organization (see Bibliography A-207).

3. *Professional growth:* The "opportunity for professional growth" ranks third. Personnel express the need for real career growth measured by promotional opportunities, salary advances, learning of new skills and techniques, and professional recognition. A particular challenge exists for management in limited-growth or zero-growth businesses to compensate for the lack in promotional opportunities by offering more intrinsic professional growth in terms of job satisfaction via accomplishments, recognition, and professional activities.

4. *Overall leadership:* The management ability to lead project personnel toward established organizational goals is an essential prerequisite for high productivity. It involves dealing effectively with individual contributors, managers, and support personnel within a specific functional discipline as well as across organizational lines. It involves information processing skills, effective communication, and decision-making. It is interesting to note that project personnel themselves perceive a strong need for effective leadership of their efforts and organizations. Many professionals relate their success in a particular effort to the quality of leadership obtained from their management. Therefore it is not surprising that the ability to lead project personnel toward established objectives is perceived by management as one of the most important skills for effectively managing the project team.

5. *Tangible rewards:* Tangible rewards are very important. They include financial rewards such as salary increases, bonuses, and incentives, as well as other rewards such as promotions, recognition, better offices, and educational opportunities. While most financial rewards are indeed short-term, extrinsic motivators seem to be necessary to sustain strong long-term project efforts and motivation. Furthermore, financial rewards seem to validate softer rewards such as recognition and praise, and to reassure people that higher goals are attainable.

6. *Technical expertise:* Sufficient technical expertise within project teams is important. That is, personnel need to have all necessary interdisciplinary skills and expertise available within the project team to perform the required tasks. Technical expertise comes in many facets: It includes an understanding of the technicalities of the project; the technology and underlying concepts, theories,

and principles; the design methods and techniques; and the functioning and interrelationship of the various components that make up the total system. In addition, technical expertise includes an understanding of the applications, the markets, and the business environment. It is necessary, not only for proper analytical and development work, but equally important for evaluating solutions and trade-offs, to communicate effectively within the team, assess risks, participate in search of integrated solutions, and make trade-offs among various alternatives.

To provide project personnel with the needed interdisciplinary expertise within their teams requires extensive technical skills and expertise on the part of the project manager who leads the overall effort.

7. *Assisting in problem-solving:* Obtaining assistance from management in facilitating solutions to technical, administrative, and personal problems seems to be very important. This clearly overlaps with the previously defined needs for sufficient expertise within the work unit and overall direction and leadership. If assistance to problem-solving is not provided it often leads to frustration, conflict, and demotivation of team members. It is interpreted as disinterest and indifference of management toward the effort, and was found to be one of the most severe barriers impeding a successful engineering effort.[51]

8. *Clearly defined objectives:* Communicating the goals, objectives, and outcomes of the project effort clearly to all affected personnel is another important need. Many project managers indicate that conflict develops over ambiguities or missing information regarding the what, when, and how of the effort. High motivational levels with the team are virtually impossible unless the objectives of the project effort are clearly delineated.

9. *Management control:* Proper management control is important to most project professionals for effective task performance. This also indicates one of the challenges phased by managers because it appears somewhat controversial to the needs for a stimulating work environment with freedom for decision-making and innovative thinking. It is consistent, however, with modern leadership practices.

---

[51] For detailed discussion, see H. Thamhain and D. Wilemon, "Managing Change in Project Management," *Proceedings, PMI Symposium,* Chicago, 1977.

The manager must understand the interaction of organizational and behavioral variables in order to exert the direction, leadership, and control required to steer the project effort toward established organizational goals in addition to fostering a climate conducive to the team's motivational needs.

10. *Job security:* Job security is one of the very fundamental needs that must be satisfied before people consider higher-order growth needs. Job security has many facets. Most weight seems to be placed on the stability of employment as measured by voluntary terminations, layoffs, and firings. But it also includes more intricate measures such as the ability to choose the type of work and location desired.

11. *Senior management support:* Senior management support and commitment are important for success in many project efforts. They are particularly crucial to larger, more complex undertakings. Support is viewed in four major areas: (1) financial resources, (2) provision of an effective operating charter, (3) facilitation of cooperation from support departments, and (4) provision of necessary facilities and equipment. Senior management support is often an absolute necessity when dealing with support groups on multidisciplinary efforts such as projects. Four key variables influence the project manager's ability to foster an environment favorable to senior management support: (1) the project manager's credibility, (2) the visibility of the effort he is leading, (3) the priority and importance of that effort, and (4) the manager's relationship and access to senior management. All four variables are interrelated and can be developed by the project manager.

12. *Good interpersonal relations:* Effective project teamwork[52] requires good working relationships among all supporting personnel. Good interpersonal relations foster a stimulating work environment with involved, motivated personnel, low conflict, and high productivity. Creating such an environment requires skills in team building

---

[52] Interpersonal relations are perceived most favorable in an environment that is conducive to *teamwork*. This was one of the conclusions from prior research by Thamhain and Wilemon (see Bibliography A, 260 and 263). The characteristics of such a work environment are (1) high task and result commitment, (2) availability of necessary resources and expertise, (3) clearly defined goals and objectives, (4) involved and supportive senior management, (5) good direction and leadership, (6) open communications among team members and support organizations, and (7) low detrimental interpersonal and intergroup conflict.

and conflict resolution, and above all, an understanding of the organization, its culture, and its value system.

13. *Proper planning:* Planning is helpful for any undertaking. It is absolutely essential, however, for successful management of complex project work. Effective project planning requires skills far beyond writing a document with schedules and budgets. It requires communication and information processing skills to define the actual resource requirements and administrative support necessary. It also requires the ability to negotiate resources and commitment from key personnel in various support groups across organizational lines.

14. *Clear role definition:* Multidisciplinary efforts especially can be negatively affected when role conflict exists among the team members and/or supporting organizations. Role conflict is most likely to occur when there is ambiguity over who does what within the project team and in external support groups. Clear charters, plans, and good management direction are some of the powerful tools to facilitate clear role definitions. The need for clearly defined roles and responsibilities is expressed by most project personnel.

15. *Open communications:* Poor communication is a major barrier to teamwork and project effectiveness. The need for a free flow of information both horizontally and vertically is important. It keeps personnel informed of technical and organizational developments, and functions as a pervasive integrator of the overall project effort.

16. *Minimization of changes:* In contrast to managers in more traditional businesses, the project manager has to live with constant change. However project personnel often see change as an unnecessary condition which impedes their creativity and productivity. They feel that changes of established technical, business, and organizational parameters should be avoided. In order to minimize the negative consequences of necessary change it seems to be important to communicate the new situation, its impact, and its reason to all effected personnel.

NEED FULFILLMENT AND PROJECT PERFORMANCE

Recognizing the specific professional needs of project personnel is important because it establishes the foundations for building a high-performing project team. Research studies[53] show repeatedly a significant positive correlation between the project manager's ability to satisfy the needs of his or her personnel and the manager's performance. That is, the more conducive a work environment is toward satisfying professional needs the higher is the rating of management performance perceived by superiors.

The rationale for this important correlation is found in the complex interaction of organizational and behavioral elements. Effective project management performance involves three primary issues: (1) people skills, (2) organizational structure, and (3) management style. All three issues are influenced by the specific task to be performed and the surrounding environment. The same three issues are reflected in each of the professional needs that are identified by project personnel. That is, the degree of satisfaction of any of the needs is a function of (1) having the right mix of people with appropriate skills and traits, (2) organizing the people and resources according to the tasks to be performed, and (3) adopting the right leadership style.

---

[53] For details see G.R. Gemmill and H.J. Thamhain "Influence Styles of Project Managers: Some Performance Correlates," *Academy of Management Journal* (June, 1974) and H.J. Thamhain, "Performing Effectively in Engineering Management," *IEEE Transactions on Engineering Management* (June, 1983).

23
The Power Spectrum in Project Management

THE SHARED POWER SYSTEM

Project managers often must cross functional lines to get the required support. They must build multidisciplinary teams into cohesive groups and successfully deal with a variety of interfaces such as functional departments, staff groups, team members, clients, and senior management. This is a work environment where managerial power is shared by many individuals. Furthermore, the project manager must often operate in areas with little or no formal authority. In contrast to the traditional functional organization which provides position power largely in the form of legitimate authority, project managers derive their power mostly from other sources such as earned authority: the power that comes from expertise, credibility, and the image of a sound decisions maker. Position power comes further from the reporting relationship of the program office to top management and the functional organization, and the charter and responsibilities assigned to the program office.

To understand the sources of interpersonal inference available to the project manager, we have to examine the authority and responsibility relationships prevalent in project organizations. In its mature form, project management is characterized by:

- Authority patterns defined only in part by formal organization charters and program plans.
- Authority largely perceived by the members of the organization based on earned credibility, expertise, and perceived priorities.
- Dual accountability of most personnel (a) to their functional managers and (b) to the program office.
- Two bosses, the project manager and the functional manager, controlling the activities of resource personnel. The result is dual accountability.
- Shared power between resource managers and project managers, which often leads to power struggles.
- Individual autonomy and participation greater than in traditional organizations.
- Weak superior-subordinate relationships in favor of stronger peer relationships.
- Subtle shifts of personnel loyalties from functional to project lines.
- Project performance depending on teamwork.
- Group decision-making tending to favor the strongest organizations.
- Reward and punishment power along both vertical and horizontal lines in a highly dynamic pattern.
- Influences to reward and punishment from many organizations and individuals.
- Multiproject involvement of support personnel and sharing of resources among many projects.

THE BASES OF MANAGERIAL INFLUENCE

Position power is a necessary prerequisite for effective leadership in program management. Like many other components of the management system, leadership style has undergone changes over time. With increasing task complexity, increasing dynamics of the new organizational systems, such as the matrix, a more adaptive and skill-oriented management style evolved.

The Traditional Management Style

Traditionally, management relies on only three major bases of power to influence compliance: (1) authority, (2) reward, and (3) punishment.

This management style is referred to as *system I style*. Its bases of influence are primarily organizationally derived. It is the traditional style of management that evolved with traditional organizations such as the militaries and the churches. It still works well today in organizations with a clear hierarchical structure of authority, control, and communications, a structure where interaction between its members is largely vertical.

Today's Contemporary Style

With the evolution of modern organizations, such as the matrix, and their complex environments a new management style gradually developed. This style complements the organizationally derived power bases with bases developed by the individual manager. Examples are technical and managerial expertise, friendship, work challenge, promotional ability, fund allocations, charisma, personal favors, project goal identification, recognition, and visibility. This style often augments the traditional power bases of authority, reward and punishment. This so-called style II management evolved particularly with the matrix but also has its application in other organizations that are low on traditional power such as volunteer organizations, R&D units, universities, professional interest groups, and committees. A descriptive summary of both styles is presented in Table 32. The two systems represent a polarity, not a dichotomy. There is a whole continuum of stages and combinations in between. In project management an effective style has to include both types, as will be discussed next.

Various research studies by Gemmill, Thamhain and Wilemon[54] provide an insight into the power spectrum available to project managers.

Figure 43 indicates the importance that project managers attach to each of the nine influence bases in gaining project support from their subordinates and assigned personnel. Three of these bases seem to be

---

[54] For specific titles and publications check Bibliography.

THE POWER SPECTRUM IN PROJECT MANAGEMENT 245

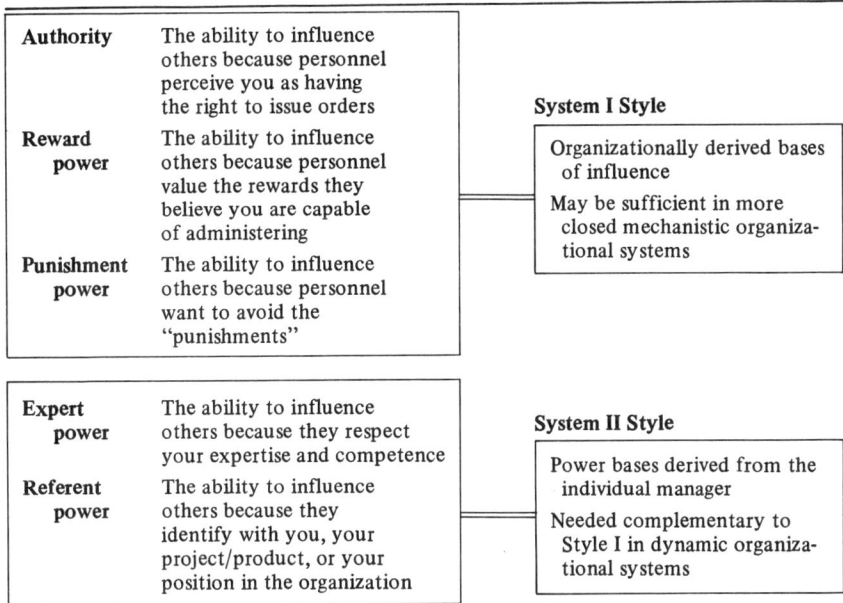

Table 32. Bases of Influence.

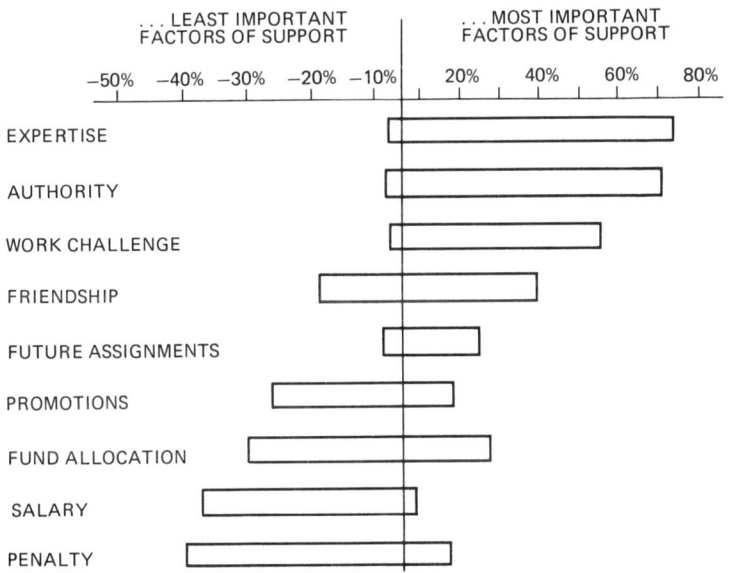

Figure 43. Power style profile. Ranking of most and least important factors in support to project management.

particularly important to managers for developing support in a project-organized work environment: expertise, formal authority, and work challenge. The three least important influence bases were fund allocation, salary adjustments, and penalty.

A similar power profile was obtained by questioning the project personnel assigned to a particular program. Specifically, they were asked to rank the reasons they usually comply with the requests of project managers, suggesting the eight influence bases of Figure 43:

1. I feel he has the formal authority.
2. I feel he can influence my salary.
3. I feel he can influence my promotion.
4. I feel he can influence future work assignments.

While the perception of project managers is basically consistent with the actual reason for compliance, one noticeable difference is authority, which seems to be overestimated by project manager. In the aggregate, formal authority takes only the fifth place when judged by project personnel while salary influences move up two positions.

Salary plays a very special role in the power spectrum. It would be a mistaken belief that because of its relatively low rank, salary is an unimportant power base. It is true, however, that adequately and fairly paid employees may make extra efforts for many other reasons than potential influence on their salaries. Frequently, the authors ask project personnel why they stayed after hours to fix a problem or worked casual overtime during weekends. The answers are invariably related to what Maslow would call the fulfillment of growth needs, such as work challenge, recognition, project goal identification, or professional pride. Few people would make these extra efforts because they got paid last Friday or try to position themselves for an 8 percent raise to be budgeted for next year.

However, the above argument holds only if personnel perceive a fair and adequate compensation. Otherwise salary becomes a barrier to effective teamwork, a handicap for attracting and holding quality people, and a source of steady conflict.

THE POWER SPECTRUM IN PROJECT MANAGEMENT 247

Lower-Ranking Influences Are Important, Too

While some of the influence bases are ranked lower than expertise, authority, and work challenge (see Figure 43), they also can be very important to project managers in eliciting support. Most likely, project managers will use several influence bases to gain support for their project. The specific influences used depend upon the authority possessed and the understanding of what motivates various project participants.

Many effective project managers "learn" what motivates or induces support from interfaces and adjust their leadership style accordingly. One person, for example, may be primarily motivated by work challenge, while another may be induced by the potentials of future work assignments derived from his satisfactory performance in supporting the project.

Finally, it is important to note that while project managers may be limited in their degree of formal authority, they nevertheless often have high degrees of reward power such as offering interesting work or future work assignments, and influencing salary and promotions. Even though the project manager may not be able to offer some of these rewards directly, he can indirectly influence them via performance feedback to the "home manager" of the functional department, which directly controls the financial rewards and often substantially influences other rewards, such as promotion and future work assignments.

24
Leadership Effectiveness in Project Management

MANAGEMENT STYLE VERSUS PERFORMANCE

While expertise, authority, and work challenge were perceived by project managers as most important in gaining project support, one cannot relate this finding directly to leadership style effectiveness.

This relationship of project management style to managerial performance is shown in Table 33. The table summarizes field research that correlates the project managers' influence bases to their personnel's degree of support, willingness to disagree (which is a measure of open communications), project involvement, and the effectiveness ratings of the project managers.* As indicated in Table 33, two influence methods are particularly favorable associated with project management performance: expertise and work challenge. The more expertise, both managerially and technically, program managers are perceived with, (1) the more support they seem to get from their personnel, (2) the better the communication seems to be, (3) the more involvement is generated, and in the end, (4) the higher is their performance rating by their superiors. The same favorable relationship exists for work challenge. Conversely, project managers

---
*The original research findings were published by Gary R. Gemmill and Hans J. Thamhain, "Influence Styles of Project Managers: Some Performance Correlates," *Sloan Management Review* (Fall, 1977).

Table 33. Power Style versus Performance (Kendall's Tau Correlation)

PROJECT MANAGER'S INFLUENCE METHOD AS PERCEIVED BY PROJECT PERSONNEL	PROJECT PERSONNEL'S			PROJECT MANAGER'S EFFECTIVENESS RATING
	DEGREE OF SUPPORT	WILLINGNESS TO DISAGREE	PROJECT INVOLVEMENT	
Expertise	0.15	0.30[a]	0	0.40[b]
Authority	−0.10	−0.20	−0.35[b]	−0.30[a]
Work challenge	0.10	0.25[a]	0.45[b]	0.25[a]
Friendship	0	0	0	0.17
Future assignment	0.25[a]	0	0	0.10
Promotion	0	0	0	0.08
Salary	−0.20	−0.10	−0.15	−0.15
Coercive power	−0.45[b]	0	0	0

Kendall's Tau:
[a] $p<.05$.
[b] $p<.01$.

who are perceived as relying strongly on authority emphasize salary and coercive measures, and do seem to get lower support, less open communications, and lower performance rating.

Management Implication

The popularity of a particular influence base is not necessarily an indication of its effectiveness.

Authority, work challenge, and expertise are cited by project managers as the three most important reasons for compliance; their project performance correlates are different, however. More specifically, project managers who were perceived by their project personnel as emphasizing work challenge and expertise as influence methods achieved not only higher effectiveness ratings on overall project performance, but also tended to foster a climate of greater disagreement and involvement among their project personnel. Conversely, the findings suggest that the use of authority as an influence method has a negative effect resulting in not only a lower level of performance but also less disagreement and involvement among project personnel. Therefore:

- The less project managers emphasize organizationally derived influence bases — such as authority, salary, and penalty — and the more they rely on work challenge and expertise, the higher they are rated in their ability to effectively manage projects.

One of the most interesting findings is the importance of work challenge as an influence method. Work challenge appears to deal with integrating the personal goals and needs of project personnel with project goals more than any other influence methods. That is, work challenge is primarily oriented toward the intrinsic motivation of project personnel, while other methods are oriented more toward extrinsic rewards without regard to the personnel's preference and needs. Therefore, to enrich the assignments of project personnel in such a way as to be professionally challenging may indeed have a beneficial effect on project performance. Additionally, the assignment of challenging work is a variable over which project managers may have a great deal of control. While in most cases the total task structure is fixed, the method by which work is assigned and distributed is discretionary.

RECOMMENDATIONS FOR IMPROVING PROJECT MANAGEMENT EFFECTIVENESS

The nature of project management, the need to elicit support from various organizational units and personnel, the frequently ambiguous authority definition of the project manager, and the temporary nature of projects all contribute to the complex operating environment project managers experience in the performance of their roles.

The findings presented in this chapter should help the professionals who operate in a project-oriented environment to understand the complex interrelationships among managerial leadership style and project management effectives.

A number of suggestions may be helpful to increase the project manager's effectiveness and ultimately improve overall program performance.

1. Project managers need to understand the interaction of organizational and behavioral elements in order to build an environment conducive to their teams' motivational needs. This will enhance active participation and minimize dysfunctional conflict. The effective flow of communication is one of the major factors determining the quality of the organizational environment. Since the project manager must build teams at various organizational layers, it is important that key decisions be communicated properly to all project-related personnel. By openly communicating both the project objectives and those of its subtasks, the project manager can minimize unproductive conflict. Regularly scheduled status review meetings can be an important vehicle for communicating project-related issues.

2. Because their environment is temporary and often untested project managers should seek a leadership style that allows them to adapt to the often conflicting demands of their project organization, parent organization, specific contributors, client requirements. They must learn to "test" the expectations of others by observation and experimentation. Although it is difficult, they must be ready to alter their leadership style as demanded by both the status of the project and its participants.

3. The project manager should try to accommodate the professional interests and desires of supporting personnel when he negotiates their tasks. Project effectiveness depends upon how well he provides work challenge to motivate those individuals who support him and matches their goals with objectives of the project and of the overall organization. Although the scope of a project may be fixed, the project manager usually has a degree of flexibility in allocating task assignments among various contributors.

4. The project manager should develop or maintain technical expertise in his field. Without an understanding of the technology he is managing, he is unable to win confidence among his team members or to build credibility with the customer community.

5. Effective planning early in the life cycle of a project is another action that may have a favorable impact on the organizational climate. This particularly so because project managers have to integrate various disciplines across functional lines. Insufficient planning may eventually lead to interdepartmental conflict and discontinuities in the work flow.

6. Finally, the project manager can influence the climate or work environment by his own actions. His concern for project team members, his ability to integrate the personal goals and needs of project personnel with project goals, and his ability to create personal enthusiasm for work itself can foster a climate that is high in motivation, work involvement, open communication, and resulting project performance.

A situational approach to project manager effectiveness is presented in Figure 44. It summarizes the effects of managerial influence style on two variables of the project environment: motivation of support personnel and position power of project manager.

Figure 44 indicates that the intrinsic motivation of project personnel increases with the project manager's emphasis on work challenge, his own expertise, and his ability to establish friendship ties. On the other hand, emphasis on penalty measures, authority, and inability to manage conflict effectively lowers personnel motivation.

The figure further illustrates that the project manager's position power is determined by such variables as formal position within the organization, the scope and nature of his project, his earned authority, and his ability to influence promotion and future work assignments. It appears to be important for sustaining continuity, resources, and organizational commitment to the project over its life cycle.

Project managers who foster a climate of highly motivated personnel not only obtain higher project support from their project personnel, but also achieve high overall project performance ratings from their superiors. In addition, the higher the perceived position power of project manager, the better is their potential for effective project performance.

Taken as a whole, Figure 44 projects some of the important elements of managerial leadership regarding project effectiveness which seem to be related to the manager's ability to foster an environment conducive to high motivation and favorable to his personal position power.

The project manager's role is a difficult one. Only by understanding those variables that contribute to more effective role performance can one develop meaningful insight into project management effectiveness.

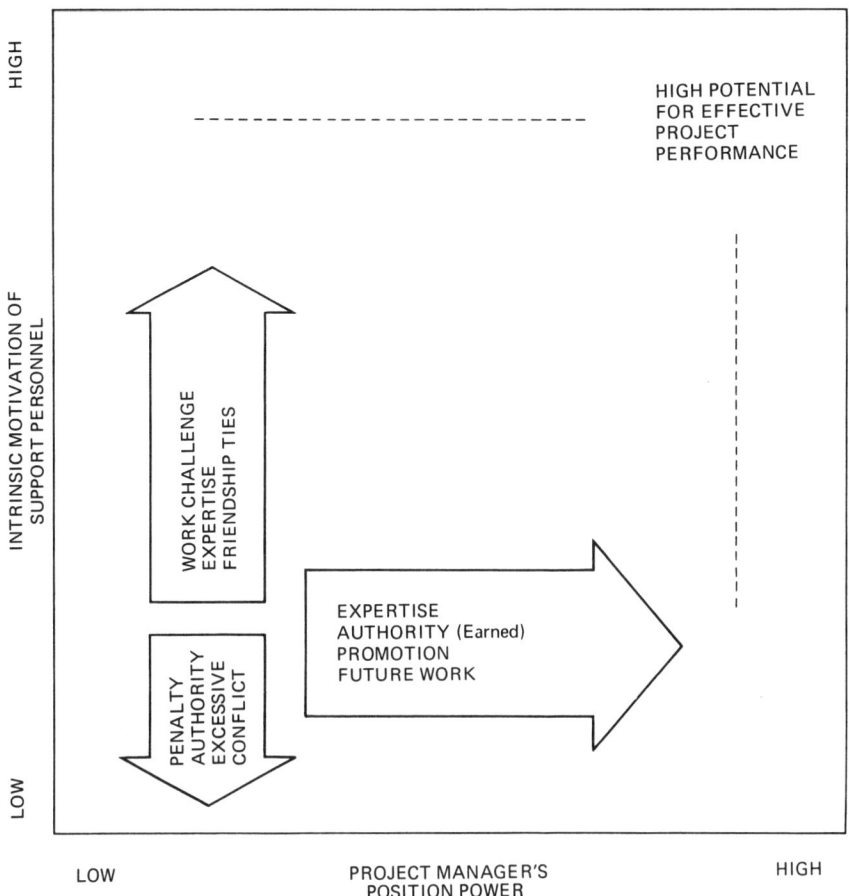

Figure 44. Variables of project management effectiveness.

25
How to Manage Change

PROJECT MANAGEMENT IS CHANGE MANAGEMENT

According to Alvin Toffler,[55] change will be one of the hallmarks of the organization of the future. In fact, many senior managers see change as the only constant in the organizational equation. Changes in technology such as computers and semiconductor LSI are constant sources of strategic and organizational design changes. Similarly, the changing energy situation, the emergence of Third World economic powers, and social currents such as minority rights and opportunities for women are another source of change that affects managerial and organizational practices. In addition, project managers have to cope with yet another layer of changes based on their contemporary work and its turbulent environment: Organizational support may wane and need reenergizing; conflict with key interfaces may develop and need prompt resolution; clients may continually change the scope of the project and thus extend task completion; and unforeseen developments may require sudden redirection of the project. Such developments can severely tax even the most experienced project leaders. Managing change also is required for building multidisciplinary teams into a cohesive groups and successfully dealing with a variety of interfaces, for example, functional departments, staff groups, team members, clients, and senior management. Each interface group

---

[55] Alvin Toffler, *Future Shock*, New York: Random House, 1970.

may have different expectations. To be effective, project managers must be able to introduce changes in strategy, technology, and organization enabling their firms to anticipate and manage changes in their business environment.

The Quandaries of Managing Change

Managing change is one of the most difficult tasks facing project managers. In contrast to the functional manager, who works in a more standardized and predictable environment, project managers must live with constant change. In their efforts to integrate various disciplines across functional lines, they must learn to cope with the pressures of the changing work environment.[56] They have to foster a climate that promotes the ability of their personnel to adapt to a continuously changing work environment. Externally the project manager has to react to the pressures from the environment such as the customer community, government agencies, unions, and functional support groups. Demanding compliance to rigid rules, principles, and techniques is often counterproductive.

The objective of this chapter is to examine the role of the project leader as a manager of change over the life cycle of the project.

The Process of Change Management

The current thinking on the process of managing change in modern organizations has been influenced by the pioneering research of Kurt Lewin.[57] His process of inducing change also applies to changing attitudes and behavior in individuals and small groups. Lewin's theory is based on the notion of countervailing forces. In the management of a project, there will be certain driving forces propelling the project toward success and certain restraining forces that may work against the project. In a steady state there is a balance between

---

[56] Machiavelli discussed the difficulty in managing change in *The Prince* (1513): "It must be remembered that there is nothing more difficult to plan, more doubtful of success, nor more dangerous to manage than the creation of a new system. For the initiator has the enmity of all who would profit by the preservation of the old institutions and merely lukewarm defenders in those who would gain by the new one...."
[57] Kurt Lewin, "Frontiers in Group Dynamics," *Human Relations,* 1, 1 (1947). Also see Lewin's *Field Theory in Social Science,* New York: Harper & Row, 1951.

the driving forces pushing for change (or success) and the restraining forces that resist change. Lewin believed that change is the result of a shifting of counterbalanced forces. In other words, if the driving forces can be increased or if restraining forces be minimized, change is likely to occur. These processes may occur separately or together.

The formal study of these forces is known as *force field analysis*. It is a simple yet powerful technique that can help a project manager to identify those forces that "drive" the projects toward success and the barriers or restraining forces that may keep a team from attaining its goal.

To understand where these driving and restraining forces originate we need to be more precise about the meaning and origin of change in project management. Change can be introduced to the project operation via many subsystems. At least four global categories can be defined:

1. *Changes introduced by the organization:* Examples of organization-introduced changes are: reorganizations, expansions, personnel turnover, layoffs, new policies and procedures, management directives, business plans, changing management support, and working conditions.

2. *Changes introduced by technical requirements:* Examples of technically introduced changes are related to project specifications and requirements, schedules, budgets, teaming, subcontracting, contingencies, technical risks, innovative requirements, and technological challenges.

3. *Changes originated by the project team:* The professional interest, abilities, motivation, and team spirit of project personnel may change over the project life cycle, impacting team performance in terms of ineffective communications, increased conflict, lower-quality decisions, less innovative thinking, and in the end, lower productivity.

4. *Changes introduced by the external environment:* Changes introduced external to the project team and its parent organization can originate at the customer community, regulatory agencies, and suppliers, or just be part of socioeconomic trends. These trends include technological changes such as in computers and robotics. But also demographic changes, the recognition of minority rights, and

and interconnected world markets are sources for constant changes from the external environment.

RECOGNIZING RESISTANCE TO CHANGE

In order to function effectively, project managers must lead in situations requiring changes agent skills. In the most fundamental vein, project managers must first be able to diagnose situations where change is needed. Second, they must be able to design strategies for accomplishing the desired change. And third, they must be able to successfully implement this change in their programs.

The way project personnel respond to implementing change seems to depend on the perceived risk-benefit factor. Each project team member has developed a psychological contract with the project office or functional organization. If the change is perceived as a violation of this contract, the individual is likely to resist its implementation. However, if the change is consistent with prior agreements, or even perceived as a potential benefit or opportunity, the individual is often quite cooperative. Other reasons for resisting change are related to the risks involved in having to perform unfamiliar tasks, requiring new skills, and dealing with new situations. This type of change is often resisted by project personnel because they fear to be asked to act beyond their capabilities. Yet, other reasons for resisting change are related to uncertainty or rumors.

HOW TO MINIMIZE THE RESISTANCE TO CHANGE

Project managers have to operate in an environment that is dynamic and constantly changing. The ability to successfully deal with change regarding organizational, human, and technical factors determines whether a project leader is successful or unsuccessful. A field study by Dugan, Thamhain, and Wilemon[58] defines specific driving forces that propel the project toward success because they foster an environment conducive to innovative work, involvement,

---

[58] H.S. Dugan, H.J. Thamhain, and D.L. Wilemon, "Managing Change in Project Management," *Proceedings of PMI Symposium,* Chicago, 1977. The study uses the concept of force field analysis, defining the driving forces that push the project environment toward change and the restraining forces that resist it.

258 PROGRAM MANAGEMENT LEADERSHIP

Table 34. Driving and Restraining Forces in Project Management.

DRIVING FORCES PROPELLING PROJECT TOWARD SUCCESS	RESTRAINING FORCES IMPEDING SUCCESSFUL PROJECT PERFORMANCE
No. 1 Good Project Direction and Leadership: • Task management experience • Proper direction • Assistance in problem-solving • Team builder • Effective communications	*No. 1 Project Leader Deficiencies:* • Inexperience • Role not delineated clearly • First project management leadership experience • Lack of self-confidence and credibility • Lack of technical knowledge • Poor project control
No. 2 Team Motivation: • Good interpersonal relations • Team's will to succeed • Integration of team and project objectives • Agreement on distribution of work • Clear role definition • Proper expertise • Professional interest in project • Achievement aspirations • Challenge of project • Project visibility and rewards	*No. 2 Lack of Motivation and Cooperation Within the Team:* • Communication barriers • Resistance to project management approach • Rewards not clear • Little commitment or ownership in project • Team members overloaded • Limited prior team experience • Poor team organization • Unequal talent distribution • Distorted objectivity of some team members
No. 3 Client Support and Commitment: • Good working relations • Clear objectives • Timely client feedback • Client support and commitment • Regular meetings/reviews • Help and concern	*No. 3 Poor Client Relationships:* • Lacking information on client needs • Lacking sustained interest • Conflict within client organization • Changing requirements • Funding problems

HOW TO MANAGE CHANGE   259

No. 4 *Senior Management Support:*
- Management interest and involvement
- Authority delegated to accomplish project; provision of charter
- Enduring commitment
- Resource provision

No. 5 *Functional Department Support:*
- Integrated functional and project objectives
- Cooperation and provision of resources; quality personnel
- Sustained support throughout project life cycle

No. 6 *Financial Resources:*
- Necessary financial resources
- Financial control capability

No. 7 *Clearly Defined Project Objectives:*
- Workable project plan
- Goals clearly defined
- Project importance recognized by team
- Clear interface relationships

No. 8 *Technical Expertise:*
- Ability to solve technical problems on project
- Ability to manage technology

No. 4 *Lack of Senior Management Support:*
- Insufficient direction and leadership
- Senior management indifference
- Excessive preoccupation with minor details
- Priorities unclear
- Waning support
- Unresponsive management
- Improper project organization
- Insufficient reporting and reviews
- Continued change in scope of project

No. 5 *Lack of Functional Department Support:*
- Poor relations with functional departments
- Roles and responsibilities unclear
- Rewards unclear
- Resistance to project objectives
- Conflict over project priorities

No. 6 *Resource Limitations:*
- Budget restraints
- Lack of authority to commit funds
- Manpower problems
- Facilities unavailable
- Insufficient planning

No. 7 *Changing Project Requirements:*
- No agreed-on project plan
- Changing requirements
- Client not knowing what he wants
- Power plays
- Technical problems

No. 8 *Technical Difficulties:*
- Lack of technical information
- Technical problems requiring complex solutions
- Inexperienced project personnel
- Inability to cope effectively with rapid technological changes

trust, and a low resistance to change. The principal driving forces, summarized in Table 34, are (1) good project direction and leadership, (2) team motivation, (3) client support, (4) senior management support, (5) functional department support, (6) financial support, (7) clearly defined project objectives, and (8) technical expertise. The study further defines the major restraining forces that impede successful project performance ranging from (1) project leader deficiencies to (8) technical difficulties. The specific underlying causes for each driving or restraining force are listed in Table 34.

GUIDELINES FOR SUCCESSFUL MANAGEMENT OF CHANGE

A number of suggestions may be beneficial for developing change-agent skills needed by project leaders to perform effectively in today's dynamic environment. First, many of the driving forces noted in the force field analysis (Table 34) can be used to monitor the state of a particular project team as it progresses through its project life cycle. For example, in the project formation phase project leaders frequently indicated that the need for accomplishment, motivational attitudes, clearly defined objectives, and senior management commitment are important ingredients for effectively launching a project. By contrast, an uncooperative and unmotivated team, poor project leadership, technological limitations, and severe financial constraints may be early warning signals for project failure. Thus, the data presented may be used as a comparative barometer of anticipated project performance over its life cycle.

Second, the project managers can use the force field analysis as a framework for auditing their project on an ongoing basis. A project manager may, for example, periodically assess the overall strengths of the team and the project, then define the existing driving forces and their potential for improvement so that the team can focus on the major areas of concern, for example, the barriers. A benefit of increasing a driving force is not always assured and should be carefully considered. In some instances, the increase of a driving force may cause the opposite reaction intended. For example, a project team may feel it has the support and visibility of senior management. A further increase in this driving force may be viewed as unnecessary and unwarranted meddling and interference by senior management, or jealousy might arise with functional support departments since they may feel that too many resources and attentions are already being devoted to the project.

To minimize the identified restraining forces or barriers the project manager may want to assess their potential for change, that is, to find ways to minimize, neutralize, or even turn the restraint into a driving force. For example, a negative support attitude of a strong functional manager may be identified as a restraining force early in the project life cycle. Unless the functional manager's attitude and behavior toward the project are changed the project may suffer. Knowing this possibility, the project manager should attempt to change the functional manager's resistance to project support through rational problem-solving approaches. The conflict issues should be discussed in detail and the importance of the project to the overall organization should be emphasized.

Involving the project team in a force field exercise can be conducive to team building. Such an approach involves the team members in an audit of, "What's going right, and what do we need in the management of the project?" When force field analysis is used as an integral part of team building, the project leader should actively seek the team's advice on dealing with the identified issues.

Third, the findings have important implications for senior management. In each life cycle phase the role of senior management is being clearly identified. The support of senior management is perceived by the project managers as an important driving force necessary for project success, while the lack of it is viewed as a detriment. Senior managers should continually reevaluate their roles and relationships to their project teams. They must establish the necessary climate for their project management groups by maintaining a balance between necessary direction, advice, and feedback without preempting the project leaders' responsibility. Finally, senior management should be selective in terms of whom they select as project leader. As identified, the deficiencies in project manager leadership are an important restraining force. A more careful selection and training of project managers may reduce leadership problems and the lack of team motivation significantly.

In summary, project leaders need to understand the principles of managing change. At any given point in the life cycle of a project, there will be certain driving forces at work that help propel the project toward success. At the same time, barriers will be present. Understanding these forces may help the project manager to build an environment that can react properly to changing needs and requirement. Without such knowledge, the project leader's effectiveness will be suboptimal.

26
Skill Requirements for Program Managers

THE ARRAY OF SKILLS NEEDED

Programs are often complex and multifaceted. Managing these programs represents a challenge requiring skills in: team building, leadership, conflict resolution, technical expertise, planning, organization, entrepreneurship, administration, management support, and the allocation of resources. This chapter examines these skills relative to program management effectiveness. A key factor to the good program performance is the program manager's capability to integrate personnel from many disciplines into an effective work team.*

To get results, the program manager must relate to (1) the people managed, (2) the task to be done, (3) the tools available, (4) the organizational structure, and (5) the organizational environment, including the customer community.

All work factors are interrelated and operate under the limited control of the program manager. With an understanding of the interaction of corporate organization and behavior elements, the

---

*This chapter is based on the research by H.J. Thamhain and D.L. Wilemon published in "Skill Requirements of Engineering Project Managers," *Proceedings* of 26th IEEE Joint Engineering Management Conference, Denver (1978) and *Professional Engineer Magazine* (February, 1979).

manager can build an environment conducive to the working team's needs. The internal and external forces that impinge on the organization of the project must be reconciled to mutual goals. For these reasons, the program manager must relate socially as well as technically to understand how the organization functions and how these functions will affect the program organization of the particular job to be done. In addition, the program manager must understand the culture and value system of the organization with which he is working. Research and experience show that effective program management performance is directly related to the level of proficiency at which these skills are mastered.

Ten specific skills are identified (in no particular order) and discussed in this chapter:

1. Team building
2. Leadership
3. Conflict resolution
4. Technical expertise
5. Planning
6. Organization
7. Entrepreneurship
8. Administration
9. Management support
10. Resource allocation

It is important that the personal management traits underlying these skills operate to form a homogeneous management style. The right mixture of skill levels depends on the project task, the techniques employed, the people assigned, and the organizational structure. To be effective, program managers must consider all facets of getting the job done. Their management style must facilitate the integration of multidisciplinary program resources for synergistic operation. The days of the manager who gets by with technical expertise alone or pure administrative skills are gone.

Team Building Skills

Building the program team is one of the prime responsibilities of the program manager. Team building involves a whole spectrum of management skills required to identify, commit, and integrate the various task groups from the traditional functional organization into a single program management system.

To be effective, the program manager must provide an atmosphere conducive to team work. He must nurture a climate that has the following characteristics:

- Team members committed to the program
- Good interpersonnel relations and team spirit
- The necessary expertise and resources
- Clearly defined goals and program objectives
- Involved and supportive top management
- Good program leadership
- Open communication among team members and support organizations
- A low degree of detrimental interpersonal and intergroup conflict

Three major considerations are involved in all of the above factors aimed toward integration of people from many disciplines into an effective team: (1) effective communications, (2) sincere interest in the professional growth of team members, and (3) commitment to the project.

Leadership Skills

An absolutely essential prerequisite for program success is the program manager's ability to lead the team within a relatively unstructured environment. It involves dealing effectively with managers and supporting personnel across functional lines with little or no formal authority. It also involves information processing skills, the ability to collect and filter relevant data valid for decision-making in a dynamic environment. It involves the ability to integrate individual demands, requirements, and limitations into decisions that benefit overall project performance. It further involves the program manager's ability to resolve intergroup conflicts, an important factor to overall program performance.

Perhaps more than in any other position below the general manager's level, quality leadership depends heavily on the program manager's personal experience and credibility within the organization. An effective management style might be characterized this way:

- Clear project leadership and direction
- Assistance in problems solving
- Ability to integrate new members into the team
- Ability to handle interpersonnel conflict
- Ability to facilitate group decisions
- Capability to plan and elicit commitments
- Ability to communicate clearly
- Ability to present team to higher management
- Ability to balance technical solutions against economical and human factors

The personal traits desirable and supportive to the above skills are:

- Project management experience
- Flexibility and change orientation
- Innovative thinking
- Initiative and enthusiasm
- Charisma and persuasiveness
- Organization and discipline

Conflict Resolution Skills

Conflict is fundamental to complex task management. It is often determined by the interplay of the program organization and the larger host organization and its multifunctional components. Understanding the determinants of conflicts is important to the program manager's ability to deal with conflicts effectively. When conflict becomes dysfunctional it often results in poor program decision-making, lengthy delays over issues, and a disruption of the team's efforts, all of them negative influences to program performance. However, conflict can be beneficial when it produces involvement and new information, and enhances the competitive spirit.

A number of suggestions are derived from various research studies aimed at increasing the program manager's ability to resolve conflict and thus improve the overall program performance. Program managers must:

- Understand interaction of the organizational and behavioral elements in order to build an environment conducive to their

team's motivational needs. This will enhance active participation and minimize unproductive conflict.
- Communicate effectively with all organizational levels regarding both project objectives and decisions. Regularly scheduled status review meetings can be an important communication vehicle.
- Recognize the determinants of conflict and their timing in the project life cycle. Effective project planning, contingency planning, securing of commitments, and involvement of top management can help to avoid or minimize many conflicts before they become an impeding factor on project performance.

The value of the conflict produced depends upon the ability of the program manager to promote beneficial conflict while minimizing its potential hazardous consequences. The accomplished manager needs a "sixth sense" to indicate when conflict is desirable, what kind of conflict will be useful, and how much conflict is optimal for a given situation. In the final analysis he has the sole responsibility for his program and the manner in which conflict will contribute to the success or failure of his program.

Technical Expertise

The program manager rarely has all the technical, administrative, and marketing expertise to direct the program single-handed. Nor is it necessary or desirable. It is essential, however, that the program manager understand the technology, the markets, and the environment of the business to participate effectively in the search for integrated solutions and technological innovations. More importantly, without this understanding, the integrated consequences of local decisions on the total program, the potential growth ramifications, and relationships to other business opportunities cannot be foreseen by the manager. Further technical expertise is necessary to evaluate technical concepts and solutions, to communicate effectively in technical terms with the project team, and to assess risks and make trade-offs between costs, schedule, and technical issues. This is why in complex problem-solving situations so many project managers must have an engineering background.

Technical expertise is important to the successful management of engineering projects. It is composed of an understanding of the:

- Technology involved
- Engineering tools and techniques employed
- Specific markets, their customers, and requirements
- Product applications
- Technological trends and evolutions
- Relationship among supporting technologies
- People who are part of the technical community

The technical expertise required for effective management of engineering programs is normally developed through progressive growth in engineering or supportive project assignments in a specific technology area. Frequently, the project begins with an exploratory phase leading into a proposal. This is normally an excellent testing ground for the future program manager. It also allows top management to judge the new candidate's capacity for managing the technological innovations and integration of solutions needed for success.

Planning Skills

Planning skills are helpful for any undertaking: They are absolutely essential, however, for the successful management of large complex programs. The project plan is the road map that defines how to get from the start to the final results.

Program planning is an ongoing activity at all organizational levels. However, the preparation of a project summary plan, prior to project start, is the responsibility of the program manager. Effective project planning requires particular skills far beyond writing a document with schedules and budgets. It requires communication and information processing skills to define the actual resource requirements and administrative support necessary. It requires the ability to negotiate the necessary resources and commitments from key personnel in various support organizations with little or no formal authority, including the definition of measurable milestones.

Effective planning requires skills in the areas of:

- Information processing
- Communication
- Resource negotiations
- Securing commitments
- Incremental and modular planning
- Assuring measurable milestones
- Facilitating top management involvement

In addition, the program manager must assure that the plan remains a viable document. Changes in project scope and depth are inevitable. The plan should reflect necessary changes through formal revisions and should be the guiding document throughout the life cycle of the program. Nothing outlives its usefulness faster than an obsolete or irrelevant plan.

Finally, program managers need an awareness that planning can certainly be overdone. If not controlled, planning can become an end in itself and a poor substitute for innovative work. Individuals retreat to the utopia of no responsibility where innovative actions cannot be taken "because it is not in the plan." It is the responsibility of the program manager to build enough flexibility into the plan and police it against such misuse.

Organizational Skills

The program manager must be a social architect, that is, he must understand how the organization works and how to work with the organization. Organizational skills are particularly important during project formation and start-up when the program manager establishes the program organization by integrating people from many different disciplines into an effective work team. It requires far more than simply constructing a project organization chart. At a minimum, it requires defining the reporting relationships, responsibilities, lines of control, and information needs. Supporting skills in the area of planning, communication, and conflict resolution are particularly helpful. A good program plan and a task matrix are useful organizational tools. In addition, the organizational effort is facilitated by clearly defined program objectives, open communication channels, good program leadership, and senior management support.

Entrepreneurial Skills

The program manager also needs a general management perspective. For example, economics is one area of importance that normally has impacts on the organization's financial performance. However, frequently the objectives are considerably broader than profits. Customer satisfaction, future growth, cultivation of related market activities, and minimum organizational disruptions of other programs might be equally important. The effective program manager is concerned with all these issues.

Entrepreneurial skills are developed through actual experience. However, formal MBA-type training, special seminars, and cross-functional training programs can help to develop the entrepreneurial skills needed by program managers.

Administrative Skills

Administrative skills are essential. The project manager must be experienced in planning, staffing, budgeting, scheduling, and other control techniques. In dealing with technical personnel the problem is seldom to make people understand administrative techniques such as budgeting and scheduling, but to impress upon them that costs and schedules are as important as elegant technical solutions.

Particularly on larger programs, managers rarely have all the administrative skills required. While it is important that the program managers understand the company's operating procedures and the available tools, it is often necessary for the program manager to free himself from administrative details regardless of his capabilities to handle them. He has to delegate considerable administrative tasks to support groups or hire a project administrator.

Some tools that assist the manager in the administration of his program include: (1) the meeting, (2) the report, (3) the review, and (4) budget and schedule controls. Program managers must be thoroughly familiar with these available tools and know how to use them effectively.

Management Support Building Skills

The program manager is surrounded by a myriad of organizations that either support him or control his activities. Understanding these interfaces is important to program managers as it enhances their ability to build favorable relationships with senior management. Management support is often an absolute necessity for dealing effectively with interface groups. Project organizations are shared-power systems with personnel of many diverse interests and ways of doing things. These power systems have a tendency toward imbalance. Only a strong leader backed by senior management can prevent the development of unfavorable biases.

Four key variables influence the project manager's ability to develop favorable relationships with senior management: (1) his ongoing credibility, (2) the visibility of his program, (3) the priority of his program relative to other organizational undertakings, and (4) his own accessibility. All variables are interrelated and can be developed by the individual manager. Furthermore, senior management can aid such developments significantly.

Resource Allocation Skills

A program organization has many bosses. Functional lines often shield support organizations from direct financial control by the project office. Once a task has been authorized, it is often impossible to control the personnel assignments, priorities, and indirect manpower costs. In addition, profit accountability is difficult due to the interdependencies of various support departments and the often changing work scope and contents.

Effective and detailed program planning may facilitate commitment and self-forcing control. Part of the plan is the statement of work, which establishes a basis for resource allocation. It is further important to work out specific agreements with all key contributors and their superiors on the tasks to be performed and the associated budgets and schedules. Measureable milestones are not only important for hardware components, but also for the "invisible" program components such as systems and software tasks. Ideally, these commitments on specs, schedules, and budgets should be established through involvement by key personnel in the early phases of project formation such as the proposal phase. This is the time when requirements are still flexible and trade-offs among performance, schedule, and budget parameters are possible. Further, this is normally the time when the competitive spirit among potential contributors is highest, which often leads to a more cohesive and challenging work plan.

CONCLUSION

Program managers must think in terms of integrating skill specialists from many disciplines into working teams. In addition, program managers must live with constant change and be able to cope with the pressures of the evolving work environment. They need to understand the interaction of organizational and behavioral elements in order to exert the influence required to build an environment conducive to the team's motivational needs. This will foster a climate of active participation and minimal detrimental conflict. The effective flow of communications is one of the major factors determining the quality of or organizational environment. Key decisions should be communicated properly to all project-related personnel.

Program managers also must provide a high degree of leadership capability in unstructured environments. This means that the program manager must have the capacity to deal seriously and carefully with:

- Selecting team personnel
- Establishing an environment that allows professional growth and innovative thinking
- Collecting and processing information
- Inspiring confidence and ability to solve problems

All of these skills will help the program manager to develop credibility among the peer group, team members, senior management, and customer community. As a leader with clearly defined goals and operational tactics, the program manager can convert much of the natural conflict into useful energy.

27
Effective Conflict Management

Conflict is fundamental to complex task management and is often determined by the interplay of the program organization and its support functions. Complex organizational relationships, dual accountability, and shared managerial powers are factors that contribute to a new-frontier environment where conflict is inevitable. An understanding of the determinants of conflict is important to a program manager's ability to deal with conflict effectively. When conflict becomes dysfunctional, it often results in poor program decision-making, lengthy delays over operational issues, and a disruption of the team's efforts — all negative influences on program performance. However, contrary to conventional wisdom, conflict can be beneficial when it produces involvement, new information, and competitive spirit. This is clearly a new perspective that traditional management concepts fail to recognize. This emerging new view on conflict (summarized in Table 35) provides a recognition of conflict as a potentially creative force in today's engineering organizations.

Effective managers must be able to deal with inevitable conflict effectively. Research studies[59] have found that accomplished project managers have developed a "sixth sense" to indicate when conflict is

---

[59] For details of this research study see H.J. Thamhain and D.L. Wilemon, "Diagnosing Conflict Determinants in Project Management," *IEEE Transactions on Engineering Management* (February 1975).

274 PROGRAM MANAGEMENT LEADERSHIP

Table 35. Realistic Assessment of Conflict.

TRADITIONAL VIEW	NEW VIEW
Conflict should be avoided.	Conflict is inevitable.
	Conflict is part of change.
Conflict is caused by troublemakers and prima donnas.	Conflict is determined by the structure of the system and the interplay of its components.
Conflict is bad.	Conflict may be beneficial.

desirable, what kind of conflict will be useful, and how much conflict is optimal for a given situation.

HOW TO ANTICIPATE PROBLEMS

Many project managers admit they are unprepared to deal effectively with conflict, yet conflict and its determinants are a prerequisite for effective conflict management, which is important for successful project performance.

Conflict determinants in project organizations have been investigated by Thamhain and Wilemon,[60] who delineated typical sources of conflict in seven propositions that were tested against expert opinions. Table 36 shows these propositions and the distribution of opinions gathered from project managers regarding their agreement or disagreement with each proposition. Responses are tabulated in order of decreasing acceptance of each statement.

Analyzing conflict provides insight into the project management environment and its dynamics, thus enabling managers to choose appropriate resolution modes and thereby manage disagreements more effectively. In addition, project managers can often prepare for and deal more effectively with operational problems if they can anticipate these problems and understand their specific sources. Seven potential conflict sources shown in Figure 45 are frequently responsible for major disagreements in various project life cycle phases:

1. *Conflict over schedules:* Disagreements may develop around the timing, sequencing, and scheduling of project-related tasks.

---

[60] Ibid.

EFFECTIVE CONFLICT MANAGEMENT 275

Table 36. Conflict Situations Judged by Project Managers Regarding Validity and Benefit

SITUATIONAL ASSESSMENT	PROJECT MANAGERS IN AGREEMENT	POTENTIAL BENEFIT	POTENTIAL HARM
No. 1: The less the specific objectives of a project are understood by project team members the more likely that conflict will develop.	90%	• Open exchange may develop which clarifies objectives and details of the project.	• Conflict over project goals and priorities. • Wasted motion by project team. • Inability to measure project performance.
No. 2: The more members of a functional area perceive that the implementation of project management will adversely affect their traditional organizational roles the greater the potential for conflict.	85%	• May cause functional area to relate more effectively to overall goals of the organization.	• Lack of support. • Withdrawal. • Sabotage. • Delay in project accomplishment.
No. 3: The greater the ambiguity of roles among participants of a project team the more likely that conflict will develop.	85%	• May insure that difficult project issues are responsibly covered. • May encourage constructive competition. • May foster exchange of ideas in early project phases. • Project team members assist in own role definition.	• Lack of project focus. • Conflict over various "turf issues." • Confusion. • Avoidance of responsibility.

Table 36. (continued)

SITUATIONAL ASSESSMENT	PROJECT MANAGERS IN AGREEMENT	POTENTIAL BENEFIT	POTENTIAL HARM
No. 4: The greater the agreement on top management goals the lower the potential for detrimental conflict at project level	80%	• Lowers potential for parochial conflict among departments. • Goal congruency.	• Top management goals may not be good for the organization or project. • Discourages constructive dialogue of key project issues.
No. 5: The lower the project manager's formal authority over supporting organizational units, the more likely conflict will occur.	70%	• Encourages open exchange of ideas. • Constructive criticisms and analysis of key project issues.	• Slows down decision-making process. • Uncertainty and disagreement over priorities, manpower, and resource allocations.
No. 6: The lower the project manager's power of reward and punishment the greater the potential for conflict to develop.	65%	• Encourages open exchange between project manager and supportive groups.	• May delay decision-making process. • May not be able to reward satisfactorily key contributors.
No. 7: The greater the diversity of expertise among the participants of a project team the greater the potential for conflict.	50%	• Enhances the decision-making process by providing high-quality informational inputs.	• May slow project decision-making process due to alternative problem-solving approaches suggested.

[a] Results are simplified in this table for clarity. Actual expert opinions were measured from 100 project managers on a five-point scale: (1) strongly agree, (2) agree, (3) neutral, (4) disagree, and (5) strongly disagree. For details see H. Thamhain and D. Wilemon, "Conflict Determinants in Project Management," *IEEE Transactions on Engineering Management* (February, 1975).

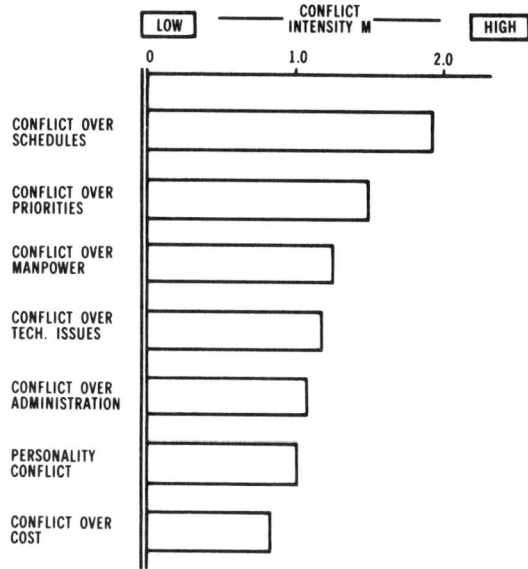

Figure 45. Mean conflict intensity profile over project life cycle.

2. *Conflict over project priorities:* The views of project participants often differ over the sequence of activities and tasks that should be undertaken to achieve successful project completion. Conflict over priorities may occur not only between the project team and other support groups but also within the project team.

3. *Conflict over manpower resources:* Conflicts may arise over the staffing of the project team with personnel from other functional and staff support areas or from the desire to use another department's personnel for project support even though the personnel remain under the authority of their functional or staff superiors.

4. *Conflict over technical opinions and performance trade-offs:* In technology-oriented projects, disagreements may arise over technical issues, performance specifications, technical trade-offs, and the means to achieve performance.

5. *Conflict over administrative procedures:* A number of managerial and administrative-oriented conflicts may develop over how the project will be managed (i.e., definition of the project manager's reporting relationships, definition of responsibilities, interface relationships, project scope, operational requirements, plan of

execution, negotiated work agreements with other groups, and procedures for administrative support).

6. *Personality conflict:* Disagreements may tend to center on interpersonal differences rather than on technical issues. Conflicts often are ego-centered.

7. *Conflict over cost:* Frequently, conflict may develop over cost estimates from support areas, regarding various project work packages. For example, the funds allocated by the project manager to a functional support group might be perceived as insufficient for the support requested.

CONFLICT INTENSITY FROM VARIOUS SOURCES

The conflict intensity experienced by project managers for each of the seven potential conflict sources was measured in a research study of 150 project managers. Figure 45 shows the relative intensity of conflict perceived by these project managers from each of the seven sources.

As indicated in Figure 45, disagreement over schedules is the most intense conflict in the project life cycle. Scheduling conflicts often occur with other support departments over which the project manager may have limited authority and control. Scheduling problems also often involve disagreements and differing perceptions of organizational departmental priorities, the second most frequent conflict source. For example, an issue urgent to the project manager may receive a low-priority treatment from support groups and/or staff personnel because of a different priority structure in the support organization. Conflicts over schedules frequently result from the cumulative effects of other areas involved in project performance, namely, technical problems and manpower resources.

Conflict over priorities ranks second highest over the project life cycle. In discussions with project managers, many indicated that this type of conflict frequently develops because the organization did not have prior experience with a current project undertaking. Consequently, the pattern of project priorities may change from the original forecast, necessitating the reallocation of crucial resources and schedules, a process that is often susceptible to intense disagreements and conflicts. Similarly, priority issues often develop into conflict with other support departments whose established schedules and work patterns are disturbed by the changed requirements.

Conflict over manpower resources is the third most important source of conflict. Project managers frequently complain that there is little "organizational slack" in terms of manpower resources, a situation in which they often experience intense conflicts. Project managers note that most conflicts over personnel resources occur with those departments who either assign personnel to the project or support the project internally.

The fourth strongest source of conflict involves disagreement over technical issues. Often the project support groups are primarily responsible for technical input and performance standards and do not have the broad management overview of the total project. The project manager, on the other hand, is accountable for cost, schedules, and performance objectives. For example, the project manager may be presented with a technical issue from a support group that involves alternative ways of solving a technical problem. Often he must reject the technical alternative due to cost or schedule restraints. In other cases, he may find that he disagrees with the opinions of others on strictly technical grounds. In either case, conflict may develop.

Conflict over administrative procedures ranks fifth in the profile of seven conflict sources. It is interesting to note that most conflict over administrative procedures that occurs is distributed almost uniformly with functional departments, project personnel, and the project manager's superior. Examples of conflict originating over administrative issues may involve disagreements over the project manager's authority and responsibilities, reporting relationships, administrative support, status reviews, or interorganizational interfacing. For the most part, disagreement over administrative procedures involves issues of how the project manager will function and how he relates to the organization's top management.

Personality conflict ranked a low sixth in intensity. Discussions with project managers indicate that while the intensity of personality conflicts may not be as high as some of the other sources of conflict, they are the most difficult to deal with effectively. Personality issues also may be obscured by communication problems and technical issues. A support person, for example, may stress the technical aspect of a disagreement with the project manager when, in fact, the real issue is a personality conflict.

Cost, like schedules, is often a basic performance measure in project management. Relative to other resources, cost ranks lowest. Disagreements over cost frequently develop when project managers, under budget constraints, negotiate with support groups who may want to maximize their part of the project budget. In addition, conflicts may occur as a result of technical problems or schedule slippages which increase costs.

WHAT TO DO ABOUT CONFLICT

An important first step in effectively dealing with the inevitable conflict situations is to recognize the potential causes and intensities of conflicts. This provides the basis for selecting the proper conflict resolution style most effective for a given situation. The next chapter will provide some insight into the complex topic of effective conflict management.

28
Conflict Resolution Approaches

When conflict situations arise, effective project managers often attempt to resolve the conflict at the project level rather than resorting to arbitration at higher management. A formal hierarchical system, however, is often established in many organizations to arbitrate conflicts that cannot be resolved at the project level. More typically, though, project personnel have straightforward meetings with other team members to address task-oriented conflicts. Such direct confrontation methods often can dispose of many problems before they become detrimental to the overall project.[61]

Five methods, defined by Blake and Mouton,[62] are frequently used to describe modes for handling conflict. These approaches are listed here in increasing order of mental involvement. Table 37 characterizes each approach summarized below:

Withdrawing — Retreating or withdrawing from actual or potential disagreements

Smoothing — Deemphasizing differences and emphasizing commonalities over conflict issues

---

[61] See P.R. Lawrence and J.W. Lorsch, "New Management Job: The Integrator," *Harvard Business Review,* 142–152 (November-December, 1967).
[62] R.R. Blake and J.S. Mouton, *The Managerial Grid,* Guld Publishing Company, 1964; and R.J. Burke, "Methods of Resolving Interpersonal Conflict," *Personnel Administration* 48-55 (July-August, 1969).

Compromising — Searching for solutions that bring some degree or satisfaction

Forcing — Exerting one's viewpoint at the potential expense of another

Confronting or Problem-Solving — Facing the conflict directly

Table 37. Five General Modes for Handling Conflict.

CONFLICT-HANDLING MODES	CHARACTERISTICS
Withdrawing	Retreating from a conflict issue. Here, the project manager does not deal with the disagreement. He may ignore it entirely, he may withdraw out of fear, he may feel inadequate to bring about an effective resolution, or he may want to avoid rocking the boat. If the issue or disagreement is important to the other party, withdrawal may intensify the conflict situation. In some cases, a project manager may elect to use the withdrawing mode as either a temporary strategy to allow the other party to cool off or as a strategy to buy time so that he can study the issue further.
Smoothing	Emphasizes common areas of agreement and deemphasizes areas of difference. Like withdrawing, smoothing may not address the real issues in a disagreement. Smoothing is a more effective mode, however, because identifying areas of agreement may more clearly focus on areas of disagreement; and further, project work can often continue in areas where there is agreement by the parties.
Compromising	Bargaining and searching for solutions that bring some degree of satisfaction to the parties involved in conflict. Since compromise yields less than optimum results, the project manager must weigh such actions against program goals.
Forcing	Exerting one's viewpoint at the expense of another — characterized by competitiveness and win/lose behavior. Forcing is often used as a last resort by project managers since it may cause resentment and deterioration of the work climate.
Confronting or Problem-Solving	Involves a rational problem-solving approach. Disputing parties solve differences by focusing on the issues, looking at alternative approaches, and selecting the best alternative. Confronting may contain elements of other modes such as compromising and smoothing.

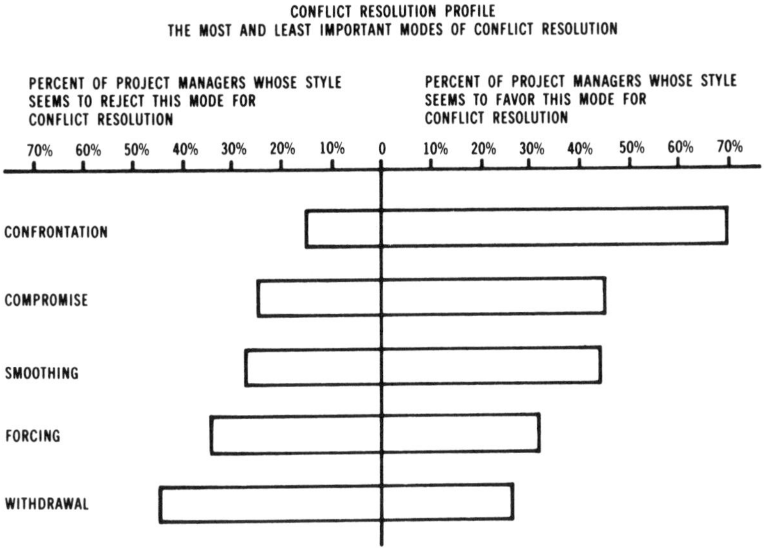

CONFLICT RESOLUTION PROFILE
THE MOST AND LEAST IMPORTANT MODES OF CONFLICT RESOLUTION

PERCENT OF PROJECT MANAGERS WHOSE STYLE SEEMS TO REJECT THIS MODE FOR CONFLICT RESOLUTION	PERCENT OF PROJECT MANAGERS WHOSE STYLE SEEMS TO FAVOR THIS MODE FOR CONFLICT RESOLUTION
70% 60% 50% 40% 30% 20% 10%	0 10% 20% 30% 40% 50% 60% 70%

- CONFRONTATION
- COMPROMISE
- SMOOTHING
- FORCING
- WITHDRAWAL

Figure 46. Conflict resolution profile — the various modes of conflict resolution actually used to manage conflict in project-oriented work environments.

WHAT CONFLICT RESOLUTION MODES WORK BEST?

Project managers are quick to point out the highly situational effectiveness of each conflict resolution mode. More specifically, a field study by Thamhain and Wilemon[63] shows that, in spite of their situational nature, certain modes are more important to project managers while others are less favored. As indicated in Figure 46 the problem-solving approaches of *confrontation* and *compromise* seem to be most important to project managers and most frequently used, while *forcing* and *withdrawal* seem to be least favored. Even more important is the finding that confrontation and compromise were found the most effective methods of dealing with conflict in most project situations, while forcing and withdrawal seem to be least effective in the management of multifunctional activities.

Some specific conclusions can be stated regarding the effectiveness of conflict resolution approaches. While the effectiveness is highly

---

[63] For details see H.J. Thamhain and D.L. Wilemon, "Conflict Management in Project Lifecycles," *Sloan Management Review* (Spring, 1975).

situational and depends upon the type of conflict to be solved, the personnel and the organization involved, and the power relationship that exists among the parties engaged over a particular problem, it appears that confrontation, the so-called problem-solving approach, not only is most frequently used but also seems to result in a higher project performance as measured by general management personnel. This holds particularly in situations of complex, unstructured decision-making which does not follow traditional lines of authority or preestablished rationales.

In contrast to studies of general management, research to project-oriented environments suggests that it is less important to search for a best mode of effective conflict management. It appears to be more significant that project managers, in their capacity as integrators of diverse organizational resources, employ the full range of conflict resolution modes. While confrontation was found as the ideal approach under most circumstances, other approaches may be equally effective depending upon the situational content of the disagreement. Withdrawal, for example, may be used effectively as a temporary measure until new information can be sought or to "cool off" a hostile reaction from a colleague. As a basic long-term strategy, however, withdrawal may actually escalate a disagreement if no resolution is eventually sought.

In other cases, compromise or smoothing might be considered an effective strategy by the project manager, if it does not severely affect the overall project objectives. Forcing, on the other hand, often proves to be a win/lose mode. Even though the project manager may win over a specific issue, effective working arrangements with the "forced" party may be jeopardized in future relationships. Nevertheless, some project managers find that forcing is the only viable mode in some situations. Confrontation, or the problem-solving mode, may actually encompass all conflict-handling modes to some extent. For example, in solving a conflict a project manager may use confrontation in combination with withdrawal, compromise, forcing, and smoothing to eventually get an effective resolution to the issue in question whereby all affected parties can live with the eventual outcome.

In summary, conflict is fundamental to complex task management. It is important for project managers not only to be cognizant of the potential sources of conflict, but also to know when, in the life cycle of a project, they are most likely to occur. Such knowledge can help the project manager avoid the detrimental aspects of conflict and maximize its beneficial aspects. Conflict can be beneficial when disagreements result in the development of new information that can enhance the decision-making process. Finally, when conflict does develop, the project manager needs to know the advantages and disadvantages of each resolution mode for conflict resoltuion effectiveness.

29
Recommendations for Improving Project Management Effectiveness

The findings presented in this chapter should help both the professionals who operate in a project-organized environment and the scholars who study and research contemporary organizational concepts to understand the complex interrelationships among managerial influence, conflict resolution approaches, and project management effectiveness.

A number of suggestions can potentially increase the project manager's effectiveness in resolving conflict and may help to improve overall program performance by creating an environment where material conflict is converted into useful energy.

1. Project managers need to understand the interaction of organizational and behavioral elements in order to build an environment conducive to their team's motivational needs. This will enhance active participation and minimize dysfunctional conflict. The effective flow of communication is one of the major factors determining the quality of the organizational environment. Since the project manager must build support teams at various organizational layers, it is important that key decisions be communicated properly to all project-related personnel. By openly communicating the project objectives and the subtasks, the project manager can minimize unproductive conflict. Regularly scheduled status review meetings

can be an important vehicle for communicating project-related issues.

2. Because their environment is temporary and often untested, project managers should seek a leadership style that allows them to adapt to the often conflicting demands of their project organization, parent organization, specific contributors, or client requirements. They must learn to "test" the expectations of others by observation and experimentation. Although it is difficult, they must be ready to alter their leadership style as demanded by both the status of the project and its participants.

3. Since the ability to manage conflict is related to the project manager's overall performance, a project manager should (a) recognize the primary determinants of conflict in his environment and know when they are most likely to occur in the life of his project; (b) consider the effectiveness of the conflict-handling approach he has used in the past to manage these conflicts; and (c) consider experimenting with alternative conflict-handling modes if he feels that better performance is warranted.

4. The project manager should try to accommodate the professional interests and desires of supporting personnel when he negotiates their tasks. Project effectiveness depends upon how well he provides work challenge to motivate those individuals who support him and matches their goals with the objectives of the project and of the overall organization. Although the scope of a project may be fixed, the project manager usually has a degree of flexibility in allocating task assignments among various contributors.

5. Project managers should develop or maintain technical expertise in their fields. Without an understanding of the technology they are managing, they are unable to win the confidence of team members or to build credibility with the customer community.

6. Effective planning early in the life cycle of a project is another action that may have a favorable impact on the organizational climate. This is particularly true as project managers have to integrate various disciplines across functional lines. Insufficient planning may eventually lead to interdepartmental conflict and discontinuances in the work flow.

7. Finally, project managers can influence the climate of the work environment by their own actions. Concern for project team members,

ability to integrate personal goals and needs of project personnel with project goals, and ability to create personal enthusiasm for the project itself can foster a climate high in motivation, work involvement, open communication, and resulting project performance.

Probably the most important research finding in the area of conflict management is that project managers who foster a climate of highly motivated personnel not only obtain higher project support from their project personnel, but also achieve high overall project performance ratings from their superiors. In addition, the higher the perceived power of project managers as derived from formal position within the organization, scope and nature of the projects, earned authority, and ability to influence promotion, the better potential for effective project performance.

PART V
TEAM BUILDING

30
Selecting Key Personnel

People are your most valuable asset. Selecting the proper key personnel is germane to successful project management. Project staffing is usually conducted in three phases. First, the project manager and the key team members are selected by senior management. Second, all personnel directly reporting to the project office are selected, committed, and assigned. Finally, during the third phase, the functional support personnel, task specialists, and individual contributors are defined, selected, and committed. This staffing process is similar whether the project organization is formed along projectized or functional/matrix lines. The only real difference is in the responsibility for project staffing, which shifts toward the functional manager in a matrix while residing with the project office in a more projectized organization. The size and depth of the project lead group depends on the size and nature of the project to be managed. Typical project management positions and their responsibilities are defined in Table 38. However, at the minimum the project management team should include: (1) the project manager, (2) the task manager of the various functional disciplines, (3) the technical director or project engineer for a technical program, and (4) a project administrator. For smaller project any one or all of these people are often shared among several projects. The important point is to have one appropriate individual responsible for each key function to be performed. Therefore, the process of selecting and

Table 38. Project Management Positions and Responsibilities.

PROJECT MANAGEMENT POSITION	TYPICAL RESPONSIBILITY	SKILL REQUIREMENTS
• Project Administrator • Project Coordinator • Technical Assistant	Coordinating and integrating of subsystem tasks. Assisting in determining technical and manpower requirements, schedules, and budgets. Measuring and analyzing project performance regarding technical progress, schedules, and budgets.	• Planning • Coordinating • Analyzing • Understanding the organization
• Task Manager • Project Engineer • Assistant Project Manager	Same as above, but stronger role in establishing and maintaining project requirements. Conducting trade-offs. Directing the technical implementation according to established schedules and budgets.	• Technical expertise • Assessing trade-offs • Managing task implementation • Leading task specialists
• Project Manager • Program Manager	Same as above, but stronger role in project planning and controlling. Coordinating and negotiating requirements between sponsor and performing organizations. Bid proposal development and pricing. Establishing project organization and staffing. Overall leadership toward implementing project plan. Project profit. New business development.	• Overall program leadership • Team building • Resolving conflict • Managing multidisciplinary tasks • Planning and allocating resources • Interfacing with customers/sponsors
• Executive Program Manager	Title reserved for very large programs relative to host organization. Responsibilities same as above. Focus is on directing overall program toward desired business results. Customer liaison. Profit performance. New business development. Organizational development.	• Business leadership • Managing overall program businesses • Building program organizations • Developing personnel • Developing new business
• Director of Programs • V.P. Program Development	Responsible for managing multi-program businesses via various project organizations, each led by a project manager. Focus is on business planning and development; profit performance; technology development, establishing policies and procedures; program management guidelines; personnel development; organizational development.	• Leadership • Strategic planning • Directing and managing program businesses • Building organizations • Selecting and developing key personnel • Identifying and developing new business

organizing the project team has three facets: defining the key functions required, selecting the proper personnel to perform, and establishing the reporting relations, a process that is discussed in the next chapter.

31
Organizing the Project Team

The following eleven-point process provides some ground rules for the selection and organization of your project team.

PART ONE: DEFINING KEY FUNCTIONS AND RESOURCES

1. *Work definitions:* Decide for each function whether personnel can be shared (S) with others or must report directly (D) to the project office (see Table 39).
2. *Reporting relations:* Decide for each function whether personnel can be shared with others who must report directly (D) to the project office (See Table 39).
3. *Job description:* Prepare job descriptions for all personnel reporting directly to the project office, regardless of whether personnel are fully dedicated to the project or shared among other tasks. This includes all task managers responsible for each major project subsystem.
4. *Personnel requisition:* Advertise your open positions company-internally and externally.

PART TWO: SELECTING PERSONNEL AND ORGANIZING THE TEAM

5. *Competency and commitment:* Select and interview candidates for all direct reports. At the interviews the job requirements, project objectives, expectations, and performance criteria should be clearly

Table 39. Project Functions Checklist.

Typical Functions That May Be Needed on Programs During Their Life Cycles

D	S	Project management
D	S	Secretarial services
D	S	Technical management
D	S	Task management (for each work package)
D	S	Project administration and coordination
D	S	Subcontracts management
D	S	Schedule control
D	S	Financial control
D	S	Contracts management/administration
D	S	Marketing
D	S	Data processing
D	S	Customer liaison
D	S	Configuration control
D	S	Documentation and publications
D	S	Site management
D	S	Proposal development
D	S	Transportation and logistics
D	S	Product assurance
D	S	Legal counseling
D	S	Personnel services
D	S	Other:
D	S	Other:
D	S	Other:

Check if function is needed and whether it should report directly to you (D) or can be shared with others (S).

stated and assessed against the candidates' experiences, skill, and prior track record.

6. *Key personnel hiring:* Negotiate offers with chosen candidates. Interviews and negotiations should also be conducted for company employees who just transfer to the project.

7. *Functional support:* Negotiate functional support personnel with either functional managers or the newly appointed task managers. In order to discuss the specific personnel requirements in an appropriate manner, the project manager must have defined the following elements for each major project subsystem: (1) task descriptions, (2) level of effort, and (3) timing. Further, the statement of work, work breakdown structure, manpower estimate, task matrix, and milestone schedule become the key tools for defining and communicating the personnel requirements across functional lines.

296 TEAM BUILDING

8. *Requirements analysis:* Familiarize all project team members with the overall project requirements. The existing project plan is often a good starting point for developing a common baseline of understanding among project team members and to develop more detailed plans, specifications, schedules, and work statements as needed. This familiarization should be a controlled effort that needs to be properly managed by the project office and all task managers.

PART THREE: ESTABLISHING REPORTING RELATIONS AND CONTROLS

9. *Reporting relations:* Define together with functional managers the reporting relationships of all project personnel. This should include the various accountabilities of personnel to both the resource manager and the project manager regarding technical aspects, quality of work, project direction, and requirements, schedules, and budgets. It should also include the performance assessment and salary review process. The agreement with the the resource managers becomes the global charter of the project manager and should be carefully communicated to all project personnel.

10. *Project controls:* The various project performance measures and controls must be defined and agreed to by all key project personnel. These include status reports, open item memos, project review meetings, and technical reviews such as critical design review. They may also include budget reports, milestone audits, technical milestone reviews, or PERT/CPM systems.

11. *Project kickoff:* Organize and conduct a formal kickoff meeting with *all* contributing project personnel present. A brief overview of the project, its requirements, applications, major milestones, and management philosophy helps to unify the team and form a common baseline of understanding of the overall requirements. Table 40 provides an agenda and list of handouts for a typical project.

ELICITING COMMITMENT

Establishing firm commitment from project personnel is important in any situation. It is absolutely critical, however, in situations where

Table 40. Checklist for Kick-Off Meeting for a Typical Project.

Agenda:

1. (5 minutes) Message from senior management
2. (10 minutes) Project overview (baseline, application, business impact)
3. (5 minutes) Key milestones
4. (10 minutes) Project organization and management
5. (5 minutes) Major criteria for success
6. (1 minute) Adjournment

Handout Material:

1. Project summary plan
   - Baseline configuration
   - Project objectives
   - Project scope
   - Management Approach
   - End Item Specifications
   - Target Schedules
   - Resource Requirements
   - Manpower/staffing plan
   - Risk areas
2. Global customer requirements
3. Work breakdown structure (WBS)
4. Statement of work (SOW)
5. Task matrix
6. Major milestone schedule
7. Budgets
8. Project personnel roster

project managers have to step across functional lines and have to deal with personnel over whom they have little or no control.[64] In such a matrix environment, project management personnel must sell each assignment primarily on the basis of professional interest, perceived career potential, and the satisfaction of higher-order needs such as the need for recognition, visibility, praise, and accomplishment. Further, the perception of how the project manager may *influence* the rewards administered by the functional organization may influence the enthusiasm of project personnel toward the new assignment.

---

[64] A low degree of formal authority is typically experienced by project managers in a matrix organization where conventional bases of influence such as raises, bonuses, and promotions are held by functional managers.

Therefore it is critical for project leaders to identify and satisfy the needs of their project personnel, involve the personnel during the project start-up, and clearly discuss the new assignment, including its requirements and career implications. This will provide the personnel with an opportunity to assess the potential for meeting their need requirements with the project. The initial job review is an important element in the process to involve, assess needs, and elicit commitment. This interview should clearly address:

- Job requirements
- Project objectives, scope, and challenges
- Specific job content in terms of techniques, skills, experience, disciplines, and degree of difficulty
- Reporting relations and project organization
- Phaseout personnel transfer/assignment policy
- Risks and challenges
- Final project outcome and deliverables
- Specific measures for final success
- Reward system

Such a dialogue will provide both parties with an insight into how compatible the requirements are with personal goals on one side and capabilities on the other. In addition, there are many side benefits to a properly conducted interview prior to the assignment. It sets the tone of how the project will be managed, recognizes the individual needs and wants, stimulates thinking, creates involvement and visibility at many levels, and establishes lines of communication for the future. If properly done, interviewing for project assignments is a highly pervasive process that provides a unifying force toward integrating and building a committed project team.

ORGANIZING WITHIN A MATRIX

Matrix-based project teams often evolve with the work during the project definition phase. In this process, project managers often end up with insufficient cross-functional coordination, while at other times too much administrative support increases overhead cost unnecessarily and may even lead to confusion and conflict.

As a basic recommendation, the project manager should designate for each functional discipline an interface person who participates in the project. For smaller projects, this interface is usually the principal contributor, with only a fraction of his or her time needed for coordination with the project office. For large programs, functional integration and interface with the program office can be a full-time job. It may require a dedicated administrator, often with the title of task manager, in each participating functional component.

Some guidelines may be helpful in determining how much interface support is needed. As a rule of thumb, the administrative portion should not exceed 15 percent of the total project effort. This figure is based on an "average" project with approximately ten functions to be integrated. Depending on the actual complexity and multidisciplinary nature of the project the 15 percent figure will certainly vary. However, if the model of Figure 47 is used, many of these factors are normalized. Figure 47 is to be used in the following way:

1. Partition the total project effort into major subsystems to be executed within corresponding functional departments. A guideline is the level 1 of your work breakdown structure.

2. Enter the estimated total effort for (1) your project and (2) its subsystems into row 10. Use man-months or dollars.

3. Calculate the percentile of total project effort to be performed by each function.

4. Start with a 10 percent administrative effort assumption for all functions and 7 percent for the project office. Enter percent figures in all corresponding boxes of row 11. Calculate the corresponding man-months of administrative support and enter at row 11.

5. For each support function, divide the man-months of row 11 by the project life cycle time. This will determine the administrative personnel level. Example: Function A requires an estimated effort of 100 man-months over a period of 20 months. Ten percent administrative effort equals 10 man-months. When distributed over 20 months, this means that we can afford $10/20 = 0.5$ or one-half of an administrator for coordination and project administration of function A.

6. Assign *actual* personnel and decide what portion should be applied to project administration. Particular attention should be

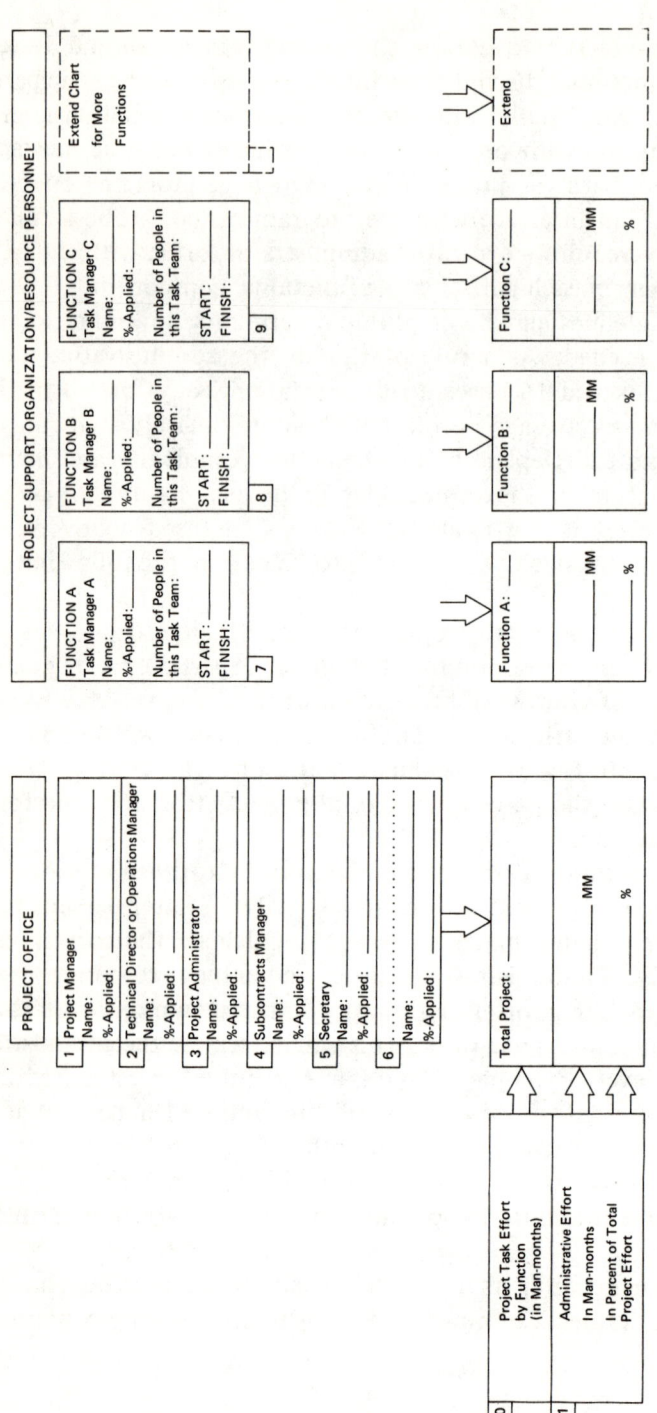

Figure 47. Planning chart for establishing project organization.

given to staffing of the project office, which may need administrative support in many areas such as secretarial, technical direction, subcontracts, and others that are not included in Figure 47. Enter names and percent of applied time into appropriate sections 1 through 9 of Figure 47.

7. Based on the actual assignments, calculate the manpower needed to administrate the project properly. Calculate the percentage figure of the administrative effort, enter in row 11, and compare against the initial target figures. If the administrative overhead looks acceptable to the project manager and senior company management, the project team is operational; otherwise the process must be repeated until a mutually acceptable solution is worked out.

32
Developing the Project Team

Building the project team is one of the prime responsibilities of the project/program manager. Team building involves a whole spectrum of management skills required to identify, commit, and integrate various task groups from traditional functional organizations into a single program management system. This process has been known for centuries. However, it becomes more complex and requires more specialized management skills as bureaucratic hierarchies decline and horizontally oriented teams and work units evolve.

TEAM BUILDING IS CRUCIAL IN PROJECT MANAGEMENT

The driving forces toward effective team building come from three specific areas:

1. *Need for multidisciplinary task integration:* Programs are often too multidisciplinary to be structured strictly along functional lines. Contemporary organizations such as the matrix necessitate the skillful collection of individuals with different needs, backgrounds, and expertise, and the transformation of them into an integrated, effective work unit directed toward the project objectives. Depending on the size and task complexities of the project, this may involve a few people or hundreds of people, organized in task groups and special support units.

2. *Increased organizational involvement:* The divided responsibility, the complex organizational relationships, the ambiguities of responsibility and authority, and the power sharing among various managerial functions results in a need for increased involvement of personnel from all levels of the organization. Therefore, organized teamwork is encouraged.

3. *Team Synergism.* The benefits of people working together can result in important synergy and creativity. An increase in task complexity and complicated environmental interfaces also promotes the development of effective teams, often leading to higher levels of job satisfaction and increased productivity.

Team building is an ongoing process that requires leadership skills and an understanding of the organization, its interfaces, authority and power structure, and motivational factors. It is a process particularly critical in certain project phases and situations, such as:

- Establishing a new program organization
- Improving project-client relations
- Organizing for a bid proposal
- Integrating new project personnel
- Resolving interfunctional problems
- Working toward a major milestone
- Transitioning the project into a new phase

AN EFFECTIVE TEAM ENVIRONMENT

To be effective, the program manager must provide an atmosphere conducive to teamwork, that is, a climate with the following characteristics:

- Team members are committed to the program.
- Good interpersonnel relations and team spirit exist.
- The necessary resources are available.
- Goals and program objectives are clearly defined.
- Top management is involved and supportive.
- Good program leadership exists.

304 TEAM BUILDING

- There is open communication among team members and the support organization.
- A low degree of detrimental interpersonal and intergroup conflict exists.

How can you build an effective and productive team? Although there is no magic formula, research findings[65] consistently show that team members have specific needs for themselves and leadership expectations from the project manager as shown below:

NEEDS OF TEAM MEMBERS	EXPECTATIONS FROM PROJECT MANAGER
• Sense of belonging	• Direction and leadership
• Interest in work itself	• Assistance in problem-solving
• Professional achievement	• Creation of stimulating environment
• Encouragement; pride	• Adaptation of new members
• Recognition for accomplishment	• Capacity to handle conflict
• Protection from infighting	• Resistance to change
• Job security/continuity	• Representation at higher management
• Potential for career growth	• Facilitation of career growth

These needs and expectations usually exist intrinsically in all teams although they are often not apparent on the surface. That is, team members do not always realize their needs and wants explicitly. However, members must feel comfortable in their work environment, have mutual trust, and be interested and involved in the work they are doing in order to form a coherent, effective team.

BARRIERS TO PROJECT TEAM DEVELOPMENT

The understanding of barriers to project team building can help in developing an environment conducive to effective teamwork. The following barriers to team building were identified and analyzed in a

---

[65] For a more detailed discussion of the research in the subject area and specific reference material, please see Bibliography section for writings by J.D. Aram, N.J. Aquilano, W.L. French, R.W. Hollman, F.E. Kate, J.L. Hayes, D.S. Hopkins, J.W. Lewis, D.E. Miller, W. O'Neil, B.E. Phillips, D.J. Streveler, H.J. Thamhain, D.J. Watson, D.L. Wilemon, and J.H. Zenger.

field study by Thamhain and Wilemon.[66] They are typical for many project environments.

Differing outlooks, priorities, and interests: A major barrier exists when team members have professional objectives and interests that are different from the project objectives. These problems are compounded when the team relies on support organizations that have different interests and priorities.

Role conflicts: Team development efforts are thwarted when role conflicts exist among the team members, such as ambiguity over who does what within the project team and at external support groups.

Unclear objectives/outcomes: Unclear project objectives frequently lead to conflict, ambiguities, and power struggles. It becomes difficult, if not impossible, to clearly define roles and responsibilities.

Dynamic project environments: Many projects operate in a continual state of change. For example, senior management may keep changing the project scope, objectives, and resource base. In other situations, regulatory changes or client demands can drastically affect the internal operations of a project team.

Competition over team leadership: Project leaders frequently indicate that this barrier most likely occurs in the early phases of a project or if the project runs into severe problems. Obviously, such cases of leadership challenge can result in barriers to team building. Frequently these challenges are covert challenges to the project leader's ability.

Lack of team definition and structure: Many senior managers complain that teamwork is severely impaired because it lacks clearly defined task responsibilities and reporting structures. We find this situation is most prevalent in dynamic organizationally unstructured work environments such as computer system and R&D projects. A common pattern is that a support department is charged with a task but no one leader is clearly delegated the responsibility. As a consequence, some personnel working on the project are not entirely clear on the extent of their responsibilities. In other cases, problems result when a project is unsupported by several departments without an interdisciplinary.

---

[66] For detailed discussion see H.J. Thamhain and D.L. Wilemon, "Team Building in Project Management," *Proceedings of the 21st Annual Symposium of the Project Management Institute* (October, 1979) and *Project Management Quarterly* (June, 1983).

Team personnel selection: This barrier develops when personnel feel unfairly treated or threatened during the staffing of a project. In some cases, project personnel are assigned to a team by functional managers, and the project manager has little or no input into the selection process. This can impede team development efforts, especially when the project leader is given available personnel versus the best, hand-picked team members. The assignment of "available personnel" can result in several problems, for example, low motivation levels, discontentment, and uncommitted team members. We have found, as a rule, that the more power the project leader has over the selection of his team members, and the more negotiated agreement over the assigned task, the more likely team building efforts will be fruitful.

Credibility of project leader: Team building efforts are hampered when the project leader suffers from poor credibility within the team or from other managers. In such cases, team members are often reluctant to make a commitment to the project or the leader. Credibility problems may come from poor managerial skills, poor technical judgments, or lack of experience relevant to the project.

Lack of team member commitment: Lack of commitment can come from several sources, such as: the team members' professional interests lying elsewhere; the feeling of insecurity being associated with projects; the unclear nature of the rewards that may be forthcoming upon successful completion; and intense interpersonal conflicts within the team.

Other issues that result in uncommitted team members are suspicious attitudes that may exist between the project leader and a functional support manager or between two team members from two warring functional departments. Finally, low commitment levels are likely to occur when a "star" on a team demands too much effort from other team members or too much attention from the team leader. One team leader put it this way:

A lot of teams have their prima donnas and you learn to live and function with them. They can be critical to overall project success. But some stars can be so demanding on everyone that they'll kill the team's motivation.

Communication problems: Not surprisingly, poor communication is a major enemy to effective team development. Poor communication can exist on four major levels: among team members, between the project leader and the team members, between the project team and top management, and between the project leaders and the client. Often the problem is caused by team members simply not keeping others informed on key project developments. Yet the whys of poor communication patterns are far more difficult to determine. It can result from low motivation levels, poor morale, or carelessness. It has also been discovered that poor communication patterns between the team and support groups result in severe team building problems, as does poor communication with the client. Poor communication practices often lead to unclear objectives and poor project control, coordination, and work flow.

Lack of senior management support: Project leaders often indicate that senior management support and commitment are unclear and subject to waxing and waning over the project life cycle. This behavior can result in an uneasy feeling among team members and lead to low levels of enthusiasm and project commitment. Two other common problems are that senior management often does not help set the right environment for the project team at the outset, nor do they give the team timely feedback on their performance and activities during the life of the project.

HOW TO OVERCOME TEAM BARRIERS

Project managers who are successfully performing their role not only recognize these barriers but also know when in the project life cycle they are most likely to occur. Moreover, these managers take preventive actions and usually foster a work environment that is conducive to effective team work. The effective team builder is usually a social architect who understands the interaction of organizational and behavioral variables and can foster a climate of active participation and minimal conflict. This requires carefully developed skills in leadership, administration, organization, and technical expertise on the project. However, besides the delicately balanced management skills, the project manager's sensitivity to the basic issues underlying each barrier can help to increase success in developing an effective project team. Specific suggestions for team building are advanced in Table 41.

Table 41. Barriers to Effective Team Building and Suggested Handling Approaches.

BARRIER	SUGGESTIONS FOR EFFECTIVELY MANAGING BARRIERS (HOW TO MINIMIZE OR ELIMINATE BARRIERS)
Differing outlooks, priorities, interests, and judgments of team members	Make an effort early in the project life cycle to discover these conflicting differences. Fully explain the scope of the project and the rewards that may be forthcoming upon successful project completion. Sell the "team" concept and explain responsibilities. Try to blend individual interests with the overall project objectives.
Role conflicts	As early in a project as feasible, ask team members where they see themselves fitting into the project. Determine how the overall project can best be divided into subsystems and subtasks (e.g., the work breakdown structure). Assign/negotiate roles. Conduct regular status review meetings to keep team informed on progress and watch for unanticipated role conflicts over the project's life.
Unclear project objectives/ outcomes	Assure that all parties understand the overall and interdisciplinary project objectives. Clear and frequent communication with senior management and the client becomes critically important. Status review meetings can be used for feedback. Finally, a proper team name can help to reinforce the project objectives.
Dynamic project environments	The major challenge is to stabilize external influences. First, key project personnel must work out an agreement on the principal project direction and "sell" this direction to the total team. Also, educate senior management and the customer on the detrimental consequences of unwarranted change. It is critically important to forecast the environment within which the project will be developed. Develop contingency plans.
Competition over team leadership	Senior management must help establish the project manager's leadership role. On the other hand, the project manager needs to fulfill the leadership expectations of team members. Clear role and responsibility definition often minimizes competition over leadership.
Lack of team definition and structure	Project leaders need to sell the team concept to senior management as well as to their team members. Regular meetings with the team will reinforce the team notion as will clearly defined tasks, roles, and responsibilities. Also, visibility in memos and other forms of written media as well as senior management and client participation can unify the team.
Project personnel selection	Attempt to negotiate the project assignments with potential team members. Clearly discuss with potential team

DEVELOPING THE PROJECT TEAM 309

	members the importance of the project, their role in it, what rewards might result upon completion, and the general "rules-of-the-road" of project management. Finally, if team members remain uninterested in the project, then replacements should be considered.
Credibility of project leader	Credibility of the project leader among team members is crucial. It grows with the image of a sound decision-maker in both general management and relevant technical expertise. Credibility can be enhanced by the project leader's relationship to other key managers who support the team's efforts.
Lack of team member commitment	Try to determine lack of team member commitment early in the life of the project and attempt to change possible negative views toward the project. Often, insecurity is a major reason for the lack of commitment; try to determine why insecurity exists, then work on reducing the team member's fears. Conflicts with other team members may be another reason for lack of commitment. It is important for the project leader to intervene and mediate the conflict quickly. Finally, if a team member's professional interests lie elsewhere, the project leader should examine ways to satisfy part of the team member's interests or consider replacement.
Communication problems	The project leader should devote considerable time communicating with individual team members about their needs and concerns. In addition, the leader should provide a vehicle for timely sessions to encourage communications among the individual team contributors. Tools for enhancing communications are status meetings, reviews, schedules, reporting system, and colocation. Similarly, the project leader should establish regular and thorough communications with the client and senior management. Emphasis is placed on written and oral communications with key issues and agreements in writing.
Lack of senior management support	Senior management support is an absolute necessity for dealing effectively with interface groups and proper resource commitment. Therefore, a major goal for project leaders is to maintain the continued interest and commitment of senior management in their projects. We suggest that senior management become an integral part of project reviews. Equally important, it is critical for senior management to provide the proper environment for the project to function effectively. Here the project leader needs to tell management at the onset of the program what resources are needed. The project manager's relationship with senior management and ability to develop senior management support is critically affected by his own credibility and the visibility and priority of his project.

SUGGESTIONS FOR HANDLING THE NEWLY FORMED TEAM

A major problem faced by many project leaders is managing the anxiety that usually develops when a new team is first formed. This anxiety experienced by team members is normal and predictable. It is a barrier, however, to getting the team quickly focused on the task. In other words, if team members are suffering from anxiety, their attention consciously or subconsciously will be focused on the resolution of their own anxieties rather than on the needs of the project.

This anxiety may come from several sources. For example, if the team members have never worked with the project leader, the team members may be concerned about his leadership style and its effect on them. In a different vein, some team members may be concerned about the nature of the project and whether it will match their professional interests and capabilities. Other team members may be concerned whether the project will help or hinder their career aspirations. Further, team members can be highly anxious about life-style/work-style disruptions that the project may bring. As one project manager remarked:

> Moving a team member's desk from one side of the room to the other can sometimes be just about as traumatic as moving someone from Chicago to Manila.

As the quote suggests, seemingly minor changes can result in unanticipated anxiety among team members.

Another common concern among newly formed teams is whether or not there will be an equitable distribution of the work load among team members and whether each member is capable of pulling his weight. In some newly formed teams, members not only might have to do their own work but they also must train other team members. Within reason this is bearable, necessary, and often expected. However, when it becomes excessive, anxiety increases and morale can fall.

Certain steps taken early in the life of a team can be effective in terms of handling the above problems. First, we recommend that the project leader at the start of the project talk with each team member on a one-to-one basis about the following:

1. What the objectives are for the project.
2. Who will be involved and why.

3. How the project is important to the overall organization or work unit.
4. Why the team member was selected and assigned to the project. What role will he perform.
5. What rewards might be forthcoming if the project is successfully completed.
6. What problems and constraints are likely to be encountered.
7. What rules-of-the-road will be followed in managing the project (e.g., regular status review meetings).
8. What suggestions the team member has for achieving success.
9. What the professional interests of the team member are.
10. What challenge the projet will present to individual members and the entire team.
11. Why the team concept is so important to project management success and how it should work.

A frank, open discussion with each team member on the above is likely to reduce his initial anxiety. As a consequence, the team member is likely to be more attentive to the needs of the project. Of course, the opposite reaction is possible, too. A frank discussion, for example, may actually increase a team member's anxiety level. Often, however, the source of the anxiety can be identified and dealt with in a timely manner.

The importance of dealing with these anxieties and helping team members feel that they are an integral part of the team can result in rich dividends. First, as noted in Figure 48, the more effective the project leader is in developing a feeling of team membership, the higher the quality of information that is likely to be contributed by team members. Team members will openly share their ideas and approaches. By contrast, when a team member does not feel part of the team and does not trust others in team deliberations, information will not be shared willingly or openly. One project leader emphasized this point:

There's nothing worse than being on a team when no one trusts anyone else.... Such situations lead to gamesmanship and a lot of watching what you say because you don't want your own words to bounce back in your face....

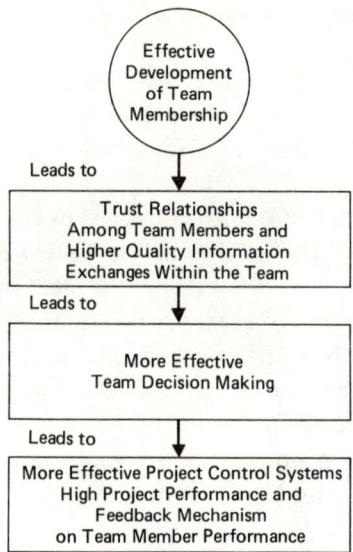

Figure 48. Team building outcomes.

Second, the greater the feeling of team membership and the better the information exchange among team members, the more likely the team will be able to develop effective decision-making processes. The reason is that the team members feel committed to the project and they feel free to share their information and develop effective problem-solving approaches. Third, the team is likely to develop more effective project control procedures. Project control procedures can be divided into two basic areas. The first is the quantitative control procedures traditionally used to monitor project performance, such as PERT/CPM, networking, and work breakdown structures. The second is the willingness and ability of project team members to give feedback to each other regarding performance. Again, trust among the project team members makes the feedback process easier and more effective. Without a high level of trust, project personnel are often reluctant to give constructive feedback to fellow team members.

TEAM BUILDING AS AN ONGOING PROCESS

While proper attention to team building is critical during early phases of a project, it is a never-ending process. The project manager is continually monitoring team functioning and performance to see what corrective action may be needed to prevent or correct various team problems. Several barometers provide good clues of potential team dysfunctioning. First, noticeable changes in performance levels for the team and/or for individual team members should always be followed up. Such changes can be symptomatic of more serious problems, for example, conflict, lack of work integration, communication problems, and unclear objectives. Second, the project leader and team members want to be aware of the changing energy levels of team members. This, too, may signal more serious problems or that the team is tired and stressed. Sometimes changing the work pace, taking time off, or selling short-term targets can serve as a means to reenergize team members. More serious cases, however, can call for more drastic action, such as reappraising project objectives and/or the means to achieve them. Third, verbal and nonverbal clues from team members may be a source of information on team functioning. It is important to hear the needs and concerns of team members (verbal clues) and to observe how they act in carrying out their responsibilities (nonverbal clues). Finally, detrimental behavior of one team member toward another can be a signal that a problem within the team warrants attention.

We highly recommend that project leaders hold regular meetings to evaluate overall team performance and deal with team functioning problems. The focus of these meetings can be directed toward "what are we doing well as a team" and "what areas need our team's attention." This approach often brings positive surprises in that the total team will be informed on progress in diverse project areas, for example, a breakthrough in technology development, a subsystem schedule met ahead of the original target, or a positive change in the client's behavior toward the project. After the positive issues have been discussed, attention should be devoted toward areas needing team attention. The purpose of this part of the review session is to focus on actual or potential problem areas. The meeting leader should ask each team member for his observations on these issues. Then, an open discussion should be held to ascertain how significant the problems really are. Assumptions should, of course, be separated from the facts of each situation. Next, assignments should be agreed upon on how best to handle these problems. Finally, a plan for problem follow-up should be developed. The process should result in better overall performance and promote a feeling of team participation and high morale.

Over the life of a project, the problems encountered by the project team are likely to change, and as old problems are identified and solved, new ones will emerge.

In summary, effective team building is a critical determinant of project success. While the process of team building can entail frustrations and energy on the part of all concerned, the rewards can be great.

Social scientists generally agree that there are several indicators of effective and ineffective teams. At any point in the life of a team, the project manager should be aware of certain effectiveness/ineffectiveness indicators, which are summarized in Table 42.

Table 42. Project Team Characteristics: Effective vs. Ineffective.

THE EFFECTIVE TEAM LIKELY CHARACTERISTICS	THE INEFFECTIVE TEAM LIKELY CHARACTERISTICS
• High performance and task efficiency	• Low performance
• Innovative/creative behavior	
• Commitment	• Low commitment to project objectives
• Professional objectives of team members coinciding with project requirements	
• Team members highly interdependent, interface effectively	• Unclear project objectives and fluid commitment levels from key participants
• Capacity for conflict resolution, but conflict encouraged when it can lead to beneficial results	• Unproductive gamesmanship, manipulation of others, hidden feelings, conflict avoided at all costs
• Effective communication	• Confusion, conflict, inefficiency
• High trust levels	• Subtle sabotage, fear, disinterest or foot-dragging
• Result-oriented	
• Interested in membership	• Cliques, collusion, isolating members
• High energy levels and enthusiasm	• Lethargic/unresponsive
• High morale	
• Change-oriented	

As we approach the next decade, we anticipate important developments in team building. As shown in Figure 48, these developments will lead to higher performance levels, increased morale, and a pervasive commitment to final results that can withstand almost any kind of adversity.

33
Financial Compensation and Rewards

Proper financial compensation and rewards are important to the morale and motivation of people in any organization. Projects are no exception. However, there are several issues that make it often necessary to treat compensation practices of project personnel separately from the rest of the organization:

- *Job classifications and job descriptions* for project personnel are usually not compatible with those existing for other professional jobs. It is often difficult to pick an existing classification and adopt it to project personnel. If not adjusted properly, the low formal authority and small number of direct reports may distort the position level of project personnel in spite of their broad-range business responsibilities.
- *Dual accountability* and dual reporting relationships of project personnel raise the question of who should assess performance and control the rewards.
- *Bases for financial rewards* are often difficult to establish, quantify, and administer. The criterion of "doing a good job" is difficult to quantify.
- *Special compensations* for overtime, extensive travel, or living away from home should be considered in addition to bonus pay for preestablished results. Bonus pay is a particularly difficult and delicate issue since often many people contribute to the

incentivized results. Discretionary bonus practices can be demoralizing to the project team.

Some specific guidelines are provided in this book to help business managers to establish compensation systems for their project organizations. The foundations of these compensation practices are based on four systems: (1) job classification, (2) base pay, (3) performance appraisals, and (4) merit increases.

JOB CLASSIFICATIONS AND JOB DESCRIPTIONS

Every effort should be made to fit the new classifications for project personnel into the existing standard classification that has already been established for the organization.

The first step is to define job titles for various project personnel and their corresponding responsibilities. Table 38 in Chapter 30 provides an overview of typical titles and responsibilities, rank-ordered from least to most senior positions. Titles are very newsworthy. They imply certain responsibilities, position power, organizational status, and pay level. Furthermore, titles may indicate certain functional responsibilities such as the title of task manager.[62] Therefore, titles should be carefully selected and each of them supported by a formal job description.

The job description provides the basic charter for the job and the individual in charge of it. Therefore, the job description should be written not just for one individual but more generally for all individuals who fit the respective job classification. A good job description is brief and concise, not exceeding one page. Typically, it is broken down into three sections: (1) overall responsibilities, (2) specific duties, and (3) qualifications. A sample job description is given in Table 43.

BASE-PAY CLASSIFICATIONS AND INCENTIVES

After the job descriptions have been developed, one can delineate the pay classes consistent with the responsibilities and accountabilities

---

[67]In most organizations the title of task manager indicates responsibilities for managing the technical content of a project subsystem within a functional unit, having dual accountabilities to the functional superior and the project office.

Table 43. Sample Job Description.

JOB DESCRIPTION: LEAD PROJECT ENGINEER OF PROCESSOR DEVELOPMENT

Overall Responsibility:

Responsible for directing the technical development of the new central processor including managing the technical personnel assigned to this development. The lead project engineer has dual responsibility, (1) to his/her functional superior for the technical implementation and engineering quality and (2) to the project manager for managing the development within the established budget and schedule.

Specific Duties and Responsibilities:
1. Provide necessary program direction for planning, organizing, developing, and integrating the engineering effort, including establishing the specific objectives, schedules, and budgets for the processor subsystem.
2. Provide technical leadership for analyzing and establishing requirements, preliminary designing, designing, prototyping, and testing of the processor subsystem.
3. Divide the work into discrete and clearly definable tasks. Assign tasks to technical personnel within the lead engineer's area of responsibility and other organizational units.
4. Define, negotiate, and allocate budgets and schedules according to the specific tasks and overall program requirements.
5. Measure and control cost, schedule, and technical performance against program plan.
6. Report deviations from program plan to program office.
7. Replan trade-off and redirect the development effort in case of contingencies such as to best utilize the available resources toward the overall program objectives.
8. Plan, maintain, and utilize engineering facilities to meet the long-range program requirements.

Qualifications:
1. Strong technical background in state-of-the-art central processor development.
2. Prior task management experience with proven record for effective cost and schedule control of multidisciplinary technology-based task in excess of SIM.
3. Personal skills to lead, direct, and motivate senior engineering personnel.
4. Excellent communication skills, both orally and in writing.

for business results. If left to the personnel specialist, these pay scales often have a tendency to slip toward the lower end of an equitable compensation. This is understandable because, on the surface, project positions look less senior than their functional counterparts since formal authority over resources and direct reports are often less than those for traditional functional positions. The impact of such a skewed compensation is that the project organization will attract less qualified personnel than the functional units. Moreover, project management may be seen as an inferior career which at best may serve as a stepping stone to get into functional management.

Many companies that struggled with this problem found a solution by (1) working out compensation schemes as a team of senior managers and personnel specialists and (2) applying criteria of responsibility and business/profit accountability to setting pay scales for project personnel in accord with other jobs in their organization. Once the proper range of compensation has been set, fine-tuning is a built-in feature. That is, hiring managers can choose a salary from the established range based on their judgment of actual position responsibilities, the candidate's qualifications, the available budget, and other considerations. Valuable guidance and perspective can be obtained from the personnel specialist.

PERFORMANCE APPRAISALS

Traditionally, the purpose of the performance appraisal is to:

- Assess the employee's work performance, preferably against preestablished objectives
- Provide a justification for salary actions
- Establish new goals and objectives for the next review period
- Identify and deal with work-related problems
- Serve as a basis for career discussions

The realities are, however, that the first two objectives are in conflict with the other three. As a result, the traditional performance appraisal essentially becomes a salary discussion the objective of which is to justify subsequent managerial actions.[68] In addition, a discussion dominated by salary actions is usually not conducive to future goal setting, problem-solving, or career planning.

---

[68] For detailed discussions see The Conference Board, *Matrix Organizations of Complex Businesses,* 1979; plus some basic research by H. H. Meyer, E. Kay, and J. R. P. French, "Split Roles in Performance Appraisal," *Harvard Business Review* (January–February, 1965).

In order to get around this dilemma, many companies have separated the salary discussion from the other parts of the performance appraisal. Moreover, successful managers have carefully considered the complex issues involved and have built a performance appraisal system that is solid on content, measurability, and source of information.

The first challenge is on content, that is, to decide what to review and how to measure performance. Modern management practices try to individualize accountability as much as possible. Furthermore, subsequent incentive or merit increases are tied to profit performance.

Although most companies apply these principles to their project organizations, they do it with a great deal of skepticism. Practices are often modified to assure balance and equity for jointly performed responsibilities. A similar dilemma exists in the area of profit accountability. The comment of a project manager at the General Electric Company is typical for the situation fad by business managers: "Although I am responsible for business results of a large program, I really can't control more than 20 percent of its cost." Acknowledging the realities, organizations are measuring performance of their project managers, in at least two areas:

- *Business results* as measured by profits, contribution margin, return on investment, new business, and income; also, on-time delivery, meeting of contractural requirements, and within-budget performance
- *Managerial performance* as measured by overall project management effectiveness, organization, direction and leadership, and team performance

The first area applies only if the project manager is indeed responsible for business results such as contractual performance or new business acquisitions. Many project managers work with company-internal sponsors, such as a company-internal new product development or a feasibility study. In these cases, producing the results within the agreed-on schedule and budget constraints becomes the primary measure of performance. The second area is clearly more difficult to assess. Moreover, if handled improperly, it will lead to manipulation and game playing. Table 44 provides some specific measures of project management performance. Regardless of whether the sponsor

Table 44. Performance Measures for Project Managers.

Who Performs Appraisal:
  Functional superior of project manager

Source of Performance Data:
  Functional superior, resource managers, general managers

Primary Measures:
1. Project manager's success in leading the project toward preestablished global objectives
   - Target costs
   - Key milestones
   - Profit, net income, return on investment, contribution margin
   - Quality
   - Technical accomplishments
   - Market measures, new business, follow-on contract
2. Project manager's effectiveness in overall project direction and leadership during all phases, including establishing
   - Objectives and customer requirements
   - Budgets and schedules
   - Policies
   - Performance measures and controls
   - Reporting and review system

Secondary Measures:
1. Ability to utilize organizational resources
   - Overhead cost reduction
   - Working with existing personnel
   - Cost-effective make-buy decisions
2. Ability to build effective project team
   - Project staffing
   - Interfunctional communications
   - Low team conflict, complaints, and hassles
   - Professionally satisfied team members
   - Work with support groups
3. Effective project planning and plan implementation
   - Plan detail and measurability
   - Commitment by key personnel and management
   - Management involvement
   - Contingency provisions
   - Reports and reviews
4. Customer/client satisfaction
   - Perception of overall project performance by sponsor
   - Communications, liaison
   - Responsiveness to changes
5. Participation in business management
   - Keeping management informed of new project/product/business opportunities
   - Bid proposal work
   - Business planning, policy development

Table 44. (continued)

Additional Considerations:

1. Difficulty of tasks involved
   - Technical tasks
   - Administrative and organizational complexity
   - Multidisciplinary nature
   - Staffing and start-up

2. Scope of the project
   - Total project budget
   - Number of personnel involved
   - Number of organizations and subcontractors involved

3. Changing work environment
   - Nature and degree of customer changes and redirections
   - Contingencies

is company-internal or external, project managers are usually being assessed on how long it took to organize the team, whether the project is moving along according to agreed-on schedules and budgets, and how closely they meet the global goals and objectives set by their superiors.

On the other side of the project organization, resource managers or project personnel are assessed primarily on their ability to direct the implementation of a specific project subsystem.

- *Technical implementation* measured against requirements, quality, schedules, and cost targets
- *Team performance* as measured by ability to staff, build an effective task group, interface with other groups, and integrate among various functions.

Specific performance measures are shown in Table 45. In addition, the actual project performance of both project managers and their resource personnel should be assessed on the conditions under which it was achieved: The degree of task difficulty, complexity, size, changes, and general business conditions.

Finally, one needs to decide who is to conduct the performance appraisal and to make the salary adjustment. Where dual accountabilities

Table 45. Performance Measures for Project Personnel.

Who Performs Appraisal:

Functional superior of project person

Source of Performance Data:

Project manager and resource managers

Primary Measures:

1. Success in directing the agreed-on task toward completion
   - Technical implementation according to requirements
   - Quality
   - Key milestones/schedules
   - Target costs, design-to-cost
   - Innovation
   - Trade-offs
2. Effectiveness as a team member or team leader
   - Building effective task team
   - Working together with others, participation, involvement
   - Interfacing with support organizations and subcontractors
   - Interfunctional coordination
   - Getting along with others
   - Change orientation
   - Making commitments

Secondary Measures:

1. Success and effectiveness in performing functional tasks in addition to project work in accordance with functional charter
   - Special assignments
   - Advancing technology
   - Developing organization
   - Resource planning
   - Functional direction and leadership
2. Administrative support services
   - Reports and reviews
   - Special task forces and committees
   - Project planning
   - Procedure development
3. New business development
   - Bid proposal support
   - Customer presentations
4. Professional development
   - Keeping abreast in professional field
   - Publications
   - Liaison with societies, vendors, customers, and educational institutions

Table 45. (continued)

Additional Considerations:

1. Difficulty of tasks involved
   - Technical challenges
   - State-of-the-art considerations
   - Changes and contingencies
2. Managerial responsibilities
   - Task leader for number of project personnel
   - Multifunctional integration
   - Budget responsibility
   - Staffing responsibility
   - Specific accountabilities
3. Multiproject involvement
   - Number of different projects
   - Number and magnitude of functional task and duties
   - Overall workload

are involved, good practices call for inputs from both bosses. Such a situation could exist for project managers who report functionally to one superior but are also accountable for specific business results to another person. While dual accountability of project managers is an exception for most organizations, it is common for project resource personnel who are responsible to their functional superior for the quality of the work and to their project manager for meeting the requirements within budget and schedule. Moreover, resource personnel may be shared among many projects. Only the functional or resource manager can judge overall performance of resource personnel.

MERIT INCREASES AND BONUSES

Professionals have come to expect merit increases as a reward for a job well done. However, under inflationary conditions, which we have experienced for many years, pay adjustments seldom keep up with cost-of-living increases. To deal with this salary compression and to incentivize management performance, companies have introduced bonuses uniformly to all components of their organizations
The problem is that these standard plans for merit increases and bonuses are based on individual accountability, while project personnel work in teams with shared accountabilities, responsibilities, and

controls. It is usually very difficult to credit project success or failure to a single individual or a small group.

Most management that found themselves in these quandaries did turn to the traditional remedy of the performance appraisal. If done well, the appraisal should provide particular measures of job performance that assess the level and magnitude at which the individual contributed to the success of the project, including the managerial performance and team performance components. Therefore, a properly designed and executed performance appraisal, which includes the inputs from all accountable managements and the basic agreement of the employee to the conclusions, is a sound basis for future salary reviews. Often more important than the actual increase is the salary adjustment relative to other employees. Paying equitably for performance and position is crucial to employee morale and satisfactory productivity, a very important area that deserves careful management attention.

34
Handling Project Phaseouts and Transfers

By definition, projects have an end point. Closing out is a very important phase in the project life cycle and should follow particular disciplines and procedures with the objective to

- Effectively bring the project to a close according to agreed-on contractual requirements
- Prepare for the transition of the project into the next operating phase such from production to field installation, field operation, or training
- Analyze overall project performance with regard to financial data, schedules, and technical efforts
- Close the project office. Transfer or sell off all resources originally assigned to the project, including personnel
- Identify and pursue follow-on business

Project success or failure often depends on management's ability to handle personnel issues properly during this first phase. If job assignments beyond the current project look undesirable or uncertain to project team members, a great deal of anxiety and conflict may develop which diverts needed energy to job hunting, foot-dragging, or even sabotage. Another problem is that project personnel engage in job searches on their own and may leave the project prematurely.

This creates a glaring void that is often difficult to patch, always costs additional time and money, and often erodes the already strained morale of the remaining project team.

Given the business realities, it is often difficult to transfer project personnel under ideal conditions for all parties involved. However, some suggestions are delineated that can increase organizational effectiveness in closing out a project and can minimize personal stress for all parties involved:

1. Carefully plan the project closeout on the part of both the project and functional managers. Use a checklist such as Table 46 to assist in the preparation of the closeout plan.
2. Establish a simple project closeout procedure that identifies the major steps and responsibilities.
3. Treat the closeout phase like any other project with clearly delineated tasks, agreed-on responsibilities, schedules, budgets, and deliverable items or results.
4. Understand the interaction of behavioral and organizational elements in order to build an environment conducive to teamwork during this final project phase.
5. Emphasize the overall goals, applications, and utilities of the project as well as its business impact. This will boost the morale of the team and enhance the desire to participate up to the final closure and success.
6. Secure top management involvement and support.
7. Be aware of conflict, fatigue, shifting priorities, and technical or logistic problems. Try to identify and deal with these problems when they start to develop. Maintaining an effective flow of communications is key to the ability to manage these problems. Regularly scheduled status meetings can be an important vehicle for maintaining effective communications.
8. If at all possible, keep project personnel informed of upcoming job opportunities. Resource managers should discuss and negotiate new assignments with their personnel and, ideally, start involving their people in the next project.
9. Be aware of rumors. If a reorganization or layoff is inevitable at the end of a project, the situation should be communicated in a professional manner. If left to their imagination, project

Table 46. Project Closeout Checklist for an Engineering Project.

OBJECTIVE: Close out the project, assure meeting all contractual requirement and financial obligations.

PART A: DOCUMENTS

TYPE	ITEM	DONE YES	NO	COMMENTS/REFERENCE
Technical	1. Engineering documentation	Y	N	
	2. Design assurance test report	Y	N	
	3. System specifications	Y	N	
	4. Product maintenance plan	Y	N	
	5. User manuals	Y	N	
	6. Field support plan	Y	N	
	7. Final technical report	Y	N	
Contractual	8. List of deliverables	Y	N	
	9. Final contract documents	Y	N	
	10. Shipping instructions	Y	N	
Financial	11. Final financial report	Y	N	
	12. Financial audit	Y	N	
Personnel	13. Manpower	Y	N	

PART B: ACTIVITIES

RESPONSIBILITY	ITEM	COMPLETION DATE SCHEDULED	ACTUAL	COMMENTS
Project Manager: Name	1. Review results of design assurance test			
	2. Complete and release engineering documentation			
	3. Establish manpower phaseout schedule			
	4. Prepare final project report			
	5. Conduct final project review meeting			
	6. Conduct project closeout meeting			
	7. Prepare personnel evaluation			
	8. Meet with customer to establish final acceptance procedures			
	9. Close out all work orders and contracts			
	10. Complete and secure project file			
	11. Close charge numbers			
	12. Close facilities, dispose equipment and materials			
	13. Identify, document, and communicate new business opportunities such as follow-ons, extensions, modifications, or new projects			

Table 46. (continued)

RESPONSIBILITY	ITEM	COMPLETION DATE SCHEDULED ACTUAL	COMMENTS
	PART B: ACTIVITIES (Continued)		
Project Engineer(s) Name	14. Finalize engineering documentation		
	15. Prepare final technical report		
	16. Conduct final technical review		
	17. Analyze and release design assurance test		
	18. Prepare for shipping		
	19. Prepare for site integration		
	20. Prepare for customer acceptance		
	21. Transfer data to field support personnel		
Contract Administration Name	22. Review and approve shipping authorization		
	23. Compile final contract documents		
	24. Verify contractual compliance		
	25. Notify customer of contract completion and shipment		
	26. Prepare accrued cost report to be billed after		
Purchasing Name	27. Prepare list of vended items in procurement		
	28. Verify final payments		
Cost Accounting/ Finance	29. Close out cost accounts including accrued and pending costs		
	30. Prepare final cost report		
	31. Prepare financial summary report		
	32. Conduct financial audit		
	33. Collect receivables		

PART C: SIGN-OFF

Project Manager: _____   Field Support Manager _____
Project Engineer: _____   Documentation Control _____
Project Engineer: _____   Contract Administration _____
Project Engineer: _____   Finance _____
Product Assurance _____   V.P. Engineering _____

Business Area Manager: _____

personnel will make the worst assumptions, resulting in a demoralized team, work slowdowns and sporadic departure of key team members.

10. Assign a contract administrator, dedicated to any company-oriented projects. He will protect your financial position and business interests by following through on customer sign-offs and final payment.

35
Career Development in Project Management

The need for identifying, selecting, and developing project personnel is very clear to the majority of senior managers in project-oriented businesses and government organizations. The issue discussed today is not so much the need but the process and its effectiveness. There are two major reasons for dealing with program management development separately from other personnel: (1) the special skill requirements needed by program/project managers to fulfill their roles effectively and (2) the high mobility of program managers regarding other programs or functional assignments, which often results in a high turnover rate.

Because of the dynamics and experiential nature of skills required, many senior managers feel that program management personnel must be trained and developed on the job. However, there are sharply different approaches being taken by organizations regarding their methods and practices. This chapter provides an insight into human resource planning and development practices in project management with focus on small and medium-sized businesses. The findings may help senior managers to define the tools and methods for selecting and developing the project management personnel needed in today's complex environment.

CAREER LADDERS IN PROJECT MANAGEMENT

Project management offers many career avenues. It provides opportunities for administrative as well as technical and business management positions. Table 38 in Chapter 30 gives an overview of typical positions and their responsibilities. Career ladders in project management usually parallel those in functional management with many crossovers on both sides. For example, an engineering professional might start his career as a designer, then take an assignment as a project engineer, later work as a project manager, and then return to a functional position as product manager. Project assignments often provide excellent opportunities for the individual to gain a better understanding of the organization and its interfaces. The project activities cut across various functional lines, which requires dealing with a broad variety of personnel. Moreover, project personnel receive management recognition and company-wide visibility for their work and accomplishments.

THE INCREMENTAL NATURE OF CAREER ADVANCEMENT

Career advances in project management usually are made incrementally. That is, assignments for a particular task or project responsibility are made for a fixed time period, namely the duration of the project. Thereafter, the individual returns to his previous position. This gives both management and the individual a chance to evaluate the past assignment regarding job performance, as well as likes and dislikes for the new assignment. This process has a built-in failsafe mechanism. In contrast to traditional management appointments, the assignment is not permanent, and reassignment to similar or higher-level responsibility depends on a mutually satisfactory assessment of the individual's performance. Moreover, career growth in project management can be effectively supported and enhanced by on-the-job training. A person interested in a project management career can be assigned a job as an assistant to a task manager, administrative assistant, or project manager. At the more junior level these assistant-to positions might have titles such as analyst, schedule project administrator, or technical assistant. At more advanced stages of the project management career, actual management and project management responsibilities are assigned. Further, assignments can vary by project size, complexity, and duration to reflect the individual's experience level and career ambitions.

A PLANNED APPROACH TO PROJECT PERSONNEL DEVELOPMENT

Successful personnel development programs usually consider the total job cycle from need identification to placement. Four specific phases should be considered. Each phase should be planned, regularly reviewed, and updated, and its results used on a perpetuating basis as inputs for the next phase.

Phase I: Identify Staffing Needs

An important first step is to identify the number and types of project management personnel needed over the next few years. Three years may be a convenient planning horizon. This phase needs the involvement of all senior management personnel. Specific management tools to aid this phase are:

1. Business plans
2. Organization charts
3. Job descriptions
4. Manpower plans

Phase 2: Define the Work Environment

Many executives of small and medium-sized businesses like to say that their project organizations evolved in a natural process, as a by-product of getting the required work done. Therefore, it is often argued, the need for formal policies, procedures, and directives is minimum. It should be realized, however, that especially in a less structured environment, such as a matrix, the various management processes must be clearly spelled out and integrated into the organization. Furthermore, these processes become a crucial input to the design of any personnel development program. Three types of processes are used to define the work environment:

- *Role specifications,* which define the authority and reporting relations. They include job descriptions, policies, procedures, directives, and organization charts.
- *Project management support system,* which provides the basis for integrated decision-making. It includes planning, bidding, reports and reviews, and controls.
- *Reward system,* which establishes the accountability and assesses performance as a basis for rewards. It includes the appraisal system, salary and bonus structure, promotional policies, and career development.

Each of these processes is operational in every organization, at least to some degree. An effort should be made to formalize and document the work environment. The management tools to be developed and updated include:

1. Job description
2. Charter of specific program office
3. Project management policies and procedures
4. Project management guidelines
5. Appraisal and reward guidelines/policy

Phase 3: Develop the Personnel Development Plan

The development plan should include all aspects, from identifying candidates to placement. Along with training, companies have learned to pay more attention to the team approach of personnel development where personnel become intrinsically interested, involved, and motivated toward taking on project responsibilities and grow with the project operations. The major facets of the development plan are:

1. Means of identifying and attracting candidates for various levels of project management positions
2. Specific training and development methods
3. Appraisal and assessment of training effectiveness; reviews
4. Personnel placement and advancement

Phase 4: The Implement Plan

To be successful, the personnel development plan must have an approved budget and the total commitment of the organization, at all levels of management. This commitment will likely develop if management was actively involved in the generation of the plan. It seems to be important to assess the effectiveness of the personnel development activity from both sides, the management and the personnel in training. If people are not attracted to the development opportunity, it is doomed to fail. Regular interviews should be held with all participants of the program being involved. The specific management tools to aid this phase are:

1. Project personnel development plan
2. Formal and informal feedback from participants
3. Review meetings
4. Independent audit

METHODS AND TECHNIQUES FOR DEVELOPING PROJECT MANAGEMENT PERSONNEL

Companies that believe in developing the project management function have a wide array of methods and techniques to choose from. Table 47 provides an overview of these methods, which break down into three categories: (1) on-the-job training, (2) schooling, and (3) organizational system developments. However, when actual management practices are analyzed, it is found that only 30 percent of the companies investigated in a field study[69] have formal project management development systems. Furthermore, companies that develop project management personnel build their systems around the experiential, on-the-job training methods supplemented by special courses, workshops, and professional activities. Table 48 indicates the relative time and effort that is being spent among the four training methods. The data indicate that, on the average, managers feel that 60 percent of the training time and effort should

---

[69] Details of this field study are discussed by H. Thamhain and D. Wilemon in "Developing Project/Program Managers," *Proceedings of the 1982 Symposium of the Project Management Institute.*

Table 47. Methods and Techniques for Developing Project Managers.

I. Experiential Training/On-the-job
- Working with experienced professional leader
- Working with project team member
- Assigning a variety of project management responsibilities, consecutively
- Job rotation
- Formal on-the-job training
- Supporting multifunctional activities
- Customer liaison activities

II. Conceptional Training/Schooling
- Courses, seminars, workshops
- Simulations, games, cases
- Group exercises
- Hands-on exercises in using p.m. techniques
- Professional meetings
- Conventions, symposia
- Readings, books, trade journals, professional magazines

III. Organizational Development
- Formally established and recognized project management function
- Proper project organization
- Project support systems
- Project charter
- Project management directives, policies, and procedures

Table 48. How to Train Project Managers.

Company Management Say Project Managers Can Be Trained in a Combination of Ways	
Experiential learning, on the job	60%
Formal education and special courses	20%
Professional activities, seminars	10%
Readings	10%

be spent on the job. Given the complexities and challenges of managing projects, it is not surprising that experiential learning is the primary method of gaining the needed skills and qualifications.

Further, on-the-job training has the advantage of teaching personnel methods and techniques hands-on while they contribute to the project, often on a fully applied basis, therefore minimizing any training cost to the organization.

HOW TO DEVELOP SENIOR PROJECT PERSONNEL

The methods described so far are relevant only for entry-level project personnel. However, this is a very critical need area. Management sees the identification and development of new project personnel as more important than that of their senior project people. The reason is that junior personnel, once successful, move on to new jobs. They leave a void that must be filled by newcomers to the project management field. Without a development program, the needed entry-level personnel are often not readily available, poorly qualified, and in the end often highly disillusioned and frustrated about project management.

Most senior project personnel, such as project managers and program directors, rely on the same methods to further their careers as described in Table 45. However, the process is less formal and is primarily based on the intrinsic motivation for professional development. In essence, it is the same process that underlies other management development activities. In addition, senior project personnel are often encouraged by their management to select and attend professional development seminars, conferences, and meetings. In the end it is a combination of skill development, hard work, and determination that will help to advance people up the organizational ladder.

RECOMMENDATIONS FOR DEVELOPING PROJECT MANAGERS

Making the project management development system work requires more than just another plan. Even in a small business organization, it requires the total commitment of management at all levels. To be successful companies must not only consider the training of their personnel but also devise systems for identifying prospective candidates, develop their project management support systems, assure equitable and attractive rewards consistent with the challenges and responsibilities involved, and have the role of project personnel delineated through charters, job descriptions, policies, procedures, and directives. Most importantly, management must foster a work environment that is professionally stimulating and conducive to teamwork. In such an environment the project management function will be self-developing to a large extent. That is, personnel from all levels and disciplines will see the professional and personal incentives of participating in project activities. There will be many volunteers who will compete for job openings in the project organization.

A number of suggestions are advanced that can potentially increase the effectiveness of a project-oriented business:

1. Carefully consider and analyze the specific needs of your project management function, including the development of project personnel, support systems, and organizations.
2. Define your work environment. Charters, job descriptions, and policies are helpful in all organizational endeavors, but they are absolutely crucial in defining and communicating the work environment, a prerequisite for training project personnel.
3. Understand your project organization, its interfaces, cultures, and value system. This will provide the basis for building a professionally stimulating work environment, the prerequisite for a self-developing project management system.
4. Plan your project personnel development in sufficient detail to make it operational. The plan should include key results, measurable milestones, budgets, and responsible individuals for each major activity.
5. Involve your management and human resource people in this organizational development, starting at the initial planning. This will develop the needed support, endorsement, and commitment.
6. Use the experiential, on-the-job training method as the cornerstone of your personnel development system.

7. Assure systematic tracking and follow-through of your development plan. Many project personnel system development programs do not achieve their anticipated results because of poor tracking and control. The initial enthusiasm and interest may evaporate quickly if progress is slow. The development program should be tracked and controlled like any other project, including status reviews and progress reports.
8. Management should tie the specific results of the development program into the performance reviews of the responsible individuals. Rewards can come in many forms, ranging from recognition for accomplishments, to incentives for higher operating efficiencies, to monetary rewards.
9. Take a multidisciplinary approach to organization development. Usually the problems are a mixture of human, technical, management, and organizational facets.
10. Avoid the label of a staff function for your organization development by involving all line and senior management.
11. Be aware of resistance to chance. Your development efforts may not be in tune with deeply rooted cultures and value systems of the organization. Your success will depend on cooperation, participation, trust, and a team spirit. Early involvement and participation of key personnel throughout the organization may help to ease this resistance to change.
12. Take a long-range approach. Organization developments are long-range rather than short-term fixes.
13. Assure that incentives and rewards for personnel are consistent with responsibilities and challenges to induce people to move in and up the project organization.
14. Do not panic if results are initially slow in coming. Complex, multidisciplinary developments are time consuming. Moreover, the results are perceived on the basis of potential benefits. If management and personnel in training see benefits in terms of their own career advancement or operating efficiencies or recognition by their peers and bosses, then the development program will be labeled successful. Continuous involvement of personnel at all levels, review meetings, short reports, and proper follow-through of action items will help to build the image of a credible and useful organization development program.

15. Assure that tangible results are produced early in the program. These results could include: actual staffing or project positions, promotions, provision of an additional service/support function, or reduction of some backlog or schedule.
16. Conduct audits of your development activity regularly, for instance semiannually. This will expose problems at their early stages where you can deal with them more readily. It will also help to build confidence and credibility for the program and your efforts.

HOW TO ADVANCE YOUR CAREER IN PROJECT MANAGEMENT

Project management provides a vehicle for fast-track career growth. Project organizations are dynamic regarding size, charter, and staffing levels. Work loads and manpower requirements fluctuate. No one has tenure in a project organization. People are recognized for their skills relevant to the immediate project needs and their real-time contributions. Responsibility and authority seem to gravitate toward those who are best suited to handle a particular job rather than being vested in a title or position. This is a work environment that recognizes job performance. High achievers usually enjoy increasing managerial responsibility and financial awards.

The person who is considering moving into or up to a career in project management should first find out what specific project job opportunities exist in his or her company, then assess the requirements, challenges, and benefits against the individual's needs, wants, and career goals. Once the individual concludes that he or she wants to pursue this career path, a specific development plan should be worked out by the individual and discussed with the superior. Although this discussion may not lead to an immediate change in responsibility and job content, it communicates to the boss the employee's career objectives and provides an opportunity for discussing the realism of the employee's ambitions. It may also offer helpful advice to the employee regarding specific experiences and skill development needed. Even if the superior does not support the employee's career plan the discussion may prepare him or her for seeking out opportunities with other organizations. Advancing a career requires a great deal of strategic vision plus skills in communications and information gathering and processing as a basis for organizing the array of career objectives and opportunities into a cohesive career development plan. Independent of the level of career objectives sought and the point in the career path, some specific suggestions may help in preparing for the next career move and in attaining continuous professional growth.

- Assess your own career needs in terms of job content, responsibilities, recognition, and financial needs.
- Assess the realities of your work environment by talking to people who already hold positions you are aspiring to. This will give you an insight into the type of work available, its challenges, and its skill requirements.
- Develop the skills needed in the new job. This can be done in part through courses, seminars, readings, and professional meetings, and experientially through your current position.
- Use your current position as a springboard. Apply the new knowledge you have gained in your current job. Seek out additional responsibilities that may prepare you for your next career move.
- Seek out specific opportunities for advancement such as participation in a bid proposal effort or the formation of a new program.
- Make your project management skills visible. Project review meetings and reports are good vehicles for showing to your management and your peers that you possess the needed skills for project planning and control. You can demonstrate that you clearly understand the management tools, such as for project scheduling and budgeting, and that you can apply them at an appropriate level.
- Give credit for accomplishment to others who participated and contributed to your project efforts. This builds a network of supporters.
- Grow with your present job. Find out about the broader business goals and objectives of your department. Seek out additional responsibilities that would support your career ambitions.
- Delegate. Utilize organizational resources and support as much as possible. You cannot take an additional responsibility unless

you delegate the work to others. This type of delegation does not require that support personnel be actually reporting to you, but simply means that you find out what technical and administrative support is available, company-internally or externally, and that you involve these support groups, plan for their participation, agree on the required resources, and subcontract with them.

Keeping Abreast and Ahead

- Trade shows
- Seminars and short courses
- Video tapes
- Trade magazines and journals
- Professional books
- Professional meetings
- New assignments
- Team interactions
- Job rotation
- Management briefings

PART VI
BIBLIOGRAPHY

Appendix A
A Project Management System Management Bibliography

1. Abt Associates Inc., *Applications of Systems Analysis Models: A Survey*. Washington, D.C.: Technology Utilization Division, Office of Technology Utilization, National Aeronautics and Space Administration, 1968.
2. Ackoff, Russell Lincoln, and Emery, Fred E., *On Purposeful Systems*. Chicago: Aldine/Atherton, 1972.
3. Ackoff, Russell Lincoln, *Redesigning the Future: A Systems Approach to Societal Problems*. New York: John Wiley, 1974.
4. Alderfer, Clayton P., *Change Processes in Organizations*. New Haven, Connecticut, Department of Administrative Sciences, Yale University, 1971.
5. Allen, Louis A., *The Professional Manager's Guide,* (USA: Louis A. Allen Associates, 1969).
6. Anthony, Robert N., Planning and Control Systems: *A Framework for Analysis*. Boston: Division of Research, Graduate School of Business Administration, Harvard Universtiy, 1965.
7. Archibald, Russell D., *Managing High-Technology Programs and Projects*. New York: John Wiley, 1976, pp. 55, 82, 176, 191.
8. Argyris, Chris, "How Tomorrow's Executives Will Make Decisions," *Think,* 33, 18-23, (November-December, 1967).
9. Argyris, Chris, "Resistance to Rational Management Systems," *Innovation,* issue 10: (1969), pp. 28-42.
10. Argyris, Chris, "Today's Problems with Tomorrow's Organizations," *Journal of Management Studies* 4: (February, 1967), pp. 31-55.
11. ARINC Research Corporation. *Guidebook for Systems Analysis/Cost Effectiveness.* Washington, D.C.: U.S. Department of Commerce, National Bureau of Standards; distributed by Clearinghouse for Federal Scientific and Technical Information, 1969.
12. Association for Systems Management. *An Annotated Bibliography for the Systems Professional,* 2nd ed. Cleveland: Association for Systems Management, 1970.

13. Avots, Ivars, "Why Does Project Management Fail?" *California Management Review* 12 (Fall, 1969), pp. 77–82.
14. Avots, Ivars, "Making Project Management Work: The Right Tools For the Wrong Project Manager," *S.A.M. Advanced Management Journal*, 40, 20–26, (Autumn, 1975).
15. Bachman, J., et al., "Bases of Supervisory Power: A Comparative Study in Five Organizational Settings," in *Control in Organizations*, A. Tannenbaum, ed. New York, McGraw-Hill, 1968, pp. 229–238.
16. Baker, Frank, ed. *Organizational Systems; General Systems Approaches to Complex Organizations*, Homewood, Illinois, R.D. Irwin Series in Management and the Behavioral Sciences, 1973.
17. Barnes, Lewis B., "Project Management and the Use of Authority: A Study of Structure, Role, and Influence Relationships in Public and Private Organizations," Ph.D. Dissertation, University of Southern California, 1971.
18. Baumgartner, John Stanley, *Project Management*, Homewood, Illinois, R.D. Irwin series, 1963.
19. Beckett, John A., *Management Dynamics: The New Synthesis*. New York: McGraw-Hill, 1971.
20. Benne, K.D. and Birnbaum, M., "Principles of Changing" in *The Planning of Change*, New York, Holt, Rinehart, and Winston, 1969.
21. Bennigson, Lawrence, "The Team Approach to Project Management," *Management Review* 61, (January 1972), pp. 48–52.
22. Benningson, Lawrence, *Project Management*, New York: McGraw-Hill, 1970.
23. Bennis, Warren G., "The Coming Death of Bureaucracy," *Think* 32: 30–35, (November-December 1966).
24. Benton, John Breen, *Managing the Organizational Decision Process*, Lexington, Mass, Lexington Books, 1973.
25. Berlinski, David J., "On Systems Analysis: An Essay Concerning the Limitations of some Mathematical Methods in the Social, Political, and Biological Sciences," Cambridge, Mass., M.I.T. Press, 1976.
26. Berrien, F. Kenneth, *General and Social Systems*, New Brunswick, N.J., Rutgers University Press, 1968.
27. Bertalanffy, Ludwig von, *General Systems Theory; Foundations, Development, Applications*, New York, G. Braziller, 1972.
28. ———, *General Systems Theory*, New York, G. Braziller, 1968.
29. Bingham, John E., and Davies, G.W.P., *A Handbook of Systems Analysis.* London, Macmillan, © 1972, 1974. Distributed in North America by Halsted Press, a division of John Wiley, New York and Toronto.
30. Blake, R.R. and Mouton, J.S., *The Managerial Grid*, Houston: Gulf Publishing, 1964.
31. Blankstein, Charles Sidney, "The Base Level Development Assistance Project: A Managerial Perspective," 1972. Cambridge, Mass: M.I.T., Thesis, M.S.
32. Block, Ellery B. "Accomplishment/Cost: Better Project Control." *Harvard Business Review* 49: (May 1971), pp. 110–24.
33. Bobrowski, T.M., "A Basic Philosophy of Project Management," *Journal of Systems Management*, May-June 1974.
34. Boulding, Kenneth, "General Systems Theory–The Skeleton of Science," *Management Science*, (April 1956), pp. 197–208.
35. Bowman, R.R., "An Analysis of Project Management Concepts in the Missile/Space Industry," MBA Thesis, Utah State University, 1967.
36. Boyatzis, R.E., "Building Efficacy: An Effective Use of Managerial Power," *Industrial Management Review*, 11, 1: 65–75, 1969.

37. ———, "Leadership: The Effective Use of Power," *Management of Personnel Quarterly,* Graduate School of Business Administration, University of Michigan (Fall, 1971), pp. 21-25. Reprinted in Richards, Max D., and William A. Nielander, *Readings in Management,* fourth edition, (Cincinnati, Southwestern Publishing Co., 1974), pp. 623-629.
38. Brandon, Dick H., and Gray, Max, *Project Control Standards,* Princeton, Brandon/Systems Press, 1970.
39. Burke, R.J., "Methods of Resolving Interpersonal Conflict," *Personnel Administration,* July-August, 1969, pp. 48-55.
40. ———, "Methods of Managing Superior-Subordinate Conflict," *Canadian Journal of Behavioral Science,* 2, 2: 124-135, 1970.
41. Burke, W.W. and Hornstein, H.A., *The Social Technology of Organization Development.* Fairfax, Virginia, NTL Learning Resources Corporation, 1972.
42. Burt, David N., "Getting the Right Price With the Right Contract," *Management Review* 24-34, (May, 1976).
43. Butler, Arthur G., Jr., "Project Management: A Study in Organizational Conflict," *Academy of Management Journal* 16, 84-101, (March, 1973).
44. ———, "Behavioral Implications for Professional Employees of Structural Conflict Associated with Project Management in Functional Organizations." Ph.D. Dissertation, University of Florida, 1969.
45. Butler, D., and Miller, N., "Power to Reward and Punish in Social Interaction," *Journal of Experimental Social Psychology,* 1, 4: 311-322, 1965.
46. Cicero, John P., and Wilemon, David L., "Project Authority: A Multidimensional View," *IEEE Transactions on Engineering Management,* EM-17: 52-57, (May 1970).
47. Chapman, Richard L. *Project Management in NASA: the System and the Men,* Washington: Scientific and Technical Information Office, National Aeronautics and Space Administration; for sale by the Superintendent of Documents, U.S. Government Printing Office, 1973.
48. Chen, Gordon K., and Kaczka, Eugene E., *Operations and Systems Analysis; A Simulation Approach,* Boston, Allyn and Bacon, 1974.
49. Churchman, Charles West, *The Systems Approach,* New York, Dell Publishing Company, 1968.
50. Cleland, David I., "Organizational Dynamics of Project Management," *IEEE Transactions on Engineering Management,* EM-13: 201-5, (December, 1966).
51. ———, "The Deliberate Conflict," *Business Horizon,* 11, 1: 78-80, (1968).
52. ———, "Project Management in Industry: An Assessment," *Project Management Quarterly,* 5, 2, 3: 19-21, (1974).
53. ———, "Defining A Project Management System," *Project Management Quarterly,* 8, 4: 37-40, (1977).
54. ———, "Why Project Management?" *Business Horizons,* 7: 81-88, (Winter, 1964).
55. Cleland, David I., and King, William R., *Management: A Systems Approach,* New York, McGraw-Hill, 1972.
56. ———, *Systems Analysis and Project Management,* New York, McGraw-Hill, 1968.
57. ———, *Systems Analysis and Project Management,* New York, McGraw-Hill, 1975. pp. 271, 371-380.
58. ———, *Systems, Organizations, Analysis, Management: A Book of Readings,* New York, McGraw-Hill, 1969.
59. Couger, J. Daniel, and Knapp, Robert W., (eds.) *System Analysis Techniques,* New York, John Wiley, 1974.

60. Crowston, Wallace B., "Models for Project Management," *Sloan Management Review,* 12: pp. 25-42, (Spring, 1971).
61. Cullingford, G. and Prideaux, J.D.C.A., "A Variational Study of Optimal Resource Profiles," *Management Science* 19: 1067-81, (May, 1973).
62. Dahl, R., "The Concept of Power," *Behavioral Science,* 2: 201-215, (July, 1957).
63. Datz, Marvin A. and Wilby, L.R., "What Is Good Project Management?" *Project Management Quarterly, 8,* 1: (March 1977).
64. Davis, Keith, "The Role of Project Management In Scientific Manufacturing," *Arizona Business Bulletin* 9: (May 1962), pp. 1-8.
65. ———, "The Role of Project Management in Scientific Manufacturing," *IRE Transactions on Engineering Management,* 9, 3, (1962).
66. Davis, S., "An Organic Problem-Solving Method of Organizational Change," *Journal of Applied Behavioral Science,* 3-21, (January, 1967).
67. Davis, Stanley, "Two Models of Organization: Unity of Command Versus Balance of Power," *Sloan Management Review,* (Fall, 1974), pp. 29-40.
68. Davis, S.M., and Lawrence, P.R., *Matrix,* Reading, Mass, Addison-Wesley, 1977.
69. De Greene, Kenyon Brenton, *Sociotechnical Systems: Factors in Analysis, Design, and Management.* Englewood Cliffs, N.J., Prentice-Hall, 1973.
70. ———, (ed.) *Systems Psychology,* New York: McGraw-Hill, 1970.
71. Delbecq, André L., Schull, Fremont A., Filley, Alan C., and Grimes, Andrew J., *Matrix Organization: A Conceptual Guide to Organizational Variation,* Wisconsin Business Papers No. 2. Madison, University of Wisconsin, Bureau of Business Research and Service, 1969.
72. Delbecq, André L., and Filley, Alan C., *Program and Project Management in a Matrix Organization: A Case Study,* Madison, University of Wisconsin, Bureau of Business Research and Service, 1974.
73. Dibble, E.T. and Suojanen, Waino, "Project Management in a Crisis Economy," *Infosystems-Spectrum,* 23: 44-46, (January, 1976).
74. Doering, Robert D., "An Approach Toward Improving the Creative Output of Scientific Task Teams," *IEEE Transactions on Engineering Management,* EM-20: 29-31, (February, 1973).
75. Earle, V.H., "Once Upon a Matrix: A Hindsight on Participation," *Optimum* 4, 28-36, 1973.
76. Eirich, Peter Lee, "An Information System Design Analysis for a Research Organization," Cambridge, Mass., M.I.T. M.S. Thesis, 1974.
77. Emery, F.E., *Systems Thinking: Selected Readings,* New York, Penguin Education, 1974.
78. Emery, J.C., *Organizational Planning and Control Systems,* New York, Macmillan, 1969.
79. Emshoff, James R., *Analysis of Behavioral Systems,* New York, Macmillan, 1971.
80. *European Conference on the Management of Large Space Programs,* (Paris, 1970), New York, Gordon and Breach Science Publishers, 1971.
81. Evan, W.M., "Conflict and Performance in R & D Organization," *Industrial Management Review,* 7: 37-45, (1965).
82. Evan, W.M., "Superior-Subordinate Conflict in Research Organizations," *Administrative Science Quarterly,* 52-64, (July, 1965).
83. Exton, William, *The Age of Systems: The Human Dilemma,* New York, American Management Association, 1972.
84. Fiore, Michael V., "Out of the Frying Pan into the Matrix," *Personnel Administration* 33, 3: 4-7, (1970).

85. Fisher, Gene Harvey, *Cost Considerations in Systems Analysis,* New York, American Elsevier, 1971.
86. Fitzgerald, John M. and Ardra F., *Fundamentals of Systems Analysis,* New York, Wiley, 1973.
87. Flaks, Marvin, and Archibald, Russell D., "The EE's Guide to Project Management," *Electronic Engineer* 27: 28+ (April, 1968); 20+ (May); 27-32 (June); 33-34+ (July); 33+ (August).
88. Forrester, Jay W., "A New Corporate Design," *Industrial Management Review* 7: 5-17 (Fall, 1965).
89. Frankwicz, Michael J., "A Study of Project Management Techniques," *Journal of Systems Management* 24: 18-22, (October, 1973).
90. French, J.R., Jr., and Raven, B., "The Bases of Social Power," in *Studies in Social Power,* D. Cartwright, (ed.), Ann Arbor, Mich.: Research Center for Group Dynamics, 1959, pp. 150-165.
91. Fried, Louis, "Don't Smother Your Project in People," *Management Advisor* 9: 46-49, (March, 1972).
92. Friend, Fred L., "Be A More Effective Program Manager," *Journal of Systems Management,* 27: 6-9, (February, 1976).
93. Fuller, R. Buckminster, *Synergetics: Explorations in the Geometry of Thinking,* New York, Macmillan, 1975.
94. Gaddis, P.O., "The Project Manager," *Harvard Business Review,* May-June, 89-97, (1959).
95. Galbraith, Jay R., "Matrix Organization Designs—How to Combine Functional and Project Forms," *Business Horizons,* February, 1971.
96. Geisler, M.A., "How to Plan for Management in New Systems," *Harvard Business Review,* September-October, 1962.
97. Gemmill, G., "Managerial Role Mapping," *The Management Personnel Quarterly,* 8, 3: 13-19, (Fall, 1969).
98. Gemmill, G., and H. Thamhain, "The Power Styles of Project Managers: Some Efficiency Correlates," *20th Annual JEMC, Managing for Improved Engineering Effectiveness* (Atlanta, Ga., Oct. 30-31, 1972), pp. 89-96.
99. Gemmill, G.R. and Thamhain, H.J., "Project Performance as a Function of the Leadership Styles of Project Managers: Results of a Field Study," *Convention Digest, 4th Annual Meeting of the Project Management Institute,* Philadelphia, October 18-21, 1972.
100. ———, "Influence Styles of Project Managers: Some Project Performance Correlates," *Academy of Management Journal,* 17, 2: pp. 216-224, (June, 1974).
101. Gemmill, Gary, and Thamhain, Hans J., "The Effectiveness of Different Power Styles of Project Managers in Gaining Project Support," *IEEE Transactions on Engineering Management* EM-20, 38-44, (May, 1973).
102. ———, "Interpersonal Power in Temporary Management Systems," *Journal of Management Studies,* (October, 1971).
103. ———, and Wilemon, David L., "The Power Spectrum in Project Management," *Sloan Management Review* 12: pp. 15-25, (Fall, 1970).
104. Gemmill, Gary and David Wilemon, "The Product Manager as an Influence Agent," *Journal of Marketing,* 36: 26-31, (January, 1972).
105. Gibson, James L., (ed.) *Readings in Organizations: Structure, Processes, Behavior,* Dallas, Business Publication, 1973.
106. Gildersleeve, Thomas R., *Data Processing Project Management,* New York, Van Nostrand Reinhold, 1974.

107. Gill, P.G., *Systems Management Techniques for Builders and Contractors,* New York, McGraw-Hill, 1968.
108. Goggin, William C., "How the Multidimensional Structure Works at Dow Corning," *Harvard Business Review,* pp. 54-65, (January-February 1974).
109. Goodman, Richard A. "Ambiguous Authority Definitions in Project Management," *Academy of Management Journal* 10: 395-408, (December, 1967).
110. Goodman, Richard A., "Organizational Preference in Research and Development," *Human Relations* 23: 279-298, 1970.
111. Goodman, R., "Ambiguous Authority Definition in Project Management," *Academy of Management Journal,* 10: 395-407, (1967).
112. Grinnell, S.K., and Apple, H.P., "When Two Bosses are Better than One," *Machine Design,* 9: 84-87, (January, 1975).
113. Grimes, A., S. Klein, and F. Shull, "Matrix Model: A Selective Empirical Test," *Academy of Management Journal,* 15, 1: 9-31, (March, 1972).
114. Gross, Paul F., *Systems Analysis and Design for Management,* New York, Dun-Donnelley, 1976.
115. Gullet, C. Ray, "Personnel Management in the Project Organization," *Personnel Administration and Public Personnel Review* 1: 17-22, (November, 1972).
116. Hall, D.M., *Management of Human Systems,* Cleveland, Ohio: Association for Systems Management, 1971.
117. Hall, H. Lawrence, "Management: A Continuum of Styles," *S.A.M. Advanced Management Journal* 33: pp. 68-74, (January, 1968).
118. Hansen, J.J., "The Case of the Precarious Program," *Harvard Business Review,* (January-February, 1968).
119. Center For, Health Research, "Health Research: The Systems Approach," New York, Springer, 1976.
120. Hellriegel, Don and John W. Slocum, Jr., "Organizational Design: A Contingency Approach," *Business Horizons,* 16, 2: pp. 59-68, (April 1, 1973). Reprinted in Richards, Max. D., and William A. Nielander, *Readings in Management,* fourth edition, (Cincinnati, Southwestern, 1974), pp. 516-527.
121. Hersey, Paul, and Blanchard, K.H., "The Management of Change," *Training and Development Journal,* 26, 1: (January, 1972); 26, 2: (February, 1972); and 26, 3: (March, 1972).
122. Hlavacik, James D., and Thompson, Victor A. "Bureaucracy and New Product Innovation," *Academy of Management Journal* 16: 361-72, (September, 1973).
123. Hodgetts, Richard M. "An Interindustry Analysis of Certain Aspects of Project Management," Ph.D. dissertation, University of Oklahoma, 1968.
124. ———, "Leadership Techniques in the Project Organization," *Academy of Management Journal* 11: 211-19, (June, 1968).
125. Hoge, R.R. "Research and Development Project Management: Techniques for Guiding Technical Programmes Towards Corporate Objectives," *Radio and Electronic Engineer* 39: pp. 33-48, (January, 1970).
126. Holland, Ted, "What Makes a Project Manager?" *Engineering* 207 262, (February 14, 1969).
127. Hoos, Ida Russakoff, *Systems Analysis in Public Policy; A Critique,* Berkeley, University of California Press, 1972.
128. Hopeman, Richard J., *Systems Analysis and Operations Management,* Columbus, Ohio, Merrill, 1969.

129. Hopeman, R.J. and D.L. Wilemon, *Project Management/Systems Management-Concepts and Applications,* Syracuse, Syracuse University/NASA, 1973.
130. Horowitz, J., *Critical Path Scheduling—Management Control Through CPM and PERT,* New York, Roland Press, 1967.
131. Houre, Henry Roland, *Project Management Using Network Analysis,* New York, McGraw-Hill, 1973.
132. Hynes, Cecil V., "Taking a Look at the Request For Proposal," *Defense Management Journal,* (October, 1977), pp. 26-31.
133. International Congress for Project Planning by Network Analysis, *Project Planning by Network Analysis,* Amsterdam, North-Holland Publishing Company, 1969.
134. Ivancevich, J., and J. Donnelly, "Leader Influence and Performance," *Personal Psychology,* 23: 539-549, (1970).
135. Jacobs, Richard A., "Project Management—A New Style For Success," *S.A.M. Advanced Management Journal,* 41: (Autumn 1976), pp. 4-14.
136. ———, "Putting Management Into Project Management," Paper presented at A.S.M. Workshops in Detroit, Tulsa, Oakland and Las Vegas (1976).
137. Janger, Allen R., "Anatomy of the Project Organization," *Business Management Record,* 12-18, (November, 1963).
138. Jantsh, Erich, *Design for Evolution; Self-Organization and Planning in the Life of Human Systems,* New York, G. Braziller, 1975.
139. Jenett, E., "Guidelines for Successful Project Management," *Chemical Engineering,* 70-82, (July 9, 1973).
140. Johnson, James R., "Advanced Project Control," *Journal of Systems Management,* 24-27, (May, 1977).
141. Johnson, Marvin M., (ed.) *Simulation Systems for Manufacturing Industries,* La Jolla, California: The Society for Simulation, Simulation Councils Inc., 1973.
142. Johnson, Richard Arvid, Newell, William T., and Vergin, Roger C., *Operations Management; A Systems Concept,* Boston, Houghton-Mifflin, 1972.
143. Johnson, R.A., Kast, F.E., and Rosenzweig, J.E., *The Theory and Management of Systems,* New York, McGraw-Hill, 1973.
144. Jonason, Per, "Project Management, Swedish Style," *Harvard Business Review,* 104-109, (Nov/December, 1971).
145. Kahn, R.L., Wolfe, D.M., Quinn, R.P., Snock, J.D., and Rosenthal, R.A., *Organizational Stress: Studies in Role Conflict and Ambiguity,* New York, John Wiley, 1964.
146. Kast, Fremont E., and Rosenzweig, James E. "Organization and Management of Space Programs," in *On Advances in Space Science and Technology,* edited by Frederick I. Ordway III, New York, Academic Press, 1965.
147. ———, *Organization and Management; A Systems Approach.* 2nd ed., New York, McGraw-Hill, 1974.
148. Kast, F.E. and Rosenzweig, J.E. *Contingency Views of Organization and Management,* Science Research Associates, 1973.
149. Kast, D. "The Motivational Basis of Organizational Behavior," *Behavioral Science,* 9, 2: 131-143, (1964).
150. Kelleher, Grace J., (ed.) *The Challenge to Systems Analysis: Public Policy and Change,* New York, Wiley-Interscience, 1970.
151. Kelley, William F., *Management Through Systems and Procedures: A Systems Concept,* New York, 1969.
152. Kerzner, Harold, "Systems Management and the Engineer," *Journal of Systems Management,* 18-21, (October, 1977).

153. Killian, William P., "Project Management—Future Organizational Concepts," *Marquette Business Review* 2: 90–107, (1971).
154. Kindred, Alton R., *Data Systems and Management: An Introduction to Systems Analysis and Design,* Englewood Cliffs, N.J., Prentice-Hall, 1973.
155. Kingdon, Donald R., "The Management of Complexity in an Matrix Organization: A Socio-Technical Approach to Changing Organizational Behavior," Los Angeles, University of California, M.S. thesis, 1969.
156. ———, *Matrix Organization: Managing Information Technologies,* London, Tavistock Publications, 1973.
157. Kirchner, Englebert, "The Project Manager." *Space Aeronautics,* 43: 56–64, (February, 1965).
158. Klir, George J., *Trends in General Systems Theory,* New York: John Wiley, 1972.
159. Koplow, Richard A., "From Engineer to Manager—And Back Again," *IEEE Transactions on Engineering Management,* EM-14: 88–92, (June, 1967).
160. Larsen, Niels Ove, "An Evaluation of Managerial Strategies for Dealing with Work Pressure in a Project Oriented Environment," Ph.D. dissertation, M.I.T., Alfred P. Sloan School of Management, 1969.
161. Laszlo, Ervin, *A Strategy for the Future: The Systems Approach to World Order,* New York, G. Braziller, 1974.
162. Lawrence, Paul R. and Lorsch, Jay W., "New Management Job: The Integrator," *Harvard Business Review,* 142, (November/December, 1967).
163. Lawrence, P.R. and Lorsch, J.W., *Organization and Environment,* Boston, Division of Research, Harvard Business School, 1967.
164. Lazer R.G., and A.G. Kellner, "Personnel and Organizational Development in an R and D Matrix-Overlay Operation," *IEEE Transactions on Engineering Management,* EM-11: 78–82, (June, 1964).
165. Ler, Alec M., *Systems Analysis Frameworks,* New York, Wiley, 1970.
166. Lewin, K., "Frontiers in Group Dynamics," *Human Relations,* 1. 1, (1947).
167. Lewin, K., "Group Decision and Social Change," in Maccoby, E.E., *et al., Readings in Social Psychology,* New York: Holt, Rinehart, and Winston, 1958, pp. 197–211.
168. Livingstone, G.S. "Weapon System Contracting," *Harvard Business Review,* (July-August, 1959).
169. Lock, D., *Project Management,* London, Gower Press, 1969.
170. Logistics Management Institute, *Introduction to Military Program Management,* Washington, D.C.: Superintendent of Documents, U.S. Government Printing Office, 1971.
171. London, Keith R., *The People Side of Systems: The Human Aspects of Computer Systems,* New York, McGraw-Hill, 1976.
172. Ludwig, Ernest E., *Applied Project Management for the Process Industries,* Houston, Texas, Gulf Publishing Company, 1974.
173. Lutes, Gerald Scott, "Project Selection and Scheduling in the Massachusetts Department of Public Works," M.S. Thesis M.I.T. Alfred P. Sloan School of Management, 1974.
174. McGregor, D., *The Professional Manager,* New York, McGraw-Hill, 1967.
175. McMillan, Claude, and Gonzalez, Richard F., *Systems Analysis: A Computer Approach to Decision Models,* Irwin, Homewood, Ill., 1973.
176. Maieli, Vincent, "Management by Hindsight: Diary of a Project Manager," *Management Review,* 60: 4–14, (June, 1971).
177. ———, "Sowing the Seeds of Project Cost Overruns," *Management Review,* 61: 7–14, (August, 1972).

178. Maier, N.R., and Hoffman, L.R., "Acceptance and Quality of Solutions as Related to Leader's Attitudes Toward Disagreement in Group Problem Solving," *Journal of Applied Behavioral Science*, 373-386, (1965).
179. Marquis, D.G., and Straight, J.R., D.M., "Organizational Factors in Project Performance," Working Paper pp. 133-65, Cambridge, M.I.T., School of Management, 1965.
180. Martin, Charles C., *Project Management: How to Make It Work*, New York, Amacom, 1976, pp. 41, 137.
181. Martin, James Thomas, *Systems Analysis for Data Transmission*, Englewood Cliffs, Prentice-Hall, 1972.
182. Martino, R.L., *Project Management*, Wayne, Pa., MDI Publications, Management Development Institute, 1968.
183. ———, *Resources Management*. Wayne, Pa., MDI Publications, Management Development Institute, 1968.
184. Matthies, Leslie H., *The Management Systems: Systems are People*, New York, Wiley, 1976.
185. Mechanic, D., "Sources of Power of Lower Participants in Complex Organizations," *Administrative Science Quarterly*, 7: 349-364, (December, 1962).
186. Mee, John, F., "Project Management," *Business Horizons*, 6: 53-55, (Fall, 1963).
187. ———, "Matrix Organization," *Business Horizons*, 70, (Summer, 1964).
188. Melchner, Arlyn J., (ed.), *General Systems and Organization Theory: Methodological Aspects*, Kent, Ohio, Kent University Press, 1975.
189. Melchner, Arlyn J., and Kayser, Thomas A., "Leadership without Formal Authority: The Project Department," *California Management Review*, 13, 2: 57-64, (1970).
190. Meinhart, W.A., and Delionback, Leon M., "Project Management: An Incentive Contracting Decision Model," *Academy of Management Journal*, 11: 427-34, (December, 1968).
191. Metz, William W., "Identification and Analysis of Research and Development Project Management Problems Based on Nonnuclear Munitions Development in the Air Force," Ph.D. dissertation, George Washington University, 1970.
192. Middleton, C.J., "How to Set Up a Project Organization," *Harvard Business Review* 45: 73-82, (March-April, 1967).
193. Miller, E.J., *Systems of Organization*, New York, Barnes and Noble Book Company, 1967.
194. Moder, Joseph J., and Phillips, Cecil R., *Project Management with CPM and PERT*, 2nd ed., New York, Van Nostrand Reinhold, 1970.
195. Mordlea, Irwin, "A Comparison of a Research and Development Laboratory's Organization Structures," *IEEE Transactions on Engineering Management*, EM-14, 170-76, (December, 1967).
196. Morgan, John, "Coping with Resistance to Change," *Ideas for Management*, Cleveland, Ohio, Association for Systems Management, 1971.
197. Morton, D.H., "The Project Manager, Catalyst to Constant Change: A Behavioral Analysis," *Project Management Quarterly*, 6, 1: 22-3, (1975).
198. Mungo, B.B. "Management Studies in the Field of Aeronautics: Management of Projects," *Journal of the Royal Aeronautical Society*, 71, 334-36; 336-38, (May, 1967).
199. Myers, S.M., Conditions for Manager Motivation, *Harvard Business Review*, 58-71, (Jan-Feb. 1966).
200. NATO Institute on Decomposition as a Tool for Solving Large-Scale Problems, Cambridge, England, *Decomposition of Large-Scale Problems*, Amsterdam, North-Holland Publishing Company, 1973.

201. Neuschel, Richard F., *Management Systems for Profit and Growth*, New York, McGraw-Hill, 1976.
202. O'Brien, James B., "The Project Manager: Not Just a Firefighter," *S.A.M. Advanced Management Journal*, 39: 52-56, (January, 1974).
203. Optner, Stanford L., *Systems Analysis for Business and Industrial Problem Solving*, Englewood Cliffs, N.J., Prentice-Hall, 1965.
204. ———, *Systems Analysis for Business Management*, Englewood Cliffs, N.J., Prentice-Hall, 1968.
205. ———, *Systems Analysis for Business Management*, Englewood Cliffs, N.J., Prentice-Hall, 1975.
206. ———, "Organizational Preference in Research and Development," *Human Relations*, 23: 279-98, (August, 1970).
207. Ouchi, W., *Theory Z*, Reading, Mass., Addison-Wesley, 1981.
208. Oyer, David William, "The Use of Automated Project Management Systems to Improve Information Systems Development, Cambridge, Mass.: M.S. Thesis, Alfred P. Sloan School of Management, M.I.T. 1975.
209. Pastore, Joseph M. "Organizational Metamorphosis: A Dynamic Model," *Marquette Business Review*, 15: 17-31, (Spring, 1971).
210. Patchen, M., *Some Questionnaire Measures of Employee Motivation and Morale: A Report on their Reliability and Validity*, Ann Arbor, Michigan: Institute for Social Research, 1965.
211. Paul, W.J., K. Robertson, and F. Herzberg, "Job Enrichment Pays Off," *Harvard Business Review*, 47, 2: 61-78, (1969).
212. Peart, Alan Thomas, *Design of Project Management Systems and Records*, London, Gower Press, 1971.
213. ———, *Design of Project Management Systems and Records*. Boston, Cahners Books, 1971.
214. Pegels, C. Carl, *Systems Analysis for Production Operations*, New York, Gordon and Science Publishers, 1976.
215. Pondy, L.R., "Organizational Conflict: Concepts and Models," *Administrative Science Quarterly*, 298-307, (September, 1967).
216. Potter, William J., "Management in the Ad-hocracy," *S.A.M. Advanced Management Journal*, 39: 19-23, (July, 1974).
217. Reeser, Clayton, "Some Potential Human Problems of the Project Form of Organization," *Academy of Management Journal*, 12: 459-68, (December, 1969).
218. Rogers, L.A., "Guidelines for Project Management Teams," *Industrial Engineering*, 12, (December, 1974).
219. Rudwick, Bernard H., *Systems Analysis for Effective Planning: Principles and Cases*, New York, Wiley, 1969.
220. Rubin, Irwin M., and Seilig, Wychlam, "Experience as a Factor in the Selection and Performance of Project Managers," *IEEE Transactions on Engineering Management* EM 131-35, (September, 1967).
221. Sadler, Philip, "Designing an Organization Structure," (publication source unknown).
222. Sapolsky, Harvey M., *The Polaris System Development: Bureaucratic and Programmatic Success in Government*, Cambridge, Mass., Harvard University Press, 1972.
223. Sayels, Leonard R., and Chandler, Margaret K., *Managing Large Systems: Organizations for the Future*, New York, Harper and Row, 1971.
224. Schaller, L.E., *The Change Agent*, New York, Abington Press, 1972.
225. Schoderbek, Peter P., Kefalas, A.G., and Schoderbek, Charles G., *Management Systems: Conceptual Considerations*, Dallas, Business Publications, 1975.

226. Schmidt, Joseph William, *Mathematical Foundations for Management Science and Systems Analysis,* New York, Academic Press, 1974.
227. Schroder, Harold J., "Making Project Management Work," *Management Review,* 54: 24-28, (December, 1970).
228. ———, "Project Management: Controlling Uncertainty," *Journal of Systems Management,* 24: 28-29, (February, 1975).
229. Seiler, J.A., "Diagnosing Interdepartmental Conflict," *Harvard Business Review,* 121-132, (September-October 1963).
230. Shah, Ramesh P., "Project Management: Cross Your Bridges Before You Come to Them," *Management Review,* 60: 21-27, (December, 1971).
231. Sharad, D., "About Delays, Overruns and Corrective Actions," *Project Management Quarterly,* 21-25, (December, 1976).
232. Shannon, Robert E., "Matrix Management Structures," *Industrial Engineering* 4, 26-29, (March, 1972).
233. Sheriff, M., "Superordinate Goals in the Reduction of Intergroup Conflict," *American Journal of Sociology,* 63: 349-358, (1958).
234. Shrode, William A., and Voich, Dan Jr., *Organization and Management: Basic Systems Concepts,* Homewood, Illinois, R.D. Irwin, 1974.
235. Shull, Fremont, and Judd, R.J., "Matrix Organizations and Control Systems," *Management International Review* 11, 6: 65-72, (1971).
236. Shull, Fremont A., *Matrix Structure and Project Authority for Optimizing Organizational Capacity,* Business Science Monograph No. 1. Carbondale, Business Research Bureau, Southern Illinois University, 1965.
237. Simmons, John R., *Management of Change: The Role of Information,* (based on a research project sponsored by the Institute of Office Management), London, Gee & Company, 1970.
238. Sivazlian, B.D., and Stanfeld, L.E., *Analysis of Systems in Operations Research,* Englewood Cliffs, N.J., Prentice-Hall, 1973.
239. Smith, G.A., "Program Management—Art or Science?" *Mechanical Engineering* 96, 18-22, (September, 1974).
240. Smith, Michael Gary, *PCS: A Project Control System,* Ph.D. thesis, M.I.T., Cambridge, Mass., 1973.
241. Smith, William N., "Problem-Solving and Bargaining as Modes of Constructive Conflict Resolution in Aerospace Matrix Organizations," Ph.D. thesis, University of California, Los Angeles, 1972.
242. Smyster, Craig H., "A Comparison of the Needs of Program and Functional Management" (unpublished masters thesis), School of Engineering, Wright-Patterson Air Force Base, Air Force Institute of Technology, 1965.
243. Starr, Martin Kenneth, *Production Management: Systems and Synthesis,* 2nd ed., Englewood, N.J., Prentice-Hall, 1972.
244. Stasch, Stanley F., *Systems Analysis for Marketing Planning and Control,* Glenview, Illinois, Scott, Foresman, 1972.
245. Steger, W.A., "How to Plan for Management in New Systems," *Harvard Business Review,* (September-October), 1962.
246. Steiner, George A., "Project Managers' Problems with the Development of High Performance Aerospace Systems," *Astronautics and Aeronautics,* 75-76, (June, 1966).
247. ———, and Ryan, William G., *Industrial Project Management,* New York, Macmillan, 1968, p. 24.
248. Stewart, John M., "Making Project Management Work," *Business Horizons* 8: 54-68, (Fall, 1965).

249. Stopher, Peter R., and Meyburg, Arnim H., *Transportation Systems Evaluation,* Lexington, Massachusetts, Lexington Books, 1976.
250. Tannenbaum, Robert and Warren H. Schmidt, "How to Choose a Leadership Pattern," *HBR Classic,* 162-180, (May-June, 1973).
251. Taylor, W.J., and Watling, T.F., *Successful Project Management,* London, Business Books, 1970, p. 32-; 1972.
252. ———, "Teamwork Through Conflict," *Business Week,* 44-45, (March 20, 1971).
253. Thamhain, Hans J., and Wilemon, David L., "Diagnosing Conflict Determinants in Project Management," *IEEE Transactions on Engineering Management,* EM-22, 35-44, (February, 1975).
254. ———, and Gemmill, Gary R., "Influence Styles of Project Managers: Some Project Performance Correlates," *Academy of Management Journal,* 17, 216-24, (June, 1974).
255. Thamhain, H.J., and Wilemon, D.L., "Conflict Management in Project-Oriented Work Environments," *Proceedings of the Sixth International Meeting of the Project Management Institute,* Washington, D.C., September 18-21, 1974.
256. ———, "Conflict Management in Project Life Cycles," *Sloan Management Review,* 31-50, (Summer, 1975).
257. ———, "The Effective Management of Conflict in Project-Oriented Work Environments," *Defense Management Journal* 11, 3: 975, (1978).
258. Thamhain, Hans J., and Wilemon, David L., "Leadership Effectiveness in Project Management," *Proceedings of Eighth Annual Symposium of the Project Management Institute,* Montreal, Canada, 1976.
259. Thamhain, Hans J., and Gemmill, Gary R., "The Effectiveness of Different Power Styles of Project Managers," *Project Management Quarterly,* 5, 1 (Spring, 1974).
260. Thamhain, Hans J., and Wilemon, David L., "Leadership, Conflict and Program Management Effectiveness," *Sloan Management Review* (Fall, 1977).
261. ———, ———, and Dugan, H.S., "Managing Change in Project Management," *Convention Record of the Ninth Annual Symposium of the Project Management Institute,* Chicago, 1977.
262. ———, and ———, "Skill Requirements of Engineering Program Managers," *Professional Engineer Magazine* (February, 1979).
263. ———, and ———, "Team Building in Project Management," *Proceedings of the 21st Annual Symposium of the Project Management Institute* (October, 1979).
264. ———, and ———, "Project Performance Measurement," *Proceedings, PMI-Internet Joint Symposium,* Boston, 1981.
265. ———, and ———, "Marketing for Project-Oriented Business," *PMI-Quarterly* (December, 1981).
266. Thamhain, Hans J., "Performing Effectively in Engineering Management," *IEEE Transactions on Engineering Management* (December, 1982).
267. Thompson, J.D., *Organization in Action,* New York, McGraw-Hill, 1967.
268. Thompson, Victor A., "Bureaucracy and Innovation," *Administrative Science Quarterly* 10: 1-20, (June, 1965).
269. Toellner, John, "Project Estimating," *Journal of Systems Management,* 6-9, (May, 1977).
270. Trower, Michael H., "Fast Track to Project Delivery: Systems Approach to Project Management," *Management Review* 62 19-23, (April, 1973).
271. Tsai, Martin Chia-Ping, "Contingent Conditions for the Creation of Temporary Management Organizations," M.S. thesis, Alfred, P. Sloan School of Management, M.I.T., Cambridge, Mass., 1976.

BIBLIOGRAPHY

272. Vaughn, Dennis Henry, "Key Variables of a Management Information System for a Department of Defense Project Manager," M.S. thesis, Alfred P. Sloan School of Management, M.I.T., Cambridge, Mass., 1976.
273. ———, "Understanding Project Management," *Manage* 19, 9: 52-58, (1967).
274. Wadsworth, M., *EDP Project Management Controls,* Englewood Cliffs, N.J., Prentice-Hall, 1972.
275. Walton, R.E., and Dutton, J.M., "The Management of Interdepartmental Conflict: A Model and Review," *Administrative Science Quarterly,* 14, 1: 73-84, (March, 1969).
276. Walton, R.E., and Dutton, J.M., and Cafferty, T.P., "Organizational Contest and Interdepartmental Conflict," *Administrative Science Quarterly,* 14, 4: 522-542, (December, 1969).
277. Webb, James E. "NASA as an Adaptive Organization," in *On Technological Change and Management,* ed., by David W. Ewing. Cambridge, Massachusetts, Harvard University Press, 1970.
278. Weinberg, Gerald M., *An Introduction to General Systems Thinking,* New York, Wiley, 1975.
279. Wetzel, John Jay, "Project Control at the Managerial Level in the Automotive Engineering Environment," M.S. thesis, Alfred P. Sloan School of Management, M.I.T. Cambridge, Mass., 1973.
280. Whitehouse, Gary E., "Project Management Techniques," *Industrial Engineering 5:* 24-29, (March, 1973).
281. ———, *Systems Analysis and Design Using Network Techniques,* Englewood Cliffs, N.J., Prentice-Hall, 1973.
282. Whiting, Richard J., "In Defense of Functional Organization," *Management Review, 58,* 7: 49-52, (July, 1969).
283. Wilemon, David L., "Managing Conflict in Temporary Management Systems," *Journal of Management Studies 10:* 282-96, (October, 1973).
284. Wilemon, D.L., "Project Management Conflict. A View from Apollo," *Third Annual Symposium of the Project Management Institute,* Houston, Texas, (October, 1971).
285. ———, "Managing Conflict on Project Teams," *Management Journal,* 28-34, (Summer, 1974).
286. Wilemon, D.L., "Project Management and its Conflicts: A View from Apollo," *Chemical Technology,* 2, 9: 527-534, (September, 1972).
287. ———, and Gary R. Gemmill, "Interpersonal Power in Temporary Management Systems," *Journal of Management Studies,* 8: 315-28, (October, 1971).
288. ———, and Cicero, John P., "The Project Manager: Anomalies and Ambiguities," *Academy of Management Journal* 13: 269-82, (September, 1970).
289. Willoughby, Theodore C. *Business Systems,* Cleveland, Association for Systems Management, 1975.
290. ———, and Senn, J.A., *Business Systems,* The Association for Systems Management, 1975.
291. Wilson, Ira Gaulbert, *Management Innovation and System Design,* Princeton, Auerbach, 1971.
292. Woodgate, Harry Samuel, *Planning by Network: Project Planning and Control Using Network Techniques,* London, Business Publications, 1967.
293. Wooldridge, Susan, *Project Management in Data Processing,* 1st ed., New York, Petrocelli/Charter, 1976.
294. Wrong, D., "Some Problems in Defining Social Power," *American Journal of Sociology,* 73, 6: 673-681, (May, 1968).

Appendix B
Competitive Bidding Bibliography

1. Anderson, R.M., "Handling Risk in Defense Contracting," *Harvard Business Review* (1969), pp. 90-98.
2. Arps, J.J., "A Strategy for Sealed Bidding," *Journal Petroleum Technology*, 1033, (September, 1965).
3. Baumgarten, R.M., "Discussion for Opbid-Competitive Bidding Strategy Model" by Morin and Clough, *Journal of the Construction Division of ASCE 96*, 88, (1970).
4. Benjamin, N.B.H., "Competitive Bidding for Building Construction Contracts," Technical Report No. 106, Department of Civil Engineering, Stanford University, June 1969.
5. Bell, L.B., "A System for Competitive Bidding," *Journal of Systems Management 20*, 26-29, (1969).
6. Bristor, J.D., "Discussion for Bidding Strategies and Probabilities, by Gates" (March, 1967), *Proceedings of the American Society of Civil Engineers Journal*, Construction Division 94, 109, (1968).
7. Bristor, J.D., "Discussion for 'Bidding-Work Loading Game' by Torgersen, *et al.*" (October, 1968), *Proceedings of the American Society of Civil Engineers Journal*, Construction Division 95, 139-140, (1969).
8. Broemser, G.M., "Competitive Bidding in the Construction Industry," Ph.D. dissertation, Stanford University, California, 1968.
9. Brown, K.C., "A Theoretical and Statistical Study of Decision-Making under Uncertainty – Competitive Bidding for Leases on Offshore Petroleum Lands," Ph.D. dissertation, Southern Methodist University, Dallas, Texas, 1966.
10. Casey, B.J. and L.R. Shaffer, "An Evaluation of Some Competitive Bid Strategy Models for Contractors," Report No. 4, Department of Civil Engineering, University of Illinois, Urbana, Illinois.
11. Christenson, C., *Strategic Aspects of Competitive Bidding for Corporate Securities*, Boston, Mass., Division of Research, Harvard, University School of Business.
12. Clough, R.H., *Construction Contracting*, Appendix L, 2nd Ed., New York, John Wiley, 1969.
13. Cook, Paul W., Jr., "Fact and Fancy on Identical Bids," *Harvard Business Review, 41*, 67-72 (January-February, 1963).

14. Crawford, P.B., "Pattern of Offshore Bidding," Society of Petroleum Engineers of AIME, Paper No. 2613, Dallas, Texas, 1969.
15. Crosby, A.R., "The Client/Contractor Syndrome," *Chemical Engineering Program 61*, 11, 44–48, (1965).
16. Edelman, F., "Art and Science of Competitive Bidding," *Harvard Business Review 43*, 53–66, (July-August, 1965).
17. Emerick, R.H., "How to Find the Unforeseen in Competitive Bidding," *Power Engineering 69*, 45–46, (August, 1965).
18. Flueck, J.A., "A Statistical Decision Theory Approach to a Seller's Bid Pricing Problem under Uncertainty," Ph.D. thesis, University of Chicago, School of Business, 1967.
19. Frey, J.B., "Competitive Bidding on General Construction Contracts," Ph.D. thesis, University of Delaware, 1962.
20. Friedman, L., "A Competitive Bidding Strategy," *Operations Research 4*, 104-112, (1956).
21. Gates, M., "Aspects on Competitive Bidding," Connecticut Society of Civil Engineers, 1959.
22. Gates, M., "Statistical and Economic Analysis of a Bidding Trend," *Journal of the Construction Division*, ASCE, Paper 2651, 13-35 (November, 1960).
23. Gates, M., "Bidding Strategies and Probabilities," *Journal of the Construction Division*, ASCE, Paper 5159, *93*, 75–107, (1967); and subsequent closure, p. *96*, 77–78 and *93*, (1970).
24. Green, P., "Bayesian Decision Theory in Pricing Strategy," *Journal of Marketing 27*, 5–14, (1963).
25. Griesmer, J.H. and M. Shubik, "The Theory of Bidding," IBM Research Report, RC-629, IBM Research Center, Yorktown Heights, N.Y., (March 1, 1962).
26. Griesmer, J.H. and M. Shubik, "The Theory of Bidding II," IBM Research Report, RC-688, IBM Research Center, Yorktown Heights, N.Y., (May 25, 1962).
27. Griesmer, J.H. and M. Shubik, "The Theory of Bidding III," IBM Research Report, RC-874, IBM Research Center, Yorktown Heights, N.Y., (January 29, 1963).
28. Griesmer, J.H., R.E. Levitan, and M. Shubik, "Towards a Study of Bidding Processes, Part Four, Unknown Competitive Costs–," IBM Research Paper RC-1532, IBM Research Center, Yorktown Heights, N.Y., (January, 1966).
29. Hanssman, F. and Rivett, B.H.P., "Competitive Bidding," *Operations Research, Quarterly 10*, 49-55, (1959).
30. Harsanyi, J.C., "Games with Incomplete Information Played by Bayesian Players, Parts I-III," *Management Science 14*, 159-182, 320-334, 486-502, (1967-68).
31. Hugo, G.R., "How to Prepare Bids for Crown Lease Sales," *Oil Week 16*, 56-60, (1965).
32. Lavalle, I.H., "A Bayesian Approach to an Individual Player's Choice of Bid in Competitive Sealed Auctions," *Management Science 13*, A584-597, (1967).
33. Moriguti, S. and S. Suganami, "Notes on Auction Bidding," *J. Opns. Res. Soc. (Japan), 2*, 43-59, (1959).
34. Morin, T.L., and R.H. Clough, "Opbid–Competitive Bidding Strategy Model," *Journal of Construction Division*, ASCE, Paper 6690; (June, 1970) and subsequent discussion, pp. *96*, 88-97.
35. Ortega-Reichert, A., "Models for Competitive Bidding under Uncertainty," Technical Report No. 103, Department of Operations Research, Stanford University, Stanford, California, January, 1968.
36. Park, W.R., "How Low to Bid to Get Both Job and Profit," *Engineering News-Record 168*, 38-40, (April 19, 1962).

37. Park, W.R., "Less Bidding for Bigger Profits," *Engineering News-Record 170*, 41 (February 14, 1963).
38. Park, W.R., "Bidders and Job Size Determine Your Optimum Markup, *Engineering News-Record 170*, 122-123, (June 13, 1963).
39. Park, W.R., "Bidding: When to Raise and When to Fold," *The Modern Builder*, Kansas City, Mo., (July, 1963).
40. Park, W.R., "The Problem of Breaking Even," *The Modern Builder*, Kansas City, Mo. (September, 1963).
41. Park, W.R., "The Strategy of Bidding for Profit," *The Modern Builder*, Kansas City, Mo. (September, 1963).
42. Park, W.R., "Better Bidding Will Beget Bigger Profits," *The Modern Builder*, Kansas City, Mo. (October, 1963).
43. Park, W.R., "How Much to Make to Cover Costs," *Engineering News-Record 171*, 168-170, (December 19, 1963).
44. Park, W.R., "It Takes a Profit to Make a Profit," *Mid-West Contractor*, Kansas City, Mo. (March 11, 1964).
45. Park, W.R., "Profit Optimization Through Strategic Bidding," *AACE Bulletin, 6*, 5 (December, 1964).
46. Park, W.R., *The Strategy of Contracting for Profit*. Englewood Cliffs, N.J., Prentice-Hall, 1966.
47. Rothkopf, M.H., "A Model of Rational Competitive Bidding," *Management Science 15*, 362-373, (1969).
48. Sakaguchi, M., "Mathematical Solutions to Some Problems of Competitive Bidding," *Proceedings of the Third International Conference on Operational Res.* (Oslo, 1963), 1964, pp. 179-191, Dunod (Paris) and English University Press (London).
49. Schlaifer, R., *Probability and Statistics for Business Decisions*. New York, McGraw-Hill, 1959.
50. Simmonds, K., "Adjusting Bias in Cost Estimates," *Opnal. Res. Quart., 19*, 325-327, (1968).
51. Simmonds, K., "Competitive Bidding—Deciding the Best Combination of Non-Price Features," *Operational Research Quarterly 19*, 5-15, (1968).
52. Stark, Robert M., "Competitive Bidding: A Comprehensive Bibliography," *Opns. Res. 19*, 484-490, (1971).
53. Symonds, G.H., "A Study of Management Behavior by Use of Competitive Business Games," *Management Science 11*, 135-153, (1964).
54. Vickrey, W., "Counterspeculation, Auctions, and Competitive Sealed Tenders," *Journal of Finance 16*, 8-37, (1961).
55. Wasson, C.R., *Understanding Qualitative Analysis*, New York, Appleton-Century-Crofts, 1969.
56. Wilson, R.B., "Competitive Bidding with Disparate Information," Working Paper No. 114, Graduate School of Business, Stanford University, October 1966.
57. Wilson, R.B., "Competitive Bidding with Asymmetrical Information," *Management Science 13*, A816-820, (1967).
58. Wilson, R.B., "Competitive Bidding with Disparate Options," *Management Science 15*, 46-48, (1969).

COMPETITIVE BIDDING REFERENCE SOURCES

Handbooks and Reference Books

Anatomy of a Win by Jim M. Beveridge, J.M. Beveridge Associates, 8448 Wagner Creek Road, Talent, Ore. 97540, 1978.

Business Guide to Dealing with the Federal Government, Drake Publishers Incorporated, 381 Park Avenue South, New York, N.Y. 10016, 1973 ($3.95).

Contract Planning and Organization, United Nations Publications, United Nations, LX2300, New York, N.Y. 10017, 1974 ($2.50).

Creating Superior Proposals by Jim M. Beveridge and E.J. Velton, J.M. Beveridge Associates, 8448 Wagner Creek Road, Talent, Ore. 97540, 1978.

Gordon's Modern Annotated Forms of Agreement by S. Gordon and S. Kuzman, Prentice-Hall, Englewood Cliffs, N.J. 07632, 1969.

Guide for Drawing up Contracts for Large Industrial Works, United Nations Publications, United Nations, LX2300, New York, N.Y. 10017, 1972 (1.50).

A Handbook for Proposal Preparation and Management by Roy Loring and Harold Kerzner, Van Nostrand Reinhold, New York, 1982.

How to Create a Winning Proposal, by J. Ammon-Wexler and Catherine ap Carmel, Mercury Communications, 730 Mission Street, Santa Cruz, Calif. 95060, 1977.

Selling to United States Government, United States Small Business Administration, Washington, D.C. 20416, 1973 (free).

What You Should Know About Contracts, by Robert A. Farmer, Arco Publishing Company, 219 Park Avenue South, New York, N.Y. 10003, 1969 ($4.95).

Periodicals and Newspapers

Briefing Papers, Federal Publications, 1725 K Street NW, Washington, D.C. 20006, bimonthly ($68.00 per year).

Commerce Business Daily, U.S. Department of Commerce, Office of Field Services, U.S. Government Printing Office, Washington, D.C. 20402 ($80.00 per year).

Forms of Business Agreement, Institute of Business Planning, IPB Plaza, Englewood Cliffs, N.J. 07632, monthly ($198.00 per year).

Government Contractor, Federal Publications, 1725 K Street NW, Washington, D.C. 20006, biweekly ($156.00).

Government Contracts Reports, Commerce Clearance House, 4025 West Peterson Avenue, Chicago, Ill. 60646, weekly ($4.00 per year).

NCMA Newsletter, National Contract Management Association, 675 East Wardlow Road, Long Beach, Calif. 90807, monthly.

362 BIBLIOGRAPHY

Directories

Government Contracts Directory, Government Data Publications, 422 Washington Building, Washington, D.C. 20005, annual ($100.00).

Government Contracts Guide, Commerce Clearing House, 4025 West Peterson Avenue, Chicago, Ill. 60646 ($17.50).

Selling to NASA, U.S. Government Printing Office, Washington, D.C. 20402 (free).

Selling to Navy Prime Contractors, U.S. Government Printing Office, Washington, D.C. 20402 ($1.00).

United States Government Purchasing and Sales Directory, U.S. Small Business Administration, U.S. Government Printing Office, Washington, D.C. 20402, 1972 ($2.35).

On-Line Data Bases

Defense Market Measurement System, Frost and Sullivan, 109 Fulton Street, New York, N.Y. 10038.

Federal Register, Capitol Services, 511 Second Street NE, Washington, D.C. 20002.

Associations and Societies

Electronic Industries Association, EIA, 2001 Eye Street, N.W. Washington, D.C. 20006.

National Contract Management Association, 2001 Jefferson Davis Highway, Arlington, Va. 22202.

National Institute of Government Purchasing, 1001 Connecticut Avenue NW, Washington, D.C. 20036.

Index

Index

Accountability, 52
Acquisition plan, 201-203
Actual earned value, 169-180
Authority, as project, 102-103
   delegation of, 102-103
   documentation of, 102-103
   representation of, 102-103

Bid board, 203
Bid proposal development, 214-221
   categorical outline, 220
   cost estimating, 220, 224-227
   RFT analysis, 220

Capture plan, 202
Career Development, 292, 331-342
   how to advance, 340
   methods for, 335
   plan for, 334
   planned approach to, 333
Categorical outline, 221
Change
   management of, 254-262
   minimizing, 257
   process of, 255-257
   resistance to, 257
Characteristics
   project management, 2-9, 27-29, 34-35, 139-140
   project manager, 37-39
Commitment, 239-241, 250-252, 296
Communications, 93-95, 107
Competitive assessment, 202

Conflict in project management, 273-285
   determinants, 273-280
   resolution approaches, 281-285
Conflict management, 273-285
   skills, 266
Contract management, 195-232
   closing the contract, 228-231
Contract procurement, 205-210
   advertised, 205-207
   negotiated, 207-208
Contract types, 205
Controlling, 152-154
Cost
   analysis, 152, 182-186
   benefit, 155
   center, 159-161
   changes, 162-165
   collection, 164
   directives, 190-191
   problems, 188-189
   requirements, 154, 156-157
Cost, as types
   functional, 166
   man-hours, 166
   material, 167
   support, 168
   variances, 169-185
Customer reporting, 185

Definitions
   interface, 69, 80
   programs, 15
   projects, 3, 13, 15-17, 79
   systems, 15-16

INDEX

Departmental organization, 58
Dual accountability, 243

Earned value, 169–185
Executive expectations, 97–98
Executive questions, 98–113
Executive role, 92–113

Financial compensation, 316

Influence style, 242–247
Integration positions, 47–52, 80

Job
   classification, 317
   description, 317
   security, 31

Leadership, 231–288
   effectiveness of leadership styles, 286–288
   skills, 265
Leadership style, 242–253
   effectiveness, 248–253
Life cycles, 19–26, 196
   phases, 19–26
Linear responsibility charts (LRC's), 107

Market predictability, 198
Matrix, 66–78, 89–91
   ground rules, 66
Merit increase, 324

Negotiations in project management, 36
Negotiations of contracts, 228–230
New business development, 193–230

Organizational
   responsibility, 52
   workflow, 47–52
Organizations
   authority, 51
   classical, 53
   conflict, 54, 56
   departmental, 58
   integrating positions, 56, 57
   line-staff, 61
   matrix, 66–78, 89–91
   product, 63
   selection, 81–82, 84

Performance appraisals, 319–324
Personnel selection, 291
Planning, 114–130, 240
   checklist, 131–133
   for business growth, 198
   guidelines, 114–119
   levels of, 162
   process, 122–124
   questions, 119–120
   reasons for, 116–117
   skills, 268
   variables, 118, 122–124
Power
   expert, 244–247
   managerial, 242
   punishment, 244–247
   referent, 244–247
   reward, 244–247
   shared, 242
   sources of, 242–247
Power spectrum, 242, 245, 249
Pricing of bid proposals, 221–227
Program acquisition, 195–197
Project control, 296
Project kickoff, 296
Project management, effectiveness, 248, 250–253
Project management positions, 292
   description of, 292, 318
Project (program) management
   approach, 2
   cause/effect, 33–35
   concepts, 5–9
   definition, 3, 13, 15–17, 79
   development, 9–13
   directives, 190–191
   environment, 8–11
   growth, 7–8, 10–11
   life cycles, 19–26
   location, 87–88
   selection, 37–39
   small company, 41–44
   sources, 38
   sponsor, 92–96
   staffing, 4, 37–39
   termination, 128–129
Project manager, 235, 242–243
   authority, 242–246
   career development, 331–342
   job description, 292, 318

Project manager (continued)
  performance evaluation, 319-324
  personal characteristics, 232-254
  responsibilities, 318
  role of, 242
Project marketing, 195
Project performance, 240, 319, 321-324
Project phaseout, 326-330
Project task
  integration, 302
Project team, 289-325
  developing the, 291-293
  environment, 303
  needs of, 304
  newly formed, 310
  organizing the, 294
  selecting key personnel, 291-293
Program plan
  definition, 138-139
  directives, 145
  preparation, 140
  types, 15-17, 143

Reporting relations, 296
Request for proposal, 204
Research and development, 18
Resource allocation, 201, 203
  skills, 271
Resource plan, 203

Responsibility, 52
Rewards, 237, 243

Salary, 244-246, 316
Schedules, 146-151
  complexity, 146-147
  detailed, 146-147
  development, 149
  guidelines, 147
  preparation, 149
Skills of project managers, 234, 263-272
Staffing, 291-301
Systems
  business, 30
  terminology, 15-16

Team building, 289-325
  barriers to, 304-309
  effectiveness in, 313-315
  skills, 264
Technology expertise, 237, 267

Win strategy, 202, 220
  pricing, 223-227
Work breakdown structure (WBS), 133-137
  definition, 133
  establishment, 133
Work packages, 134